THURSDAY-NIGHT POKER

♠ ♣ ♥ ♦

THURSDAY-NIGHT POKER

♠ ♣ ♥ ♦

HOW TO UNDERSTAND, ENJOY—
AND *WIN*

PETER O. STEINER

RANDOM HOUSE   NEW YORK

Library of Congress Cataloging-in-Publication Data

Steiner, Peter O.
Thursday-night poker : how to understand, enjoy—
and *win* / Peter O. Steiner
p. cm.
Includes bibliographical references.
ISBN 0-679-76020-2
1. Poker. 2. Poker—Rules. 3. Gambling. I. Title.
GV1251.S72 1996
795.412—dc20 95-8485

Printed in the United States of America on acid-free paper
6 8 9 7

To James V. McConnell,
psychologist, poker player, friend.
He was extraordinary in each role. Jim started
me on the project that became this book,
and would have been its co-author if
he were still alive.

Author's Note

THE FOCUS AND PLAN OF THIS BOOK

By *Thursday-night poker* I mean serious poker played by amateurs in a group that plays regularly, from once a week to once a month, for moderate but not trivial stakes. I picture a game of seven or eight players in their homes or clubs under either of two kinds of betting rules: first, a fixed-limit game where the *maximum* bet allowed is $5 or $10 or perhaps as much as $20; second, a low-ante, pot-limit game where no bet can ever exceed the size of the pot at the time it is made, and also where the maximum bet is limited to either $50 or $100. In either of these types of games a player's winnings or losings in a five-hour session will range typically from $50 to a few hundred dollars, and virtually never be as much as $1,000. My specific focus, then, is not "nickel-dime" poker nor high-stakes poker, nor poker as played in the gambling casinos of the world. Much of what is discussed in Parts I to III of this book may, nevertheless, be of interest and value to persons playing higher- and lower-stakes games, but the applications, particularly the starting strategies discussed in Part IV, would require substantial adaptation. In very-low-stakes poker it is common and sensible to play a wider number of games with variations and sometimes wild cards that add dimensionality to the play. In very-high-stakes games both the rhythm of the betting and the nature of the players require different strategies. The final chapter briefly considers casino and tournament poker to suggest the differences that Thursday-night players encounter when they choose to play in such games.

Most Thursday-night poker games permit the dealer to choose ("dealer's choice") the particular variety of game dealt. Dealers characteristically shift play among a relatively small number of different games, catering to their own tastes. At present, a small number of varieties (and minor modifications of them) seem to dominate in frequency. These are: 7-card stud, 7-card Hi-Lo, Holdem, and Omaha. These, plus the fast-disappearing older traditional forms of poker, draw poker (Jacks-or-better to open) and 5-card stud, provide sufficient variety to illustrate all the principles of sound play, and my attention will be largely limited to them.

Poker games differ from one another in important ways. While all have features in common, the differences become crucial in discussing strategy and tactics. Part I provides a survey of the varieties of games and players, and shows how particular games serve different objectives. Part II explains the basic principles that every serious poker player will want to understand, and suggests ways that they can be employed. Part III deals with the skills that distinguish good from mediocre players, skills that are needed in every variety of game and at every level of stakes. Part IV applies these principles and skills to each of six varieties of poker games. These chapters suggest the specific tactics and strategies that are appropriate for the opening rounds of betting, which is where the biggest differences among games occur. Starting strategies depend upon the game chosen, the stakes, and the nature of the opposition. These chapters are necessarily longer than the earlier, more general chapters, and each has in it exercises to permit the reader to test and hone his skills. While each of the applied chapters assumes that the reader has already read Parts II and III of the book, they are largely independent of one another. Finally, Part V provides some cautionary notes about games that may prove a good deal less friendly than the usual Thursday-night poker game.

Because poker players typically employ and relish an extensive jargon that often makes the less experienced amateur feel he is in a foreign land, I have provided a Glossary in the back of this book to allay any such insecurities. A short, select, and briefly annotated list of books about poker that I have enjoyed and/or found useful also appears at the end.

P.O.S.

Acknowledgments

My greatest debt is to the many people who have played Thursday-night poker with me for over half a century. I have learned from every one. They are too numerous to acknowledge individually, but a few whom I have outlived remain vividly in my memory; they are Andy Clark, Phil Cohen, Simon Dolan, Jim Early, Jim McConnell, Dean Patrides, Chuck Phillips, Art Rich, Al Sessler, and Bernie Weinstock.

Among my present poker-playing friends, Steve Bellock, Paul Courant, Dick Dougherty, Paul Sweeney, and Ken Warner have each read parts of this book in early drafts and have improved the final product greatly with their comments and suggestions. I thank them, but of course relieve them of responsibility for any errors or infelicities that remain.

David Steiner helped with complex computer calculations at several critical points in the analysis that preceded writing. Patricia Owen Steiner, who is a translator by profession and a sometime poker widow, read every chapter at least once and did her best to help me translate what I had written into coherent prose. More essentially she provided invaluable encouragement at every stage.

Finally, my gratitude to my editor, who liked some fragments well enough to engineer the publication of this book.

Contents

IV. APPLICATIONS AND EXERCISES
♦

V. SOME CAUTIONARY NOTES
♠

I

THESE GAMES CALLED POKER

1

INTRODUCTION

You are playing in your regular Thursday-night poker game, dealer's choice, and the game is 7-card stud, high only. You have a pair of Aces showing, the second received as the fifth card. You have been making normal-size bets, and after the seventh card has been dealt, there are still three others in the hand. You find that despite a number of possibilities, your hand has not improved. You consider making a bet to suggest you have at least two pair but decide instead to check. There is $50 in the pot. Duke, sitting to your left, also checks, but Bill bets the maximum allowed, and Ty folds. Now it's up to you. You . . .

Do you fold, call, or raise? That depends on several crucial pieces of information, some of which you would already have as a player, though they were not mentioned above.

First, how big is the bet, and what are the betting rules? On the one hand, if Bill bet $2 because this is a $2-limit poker game, that is a small amount to spend to possibly win $52. Because a pair of Aces or worse will prove to be the winning hand in more than one twenty-sixth of all deals in 7-card stud, it would be foolish to fold in the face of what might be a bluff. On the other hand, if the game is pot limit, and the bet is $50, you would be risking $50 to possibly win $100, and the probability of a pair of Aces being the high hand is far less than one in three. This illustrates one of the guiding principles of playing poker: **pot odds are crucial to**

determining what to do. In turn, this means that you have to pay attention to the relationship among the **probability** of holding the winning hand, the **amount you expect to spend** to be in on the call, and the **amount you expect to win** if you have the winning hand. The last two of these factors depend crucially on the betting rules and the **stakes** of the game. Anyone who tells you that you should *always* call or *always* drop with a given hand can't be right—though it may be sound advice for a beginner if it is *usually* right.

The second kind of information concerns who the other players are and their styles of play. Even a $2 bet by a very conservative player may lead you to fold if he virtually never bluffs and you know he would never bet into the two pair you may well have. But if your opponent is a regular bluffer, a big bet of $50 may be an attempt to steal the pot with a hand that was aiming for a straight or a flush and never made it. After all, in this situation his only chance of winning the $50 is to have everyone else drop out, and he may judge it worth $50 to try to win $50. This depends, of course, on how he evaluates you and anyone else still in the game. The important principle here is that **poker is played against people,** and each person plays differently. This being so, your actions and reactions must take into account the nature of your opponents.

The third consideration has to do with what the other players were looking for and how likely it is that they succeeded. After all, they did pay to get sixth and seventh cards even though you had a pair of Aces showing. Your judgment here will depend on what cards the other players are showing, the cards that have been folded, and how the betting has proceeded. There is information in each of these elements. The important but sometimes overlooked principle here is to **pay attention to all the information that is available to you.**

Fourth, *how* you play depends to a significant extent on *why* you play. While this may seem a relatively minor consideration in how you play a particular hand, it does affect your whole strategy and outlook. I do not agree with a recent book on poker that gives as the *first fundamental principle* of poker that "The only purpose in playing poker is to win money."[1] People differ in why they play poker—why they invest time, and possibly also some of their income and assets, in a game. (People *play* poker, they don't engage in it, or work at it, or suffer through it.) The motives of the professional poker player are not those of the typical Thursday-night player; those of the compulsive gambler are not those of the conservative family man seeking a night out with the boys. That, you may say, may well be, but these are differences of degree; after all, among adults poker is always played for money, and making money—or at least not losing it—is the objective of everyone who plays poker.[2] For many Thursday-night poker players, making money is not their primary objective. Yet poker *is* played for money. So what, then, is money's role?

THE ROLE OF MONEY

Three considerations suggest why, among the vast majority of poker players, money is not the dominant objective. First, because poker is what mathematicians call a zero-sum game—a game in which aggregate winnings and losings balance out[3]—most players cannot expect realistically to win money over the long run. Second, even regular winners will have invested time in the activity, and few amateur poker players' winnings will seem significant if reduced to a

1. Edwin Silberstang, *Winning Poker for the Serious Player* (New York: Cardoza Publishing, 1992), p. 10.
2. Strip poker, which isn't really poker at all, once had an age-specific appeal, but I imagine that modern sexual mores have rendered it wholly obsolete.
3. This assumes there is no fee to play; when there is, poker is a negative-sum game.

dollars-per-hour "wage." Third, and most important, the vast majority of amateur poker players play with their friends and do not make their livings that way, nor do they wish to impoverish their opponents.

For many, perhaps most, amateur players, poker is something they do as a leisure activity for a combination of the following reasons: as a form of male bonding,[4] as a night out, as a release of aggressions through the legitimatized use of hostile and self-serving behavior that may be frowned upon in everyday pursuits, and as a controlled form of gambling in which skill plays a part while luck remains to explain or rationalize less than complete success.[5] It is primarily a limited and controlled form of competition that is both exciting and forgiving, and in which most of the inherent sources of advantage that one human being may have over another are not highly relevant. All poker players are created equal, even if all do not prove equally skilled.[6]

---

4. It is an unmistakable fact that poker has long been primarily a male game. Doyle Brunson, a top professional, says, "I've never met a woman who was a really top player. Maybe that's because there aren't a lot of women players." (Doyle Brunson *et al.*, *How I Made Over $1,000,000 Playing Poker* [Las Vegas: B & G Publishing, 1978], p. 24.) This seems to be changing, for today there are, in fact, some exceptionally good and avid female players; indeed, two women reached the semifinal round of twenty-seven in the 1993 World Series of Poker, one reached the final ten in 1994 and one the final five in 1995. Still, compare the relative presences of women in poker and in bridge. I will not venture to hypothesize on why women poker players have been relatively rare, why women's regular home poker games are a rarity, and thus why poker night is a predominantly male affair, but I shall recognize this fact by using the male pronoun throughout, and without apology other than this footnote.

5. Even a poor poker player wins some of the time and is likely to both remember and depend on his triumphs. Remember how often you hear a loser say, "I would have come out ahead except for that hand in which . . ." It is in this way that poker is easier to play poorly than, say, chess, bridge, or golf.

6. It is a curious phenomenon, one that may be observed in virtually every country club, that the same four players who golf in the afternoon, giving and accepting handicaps to offset the differences in skills, sit down to play poker in the evening without handicapping those of proven greater skill. Apparently it is acceptable to admit you are a below-average golfer, but not a below-average card player.

The role of money as an objective of poker players is implicit in most of the "How to Win at Poker" books, of which there are many. Examined carefully, they assume the reader's objective to be one of the following:

1. make as much money as possible, with virtually no risk;
2. make a sure and steady profit by playing a sounder, less risky game than your opponents;
3. pursue the strategy of *minimax*, which is game-theory jargon for seeking to minimize the maximum amount of money you risk.

Because poker is a zero-sum game, the sum of the participants' winnings and losings must balance out. That being the case, the first and second of these objectives suggest that the player must succeed in doing what *all* players cannot do: be better than average. While we may all want to be that, we cannot all expect to fit in that category. The first goal can be met by cheating (using marked cards, dealing off the bottom, etc.) or being a cardsharp who seeks and finds gullible players and exploits them. The key tactical questions such people face are how to conceal their objectives and methods from their victims. There are such people, and they are skilled in knowing how best, and how quickly, to exploit their pigeons. Closely related to this is a less blatant strategy: choosing games in which there are a sufficient number of weak players that the others' weaknesses assure one of being a winner.[7]

The second objective can be more honorably pursued and does characterize some winning poker players. It requires playing a conservative and often boring game. If the rules of the game do not require large antes, this sort of

7. Silberstang defines a "good game" as one in which "you are the top player, or among the top, with several weakies in the game" (*Winning Poker,* p. 16).

player can fold and fold, simply waiting for the hand where the probability of being beaten is very small.[8] This tack does characterize some amateur poker players and almost surely characterizes many small-time professionals, but I can't imagine that it would be much fun to be part of a game in which everyone played this way. Moreover, guys who play this way in typical Thursday-night games are neither greatly admired nor welcomed. Most amateurs do not play this way not because they cannot, but because they do not choose to.

The third objective, "minimax," has received much attention because it appears to introduce the highly esoteric theory of games into the game of poker, which is itself by no means esoteric.[9] Game theory is extraordinarily pessimistic in its outlook; basically it assumes that the other guys are always smarter than you are, and that you had better be defensive. Strategies built on "minimax" are designed to show you how to break even in the long run. But if breaking even is your sole objective, no complex strategy is needed; just *don't play* and you'll break even in both the long and short runs![10]

Being satisfied with breaking even in poker may well be a reasonable attitude, but it must characterize people who de-

---

8. Spanier quotes the actor Jimmy Stewart advising Richard Nixon on how to play draw poker: Never stay unless you *know* you have everyone beaten at the time of the draw (David Spanier, *Total Poker* [New York: Simon and Schuster, 1977], p. 72). For many reasons this is *not* sound advice, but even if it were, to follow it means a long, dull evening of watching other people play poker.

9. See, for example, Nesmith C. Ankeny, *Poker Strategy: Winning with Game Theory* (New York: Basic Books, 1981).

10. Long before he achieved Watergate-era fame, Daniel Ellsberg sketched the folly of "the reluctant duelist" (Ellsberg, "The Theory of the Reluctant Duelist," *American Economic Review*, vol. XLVI, 1957). Game theory, though a poor approach to playing poker, is of course highly relevant to many situations, such as international diplomacy, where one does not have the option of not playing and, therefore, knowing how to minimize one's maximum loss may be vital.

rive other pleasures from playing—pleasures that justify their taking some risks of losing money. After all, they are investing time in playing, time that could be spent in other activities. The usual way of controlling one's maximum monetary losses is by choosing with whom one plays and the stakes and ground rules of the games played.

IF NOT MONEY, WHAT?

The attitude of most amateurs toward winning or losing money in serious poker games might be stated as: to make as much money as possible, *other things being equal.* This formulation correctly recognizes money-making as secondary to the "other things" they are playing to achieve. Because these things are important, a player will be willing to pay a price (in forgone winnings) to achieve them.

Money dominates the discussion of poker games not because making it is the dominant objective but because it is the *means of keeping score.* It is the measure of winning or losing. Indeed, in many Thursday-night poker games the stakes are such that the maximum winnings or losings are roughly the cost of dinner at a moderate restaurant, and even in so-called big games among friends, rarely is the maximum loss as much as 1 percent of the player's annual income.

Are there not other ways of keeping score? Why is poker not played for nonredeemable chips? The answer is that it is necessary to get the players to take every hand seriously. One could not behave in the ways that make poker fun, such as bluffing or manipulating one's opponents, if everyone routinely called every hand. Poker requires that every action be potentially costly. Unlike other games, the typical friendly poker game has no measure that is independent of its monetary yardstick. The board game Monopoly, by contrast, uses money, but the payoff comes in being *the* winner, not in walking off with bulging pockets.[11]

Could poker be structured along the lines of bridge, to have duplicate tournaments and give master points to those who performed best *relative to the hands they were dealt?* The answer is no, because in poker, unlike bridge, the best outcome for a given player on a given hand is never independent of the other players in the game. **You play poker with cards, but against people.** When played by skilled players, bridge is primarily played against the cards dealt, and only to a small degree against specific opponents. Psychological and interpersonal considerations play a much greater role in poker.

Motives are important because the right way to play a given hand—at a given time, on a given evening, against

---

11. This is also the case in computer poker, as well as in tournament poker, where the objective is to survive and be the ultimate winner. The so-called World Series of Poker is structured this way. Originally it was a winner-take-all contest, but as the number of entrants has grown to the hundreds, prize money is scaled to the order of finish, until in 1993 the top twenty-seven players shared in the pot. Every entrant puts up a $10,000 entry fee, and is given chips representing that amount. He or she plays until this amount is gone. Does the size of the entry fee not mean that this is really a game about money? The answer is no. The big-time professionals (from among whom top finishers virtually always emerge) can and do make more money in less time in the side games. They are playing for pride, for the love of competition, and with the hope of being thought of and labeled "World Champion." Tourists can do much better, in a probabilistic sense, at roulette, blackjack, or even slot machines. Those who enter are spending their ten grand in thrills, and in future conversations, not in the expectation of doing other than losing their entry fee. The high entry fee does play an important role: it keeps the number of entrants to a manageable number. There were 273 entrants in 1995, about as many as it is comfortable to handle in an elimination tournament. As this number grows, one may expect to see the entry fee rise, with the expectation that it will limit the entrants more than the increased prize money will encourage them. Among the accounts of this tournament are A. Alvarez's *The Biggest Game in Town* (Boston: Houghton Mifflin, 1983), Anthony Holden's *Big Deal* (New York: Viking, 1990), and A. Alvarez's "No Limit," *The New Yorker*, August 8, 1994.

particular opponents—depends on what you are trying to do with your investment of time, energy, and, to some extent, money. Not all individuals have the same objectives, and it is important that you temper any strategic and tactical advice in any book about poker (including this one) with an understanding of what you are trying to do.

2

♠ ♣ ♥ ♦

STAKES

The inscrutable Oriental puffed on his pipe, pressed his five cards close to his robe, and pushed his whole pile, about $45,000, to the center of the table. Bond fingered the $8,000 in front of him, wondered if they'd take his marker, glanced wistfully at his three aces, and slowly folded his cards. "I'd love to stay longer, gentlemen, but I have a pressing affair," he said and rose from the table.

"It's the start of the World Series of Poker, folks, and 260 assorted optimists are taking their places. Each has ventured $10,000, and by Thursday night, we'll know which one has captured all the chips. The favorite is Phil Helmuth, Jr., but about twenty others are given a good chance."

"Seven-card stud Hi-Lo, with the Joker and one-eyed Jacks wild. Quarter ante, $2 limit, with four raises. Cards speak."
  "Come on, Stan, let's play real poker."

There is no such thing as "real poker." There are many different varieties of poker games, played for widely different stakes, and for a variety of motives. There is nothing inferior or superior about one kind of game except in the tastes of a particular individual. Many varieties of poker are interesting, require and reward skill, and can be played for pleasure by persons of varying degrees of talent, wealth, and time to commit to the activity. Two keys to the variety of poker games are the stakes of the game and the nature of the players. They are the focus of this chapter and the next one.

When sitting down to play poker, it is essential to know and understand the stakes for the game being played. Rules covering antes and maximum and minimum bets and raises determine whether or not you can afford to play in a particular game. They also affect the varieties of poker that will be interesting to play, and they affect how you should play a given hand—or, indeed, a given session. Beyond the rules themselves is the "culture" of the game. For example, are the players restrained or aggressive in their betting? Are multiple bets and raises a typical feature of the early rounds of betting, or does the heavier betting only develop late in most hands? These factors, along with the rules, determine the effective "stakes of the game."

BETTING RULES

Except in the movies, virtually all high- and moderate-stakes poker games are *table stakes,* which means that a player can never be squeezed out of a hand because he lacks the resources to call a bet.[1]

Table stakes combines with other rules to determine the betting limitations. If there are more than two players in a hand when one player is *all-in* (that is, he has no more chips or money on the table), subsequent bets are segregated into

---

1. Thus, situations such as the entertaining sequence in the movie *A Big Hand for the Little Lady* do not arise. In the film, a poker player suffers an apparent heart attack while facing a huge bet he has yet to call. After tending to him and looking at his cards, his distressed wife rushes to the bank to float a loan, using his cards as collateral, in order to be able to call and then raise the outstanding bet.

a side pot, which is contested only by those who have paid the required amounts to call.[2] (Occasionally there may be more than one side pot, as successive players are forced to go all-in while other players are still betting.)

In low-stakes poker games played outside of casinos, table-stakes protection is not usually required and a player may be allowed to "play light" for the remainder of a given hand.[3]

No-Limit Poker

In no-limit poker, bets are wholly independent of the amount of money in the pot and are limited only by table stakes.[4] No-limit poker is inevitably accompanied by a rule that requires a sizable minimum *buy-in*—the amount a player must start with, or reenter with if he goes all-in and then loses—and a rule against *rat-holing*—taking funds off the table in a table-stakes game to protect one's winnings from being at risk on a subsequent hand. Psychology and nerve are the key ingredients of no-limit poker, and cards and probabilities are of almost incidental concern. This is the realm of Bet-a-Million Gates, and his modern-day poker-playing counterparts, such as Doyle Brunson and other big-time professional gamblers who are also poker players. It is not a game that amateurs often play—nor should they unless they have more money than they know what to do with. To see why, consider sitting down at a poker table where the first time you bet, the person across

2. If the all-in player wins the main pot, the best of the other hands wins the side pot.
3. This is accomplished by borrowing chips from the pot and making up the debt when the hand is completed. It is a practice I do not recommend. It causes confusion and delays the game, and a careless or unscrupulous player can fail to pay his full share of the required bets or raises by dragging chips out and then playing them back in at the next opportunity.
4. Some writers use the term *table stakes* to refer only to no-limit table stakes.

the table looks you over slowly and then raises by the amount of your entire stake. If you are not prepared for this, you should not play no-limit poker, for it will surely happen. No-limit poker is a game of bluffing and intimidation *par excellence*. It is suitable to a tournament such as the World Series of Poker, where it is employed, but not to games among amateurs.[5]

Pot-Limit Poker

This form of poker is played both by professionals and by amateurs, and is increasingly popular among better players, even of moderate means. In pot-limit, no bet or raise can be larger than the sum of the money already in the pot at the time the bet is made. For example, if the antes total $5, the first bettor can bet a maximum of $5; the next player may call the $5, making a pot of $15, and then raise a maximum of $15. If he does so, there will be $30 in the pot; the next player may either fold, call the $20 previously bet, or raise. If he chooses to raise, he can call the $20 *and* raise up to $50 since by now there will be $50 in the pot. The size of the pot can build up quickly, even on a single round, and in games where there are several rounds of betting, the possibility for very large bets exists.

Modified forms of pot-limit are sometimes used—for example, half-pot-limit, or pot-limit but with a maximum bet (of, say, $50 or $100). Such modifications limit the maximum size of pots but do not change the fundamental characteristic of pot-limit poker—namely, that betting limits are small at first, but rise sharply as a hand progresses.

While pot-limit poker may lead to a high-stakes game, it may also be kept relatively modest. The effective size of the maximum bets in pot-limit poker is controlled, first of all,

---

5. I shall not discuss it further in this book, but see Doyle Brunson *et al., How I Made Over $1,000,000 Playing Poker* (Las Vegas: B & G Publishing, 1978).

by the size of the players' antes and, second, by the presence or absence of required blind or forced bets. It is also affected by the culture of the particular game and its players, which I'll discuss at the end of this chapter.

Size of ante. The *ante* is a fee for playing a hand, paid by each player before any cards are dealt. The function of the ante is to make it expensive for a player who chooses to sit and wait for a hand that has a high probability of being the winner. Significant required contributions are necessary when playing with conservative players, or ones for whom making as much money as possible is the dominant objective. Since such players are always present in casino games, high required contributions are the rule there. The higher the ante, the more expensive, and thus less attractive, a "sit and wait" strategy becomes. In typical Thursday-night games, where players tend to play looser poker than most casino players (because they came to play rather than to watch), the size of the ante is less critical, and is often nominal in games with several rounds of betting, such as 7-card stud. In fact, it is not uncommon to have only the dealer ante so as to avoid the necessity of each player anteing every hand. In draw poker, however, a significant ante is required if there is to be any action at all.

Blind betting. In *blind betting* there is no option to fold. A designated position, usually the first hand to the left of the dealer, is obliged to bet, and often the next hand is obliged to raise, both by fixed amounts. For example, the first player may be required to bet $2 and the second to raise to $5. This is done instead of an ante, and the circulating nature of the deal spreads the fixed levy around.[6] (The

---

6. Where this is the practice, players who leave the table and miss their blind bets must be required to sit out an entire round or pay a tax to get back in.

players making the blind bets are usually permitted to raise when the betting comes around to them again even if no one else has raised.) In a different form of blind betting, appropriate for stud poker, the player with the worst showing card (the highest non-Ace in lowball, the lowest non-Ace in high) is required to bet—"to *bring in* the hand"—for a fixed amount on the first round. This, too, is like an ante, but the burden falls randomly, instead of systematically. Having a bet by the worst hand showing gives better hands a chance to raise at the outset.

Forced betting.   In *forced betting* there is no ability to *check*—that is, to pass up the opportunity to make the initial bet in any round. One must either make at least a specified minimum bet or fold. The size of the required forced bets usually rises as betting rounds progress—for example, $2, $5, and $10 for the first three betting rounds of a 7-card stud game. Forced bets eliminate checking while assuring that there are no free rounds and that by the late rounds there is a certain minimum-size pot even if only two players remain.

In pot-limit poker the sizes of the ante, blind bets, or forced bets are critical, not only in determining how tightly people play, but also in affecting the size of the pot in the later rounds. A small enough ante keeps the initial round of betting small, and this in turn keeps the subsequent rounds smaller. Consider two otherwise similar pot-limit games, with the same general class of players, but in one of the games only the dealer antes a dollar while in the other each of eight players antes fifty cents. This seemingly small difference in games (where each player usually has at least $100 on the table) can have striking consequences. Typical pots in the latter game are more than three times as large as in the former. To see why, suppose that on the first betting round in each game there is one bettor and then a raise,

which is called by a third player as well as the original bettor. In the game where the aggregate ante is $1 before the
betting and raising, the maximum pot at the start of the second round is $13: each player has contributed $4, the sum
of the maximum first bet ($1) and maximum first raise ($3).
In the other game, the aggregate ante of $4 plus a $4 initial
bet followed by a $12 raise leads to a pot of $52 at the start
of the second round. While nothing requires that bets be at
or near the permitted maximum, actual bets are generally
affected by that standard.

Fixed-Limit Poker

In fixed-limit poker (hereafter called simply *limit poker*) the
maximum size of the bet is specified for each betting round.
The limit is generally two-tier; that is, it is at one level for
the initial rounds of betting and at a higher level at some
well-defined later point. If the limit is stated as $5/$10, the
maximum bet or raise in early rounds is limited to $5, and
in the last round or two of betting to $10. Checking is per-
mitted, and usually there is no rule against later raising,
though occasionally games prohibit such *sandbagging* and
others frown on it. Limits can vary from the trivial ("nickel
and dime") to very substantial amounts, thus fitting the
tastes and pocketbooks of the players. Limit poker has tra-
ditionally been the most common form of Thursday-night
poker, although pot-limit poker seems to be increasing in
popularity among better players.

In gambling casinos (though not elsewhere) the stated
limits are usually both a maximum *and* a minimum. For example, in $5/$10, the size of any bet or raise is neither
more *nor less* than $5 for the first rounds of betting, and
$10 for the subsequent rounds. Such games can be for quite
small stakes (say, $1/$3) or much larger stakes ($200/
$400). The use of fixed betting sizes is explained by the
casinos' need to monitor closely the players' behavior in

calling bets, and by their need to limit opportunities for collusive signaling.[7]

There is usually a limit imposed on the number of raises that will be permitted in any single betting round when there are more than two players; this is to provide an effective limit on total betting for a player caught in a betting war between two players, each of whom is confident of winning. (Further, without such a limit, two players in illicit partnership could of course squeeze a third player mercilessly whenever one of the colluders had a sure winner.) A limit on the number of raises is essential in games with more than one winner, such as Hi-Lo poker.

HOW BETTING RULES AND THE CULTURE OF THE GAME AFFECT PLAY

Betting Rules

The size of the ante (or of its equivalent, such as blind bets) should affect how you play poker. At one extreme, if there were a $10 ante and a ten-cent maximum bet, it would be sensible to stay in every hand as long as there was the slightest possibility of ending up the winner; at the opposite extreme, with a ten-cent ante but a $100 minimum bet, there are a great many hands dealt to you that you would throw away without regret.

Other betting rules and habits similarly affect strategy about staying or folding. Whether to play relatively loosely (that is, to stay in with hands that have some prospects of winning but are not the favorites to do so) or to play tightly (that is, to fold hands unless they are highly favored to turn out to be winners) depends critically on the pattern

7. See Chapter 17; just as in bridge, "telling" one's partner the quality of your hand may be critical to partnership success, and varying the size of one's bet gives almost unlimited opportunity for communicating.

of betting that is expected to prevail. To see this quickly, suppose you expect to have to spend $80 to see the showdown of a hand of 7-card stud that will give you a profit of $200 if you win. It matters greatly whether you will have to pay $50 to see the fourth card and $10 for each of the final three cards, or whether the fourth, fifth, and sixth cards will cost $10 each and the last card $50. With each additional card you will learn more about your own hand, about the number of your competitors, and about their holdings. In the first case you are paying a lot to get the information the fourth card provides. If all of this information adds up to bad news, you can of course fold, but you are already out $50. In the second case, you can get that same information for only $10, and even if it is bad news, you are out only $10. Obviously, there are some situations where getting this kind of information is worth more than $10 but less than $50. When that is the case, you would choose to stay in the second betting pattern but fold in the first.

The critical aspect of betting patterns in determining how tightly or loosely you will want to play is the ratio of early-round betting to later-round betting. The larger the fraction of your expected ultimate contribution to the pot you have to put in early (when you are typically less sure about how good your final hand will be), the more conservative you will want to be, and thus the fewer hands you will stay in on. *Other things being equal,* this ratio is directly affected by the betting rules. Generally the early-round bets in limit poker are a larger fraction of the total bets than in pot-limit. Similarly, a single limit, say $10, has a higher ratio of early-to-late-round bets than an escalating limit of, say, $10/$20. Thus there is a tendency for single limits to lead to tighter play than escalating limits, and for both of them to lead to tighter play than with pot-limit rules.

Culture of the Game: Four Prototypes

The "other things" assumed equal in the previous paragraph need not be equal. Here the culture of the game plays a critical role. In games with a regular group of players, a certain betting rhythm usually develops. If players tend to play in a restrained manner and check or merely call until they are convinced they have the strongest hand, the size of the pot when the raising starts is likely to be much smaller than when players with strong starting hands raise and reraise early. The appropriate tactics change accordingly. The effective stakes of a game can be radically transformed with no change in the rules if a new, aggressive player enters it and routinely raises in the first round, or always bets or raises the maximum permitted, when that was not the former practice.[8]

The reverse problem, of pots that are too small because players are conservative until they have hands that are well defined, may lead to the use of blind betting or forced betting to start hands. Pot-limit poker with blind or forced bets virtually assures that the last- and next-to-last-round bets in contested hands will be large relative to the cost of seeing another card in the early going.

It will be useful here to define four prototype games, each of which produces different betting patterns. First is the game in which there is heavy betting at the start and relatively light betting later.[9] This pattern characterizes an *ag-*

8. I have known games that have broken up because no one can control such a newcomer, and the effective increase in the stakes makes the game uncomfortable, or even impossible, for some of the old hands. To prevent this, it is generally a good idea that a person not become a regular in a game until he has been a visitor for a couple of sessions, and then must be voted on by the regulars. If it is impossible to get rid of the spoiler, the best tactic in such a situation is to vote to lower the ante, and to reduce or eliminate blind and forced bets.

9. This is characteristic of games professionals play, but is less common in Thursday-night poker.

gressive limit game, where players bet and raise aggressively on the initial round, usually reducing the number of players to two or three, the bets and raises being moderate thereafter. Second is the game in which the betting is light at the outset, with raises a rarity, at least until the next round or two let players define the potential of their holding, and moderate thereafter. This is the pattern of many Thursday-night limit games, and will be called a *restrained limit game.* In the third type of game, the betting is light at the start but gets much heavier as the betting rounds proceed. This pattern characterizes a *restrained pot-limit game.*[10] Fourth is the game where the betting is often so intense at the start that either one player wins right there, or there are only two players after the opening round, one of whom has gone all-in, and the hand becomes showdown thereafter. This pattern describes an *aggressive pot-limit* (or *no-limit*) *game* of the kind often seen in tournament play.

To illustrate the significant differences among these games, imagine a simple two-round poker game where there is an aggregate ante of $10. In the limit games, the first-round bets and raises are limited to $10 each, and those in the second round to $20. There may be up to four raises in each round. The accompanying table outlines betting scenarios for each game.

The last row in this table calculates the ratio (as a percentage) of the first-round bet to the ultimate profit that the winner receives. It is this ratio that dictates the appro-

---

10. I am focusing here on the ratio of the later-round bets to the earlier ones. There are, of course, other relevant aspects of different games, among them the number of players, how loosely they play, and how skillful you are relative to them. As a general rule, the more players and the looser their play, the bigger the pot will be. Thus the better the pot odds and, as will be seen, the weaker the holdings you can play with at the start. Greater skill than your opponents can work in the same direction, because you are more likely to be able to "put them on a hand" (that is, infer what cards they're holding) and thus make intelligent decisions later in the play.

Table 2.1   The Effect of Betting Patterns

	Fixed-Limit		Pot-Limit	
	Aggressive	Restrained	Restrained	Aggressive
Ante	$10	$10	$10	$10
Bets and Raises:				
1st round	$50	$10	$10	$70
2nd round	$20	$20	$60	$0
Number of Callers:				
1st round	3	5	5	2
2nd round	2	4	2	2
Total pot	$200	$140	$180	$150
Amount to call	70	30	70	70
Profit to winner	$130	$110	$110	$80
First-round bet as percent of profit	38.5%	9.1%	9.1%	87.5%

priate playing strategy. Where the ratio is high, it is expensive and often foolish to pursue possible but not probable winners. Where it is low, it is not expensive and thus often sensible to see another card or two, even on hands that are not currently the best if they have prospects of improving. All of this will be discussed at length in Chapter 6 and in the applied chapters of Part IV. As can be seen from the table, you can play a much looser style in the games that I have labeled *restrained* (either limit or pot-limit), than in the forms of the games labeled *aggressive*.

These distinctions are of particular relevance in interpreting the "how to" advice given in poker books. Most of these books are written by professionals who play in highly aggressive games such as those in the two outer columns of the table. They are advising others how to play in such games, and against aggressive players, and the advice they give is wholly appropriate *for those circumstances*. But it is too conservative for the sort of restrained game that is typical of Thursday-night poker. If you play too tightly in such games, you are not only missing lots of opportunities to win, but you are spending too much time watching rather than playing poker.

Because the strategies and tactics that are appropriate for games change with different rules about betting patterns, such often-stated rigid rules as "Never draw to a low pair" and "Bluff only twice a night" are invalid. Advice like this may be correct for one set of rules or playing conditions and quite wrong for another.

3

♠ ♣ ♥ ♦

PLAYERS

Everyone knows Doyle Brunson is today's greatest big-limit player.

—MIKE CARO

Old Chinese saying: When no tiger in mountain, then monkey is king.

—HERBERT YARDLEY

No one knows how many people play poker in the United States, but it is a very large number. Anthony Holden's estimate is between 50 and 60 million,[1] but even if, as I suspect, this is wildly overstated, there are surely many millions who play more or less regularly. Suppose there are even five million who play once a month or more. Some of them play poker as *work* and should be considered professionals, or *pros*. Others, the vast majority, *play* poker—that is, they do it as recreation. They are called amateurs, which is not to demean them in any way (after all, the word is French for "one who loves") but rather to recognize that they have different objectives.[2]

1. Anthony Holden, *Big Deal* (New York: Viking, 1990), p. 61.
2. Different definitions of *amateur* are possible. The *Las Vegas Sun* defines an amateur as one whose *primary* source of income comes from something other than gambling. I would apply a sterner test: income from poker should be no more than an incidental part of an amateur's income and wealth.

How you play depends a great deal on who your opponents are. The vast majority of American poker players play in a wholly different environment than do the pros. Most amateurs play in each other's homes or clubs, where poker is neither the source of nor a threat to their economic fortunes. They play among friends, often on a regular Thursday night for months or years at a time. Some do so casually, for very small stakes; some do so as couples, as an alternative to bridge. An unknown but large number do so rather more seriously, and they are the subject—and the objects!—of this book.

The great bulk of poker literature, it turns out, is not about these poker players or their usual games, but about professional poker players and the games in which they play with each other and with the amateurs who choose to play with them in casinos and other places where pros are to be found. And although the major focus of this book is on the Thursday-night poker game and its players, it is worth giving some preliminary notice to other kinds of players and other kinds of games. One reason to do so is that these "others" sometimes join a Thursday-night game. Another is that home poker players sometimes venture abroad into different environments. An even more important reason is to make clear why much of the advice that comes from the voluminous poker literature (which implicitly assumes play in casinos) is of only marginal relevance to the Thursday-night poker player in his regular game.

The two groups, amateurs and professionals—and the subgroups within them—do not play the same game, though there are superficial similarities. An analogy may be made to golf, also played by millions, where the tournament professionals are only superficially playing the same game as the millions of country club and pub-links hackers. But the similarity between professional and amateur golfers is much greater than that between poker pros and the typical Thursday-night players. Fundamentally, poker is played against other people, not against oneself and a fixed course. While pro and amateur poker players use the same fifty-two-card deck, and the same ranking of hands, almost everything else is different, including the rules that govern the games played and the objectives of the players.

The differences between golf and poker are large enough that there are other flaws in the analogy. Whether professional or amateur, every golfer wants to save strokes, but not every poker player wants to squeeze every dollar from his opponents, nor to do so as efficiently as possible. Unlike in golf, where the eighteen-handicap golfer can improve his game by watching Lee Trevino's golf tips or by taking lessons from a teaching professional, the Thursday-night poker player gets little guidance from the war stories or precepts of a Herbert Yardley or a Doyle Brunson, though he may well thrill to their adventures. He is playing a wholly different game. Indeed, the strategies appropriate to surviving in a game with professionals are likely to make such a player an unwelcome regular in an amateur group. All of this is important because *why* a person plays, and *with whom* he plays does—and should—affect *how* he plays.

PROFESSIONALS

Perhaps a few thousand people in the United States play poker for a living. While for all of them playing poker is their occupation, they do not make up a homogeneous group.

Tournament Pros

Very few of the professional poker players—probably less than a hundred—are highly skilled, big-time gamblers who live for the excitement and challenge of betting whole fortunes, sometimes hundreds of thousands of dollars, on the turn of a card or the outcome of a fight or football game. These people are both big-time gamblers and highly skilled poker players, attributes that are more frequently found separately than together. For this group of players, poker is the sport of choice, being the one where their skill and nerve permit them to earn enough money to support a flamboyant lifestyle of conspicuous consumption.[3] Indeed, in recent years about twenty of them have become famous names and media personalities—among them, Johnny Moss, "Amarillo Slim," and, currently, Phil Helmuth, Jr. Their celebrity status has been enhanced by the television coverage of the World Series of Poker, which is an effort to make poker a spectator sport.[4] A number of books have been written by and about them. These often "as told to" accounts are not unlike the biographies of movie stars in an earlier era, and of major sports personalities today.

It might seem that these tournament pros are the poker-playing equivalents of leading tournament golfers like Fred Couples and Greg Norman. In some ways they are; each group's members have skills almost beyond the comprehension of the rest of us, are exhilarated by the competition, and have learned to play for very high stakes without it adversely affecting their play. But in two crucial ways poker players differ from their golfing counterparts: first, they risk not only their time and energy but their own fortunes in every encounter; second, they do not make their living in the tournaments they play in, but "on the side." Tournament golfers play for shares of a pie that is provided by spectators, sponsors, and television revenues; they are engaged, fundamentally, in an entertainment industry. Tournament

---

3. Many of them spend large fractions of their poker winnings betting on golf, football, and horse racing, arenas in which they have no special skills.
4. Winning a large viewing audience for poker will be an uphill struggle, because one cannot see the players' cards while the action is going on, and because a great many hands are decided by the next-to-last player folding, so that there is no showdown.

golf is a *positive-sum game;* that is, the sum of the winnings of all the players is greater than zero. At least a hundred or more players are good enough to count on a regular income for years at a time. They compete against one another, to be sure, but all can be winners, though to different degrees.

By contrast, top professional poker players play for a pie that is provided by themselves and their competitors, amateur and professional, who must be separated from their funds by all sorts of intimidation, and by skills that are more intellectual and psychological than physical.[5] Survival and dominance of the top poker pros is due largely to their ability to take risks that seem all but unthinkable to most people, without letting it adversely affect their game.

Second-Line Pros

Behind the superstars are several hundred very good professional poker players who are not at the same time big-time *gamblers,* since they do not particularly enjoy taking risks. Many of them hold casino-related jobs, such as card-room managers, but count on making a significant part of their annual income playing in the small- and middle-size games that flourish at casinos. Some of them dream of being in the first category and often invest a good part of their income competing with the top pros for the challenge it presents, and as a learning experience. It was said of one of them, Eric Drache, a card-room manager, that he was the seventh-best 7-card stud player in the world and only enjoyed himself thoroughly when playing against the other six.

These second-line professionals are well known in the poker-playing centers of the world, and are somewhat anal-

---

5. There is a physical dimension in terms of stamina and the ability to maintain one's concentration hour after hour, often on a few hours' sleep. It is like the stamina required of a top chess competitor and seems to deteriorate beyond middle age.

ogous to golfing's club pros, though the services they provide are not in teaching poker but in servicing the games that cater to an important amateur clientele. They enter and often finish in the money in the smaller tournaments that are common fare in Las Vegas and other gambling centers. They stay in the penumbra of the big-time poker players by being regulars in the side games that attract wealthy tourists and other thrill seekers who come on gambling junkets.

Small-Time Pros

A third category of poker professionals is by far the largest and the least well understood. It consists of several thousand players who earn a regular though modest living by playing a full work week of tight, conservative poker in the myriad small-limit poker games found in legitimate gambling casinos. These are the professionals (called *locals* by the other pros) studied and reported on by David Hayano, an anthropologist who lived among them for several years.[6] They work long hours and play low-limit poker. They lie in wait for the occasional tourists who wander into their web, play for a few hours, lose a modest stake, and then head on to other activities. Probably a good half of the players in every house-run, low-limit poker game are these small-time pros. They play the percentages, fold, fold, fold, and count on the occasional pots that come their way as a regular matter of probability. Professor Hayano artfully profiles these professionals, whose ranks include many women and retired men. He came to admire the perseverance and ability of the survivors in regularly coming out ahead despite the fees required to play. Anyone with the time to invest and a small stake can try to join their ranks, and while some fail, many

6. David Hayano, *Poker Faces* (Berkeley: University of California Press, 1982).

people possess the talent and patience to do better than break even, despite the house take. These pros invest their time, but for many who are retired or otherwise not employed, that time is not otherwise in demand.[7] Because the skills required are modest and entry is easy, the rewards are also modest, and few of them do better than earn a subsistence wage.[8]

Hustlers

Finally there exist an unknown number of cardsharps, or hustlers, who spend time and energy assembling sheep and then fleecing them.[9] Some do it honestly by using their superior skills, often deliberately concealed in the manner of the pool hustler, to lure people into a "friendly game" that often proves less friendly as it goes on; others do it by a variety of dishonest aids that include card manipulation, collusion, marked cards, and dealer accomplices.[10]

These categories of professionals are to some extent overlapping. Some of those who do not hesitate to fleece tourists are also good poker players in their own right, and look at the earnings they get as providing the safety net that their risky profession requires; some of the small-time pros cheat by colluding.

---

7. Indeed, for many of them the time involved is a benefit since they have nothing better to do. Poker for them is, literally, a pastime.
8. One of them, intending to flatter me, once asked if I intended to move to Las Vegas and play poker in my retirement. "You could," he said, "probably count on clearing $1,000 to $1,500 a month."
9. Poker professionals call them "geese."
10. In his account of Mafia activities, Vincent Teresa gives vivid examples of the kinds of dishonest games that are regularly organized to take advantage of the legion of suckers born and reborn every year. (Vincent Teresa with Thomas C. Renner, *My Life in the Mafia* [London: Grafton Books, 1974].)

AMATEURS WHO SUPPORT THE PROS

Taken all together the professional poker players are small in number and a minute fraction of those who play poker, and one would have to learn to play *their* games if one's objective were to make a living at poker. However, this seldom is the amateur's goal. One might wish to learn to play the way the pros must play, if that style related closely to the the objectives of amateurs in their own games. And although there are several kinds of amateurs, this is only rarely the case.

For there to be a few thousand professionals who make a decent living playing poker, there must be a stream of others who fuel the system. At this time there are virtually no commercial sponsors or television advertisers who put up prize money for the game. Commercial poker is a *negative sum game;* that is, the aggregate of the winnings is less than the aggregate of the losings, because casinos must be repaid for the services they provide: space, dealers, complimentary food and drink, and so on. This payment usually occurs either in the form of an hourly fee to play, or by the house taking a cut from every pot. Who supplies the fuel?

Wing Testers

Among amateur poker players there are some who want to test their skills by playing with the pros, and they pay for this privilege, just as amateur golfers pay sizable entry fees to play in pro-am tournaments. Of the over 200 entrants in the annual World Series of Poker, where a $10,000 entry fee lets you rub shoulders for a while with Phil Helmuth, Jr., perhaps half are thrill seekers with no realistic hope of winning. After ten years of working his way up and watching, Anthony Holden, a journalist and good amateur poker player, took great pride in finally entering and finishing ninetieth—far out of the money, which was shared by the top nine. The next year, after laboring to polish his game, he again finished in the middle of the pack. The writer A. Alvarez had a similar experience. Few amateurs could expect to do as well, but, unlike the pros, those who enter have little or no expectation of making money, even in the long run. They have other objectives, even if they are not, like Holden and Alvarez, able to recoup their entry fees by writing about the experience.

High Rollers

Some of the fuel for the industry of commercial poker-playing comes from the often huge losses of high-rolling amateur gamblers, of whom wealthy Japanese are lately the most chronicled. They also include businessmen, criminal types,[11] and some athletes and entertainers who have more money than they can easily spend and are prone to gamble, if only for the excitement it provides. Other amateurs, possibly a few thousand, play occasionally in high-stakes commercial poker games or go on poker cruises because they are gamblers. Some of them are compulsive gamblers, and such addicts are the prey of many of the professionals.

Tourists

Far more numerous, more anonymous, and as a group more important are those for whom a casino-gambling trip is vacation time and who wish to gamble a few hundred dollars relatively slowly by playing poker rather than mindlessly playing slot machines or gambling quickly at roulette or craps.[12] In poker, skill *is* a factor, and the illusion of control

11. Gambling is not a bad way to launder money that has been obtained illegally, especially if the launderer is willing to pay taxes on the revenues he pockets.
12. Holden speaks of "the few grand I took with me as my birthday treat" (*Big Deal*, p. 7).

is important to many who play in casinos. The games these tourists play vary from those with a very low limit right up to the biggest ones. Casinos provide games with stakes for every pocketbook, as well as variety in the kinds of games that are available.

Interestingly, tourists are viewed by the professionals not as valued customers, but as geese, suckers to be exploited. From an economist's perspective, this view is misguided. While professional poker players may think of themselves as unproductive (if they give the subject any thought at all), they are in fact providing a valuable service: they make available the poker games in which tourists can find entertainment at almost any level of stakes, at almost any hour of the day or night. Far from exploiting the tourists whose losses finance their modest earnings, these professionals are serving them by providing an ever-open bazaar for them to buy a few hours' entertainment. They are a rough equivalent of convenience-store operators, or all-night cafe waitresses. The demand for such services draws tourists to gambling houses in Las Vegas, Los Angeles, Atlantic City, and elsewhere. The visitor who sits down with $100 to play poker for a few hours may well have a better than 70-percent chance of losing his stake, but even at $25 an hour this is no more expensive than dinner and the theater or attending a major sporting event. Besides, sometimes the tourist goes home a winner.

Poker rooms are not as profitable a use of space for gambling casinos as slot machines or crap, roulette, or blackjack tables because the action is slower, which explains why many casinos do not offer poker.[13] A great variety of low-

13. From the casino's point of view, poker is a relatively inefficient way of separating big-time gamblers from their money since it takes longer to do so than roulette, baccarat, craps, or even blackjack. But big-time casinos run both high- and low-stakes poker games as a kind of loss-leader that brings people in to play, or to watch, just as do cheap meals, lavish floor shows, and accommo-

stakes poker games is offered in some of the biggest casinos to attract poker players in the hope that they will also engage in other casino gambling.

From the many millions of Americans who play poker, all of the foregoing types account for only a tiny fraction.[14] And this fraction will seem to be the norm only if you live in Las Vegas or similar environments.

AMATEURS WHO PLAY
WITH OTHER AMATEURS

Most poker players have neither seen a poker-playing professional nor visited the poker room of a casino. Yet while they have this in common, they are not all the same. The way you play a given hand depends crucially on who is playing or betting against you. A sophisticated ploy doesn't work against the player who notices nothing, nor against a master who sees through your every move. There are a number of characteristics that can be helpful in defining your opponents, and they can be converted into some stylized personalities—caricatures, really—that will be familiar to most poker players. Here are seven you may know from your Thursday-night game; you'll meet them repeatedly in my illustrations in the chapters that follow.

---

dating hostesses. The expectation (and the reality) is that the gamblers will drop their money, one way or another, before they leave the casino. Of particular relevance is sports betting, which most regular poker players seem unable to resist. It is no coincidence that the poker room is virtually always placed adjacent to the sports betting parlor.

14. One indication of how many may be suggested by the fact that the magazine *Card Player*, which is primarily addressed to casino poker players, has a biweekly production run of 45,000 copies, many of which are distributed free of charge in the poker rooms of gambling casinos.

Dramatis Personae

Tyrone ("Ty") Tass: Ty is a broker at Paine Webber with a clientele that depends on his conservative investment advice. His clients probably don't know that he plays poker regularly, and wouldn't approve if they did. But they needn't worry. Ty is known as a *rock*, a poker player who almost never bluffs, folds a lot even in the face of modest betting, and is content to sit and watch many hands in which he has no part. He does not like to take risks either in business or in poker—that is, he is *risk-averse*. When he stays in a hand, you can be sure he has something more than vague hopes, and when he bets, watch out. This guy never bets his hand unless he must do so to stay in, or until he has a sure thing (called a *lock*, or the *nuts*, or an *immortal*) after the last card has been dealt. He checks often, and passively calls other players' bets even when he has a very strong hand. He lets other people build the pots, or fail to. He makes his killings when someone like Bill (see below) makes a big bet into his sure thing. Whether he wins or loses in a given evening depends on how many people walk into his sandbags.

Ty Tass needs only two or three such killings a night to come out a winner. In most sessions he gets them, and thus is a steady but relatively modest winner in a long evening. He plays what seems to many to be boring poker, and in a game populated by many players like him you will be forced to play the same way if you want to break even. More likely it'll prompt you to find a different group to spend your Thursday nights with.

Ty thrives on the loose play of poor poker players, on people who are playing to pass the time of day, and on those who do not adjust to him. Better poker players know his game and tend to avoid confrontations with him. The more they do, the less his winnings. He gets bluffed out often but doesn't seem to mind.

William (Buffalo Bill") Baxter: Ask about his occupation and he'll tell you he's "in oil." Actually he is a former manufacturer's representative for a company that makes peanut oil who has recently been appointed regional sales manager and moved into town. Bill has added spice to the game. Anytime he has a credible winning hand with his showing cards, he'll bet it to the hilt. He is unembarrassed by being caught bluffing, and gets enormous satisfaction when he gets away with one, which he always lets you know about one way or another. Bill loves to gamble and is a *risk-seeker.* He is a frequent victim of Ty's sandbags, but he not only wins some bluffs but gets called a lot when he has a winning hand.

Bill talks all the time and never tells the truth. If he says, "Gimme a heart," you know he doesn't have a heart flush going, but is looking for a card that pairs him. He intends to mislead, but his consistent lying is, in fact, informative. Talking about your hand is not a problem in itself, as long as it doesn't give away information.[15]

Charles ("Duke") Steele: He is known as Mr. Steele to the teachers at the high school where he is principal, and as Coach to the kids on the tennis team, which he coaches, but to everyone else he is Duke, as in John Wayne. His high moral standards are well known, in no small part because he makes a point of telling you about them regularly.

Duke will not be bluffed out, and can be counted on to "keep people honest" whenever he has an above-average hand. He assumes the bettor is bluffing at least half of the time, and regards his losing calls as a small price to pay to

15. An interesting sidelight: table talk is intended to mislead one's opponents, and even good players believe the way to do this is not to tell the truth most of the time. As an experiment one night, I told the truth every time I talked about my hand, and did so often. No one noticed.

avoid the humiliation of folding what turns out to be the winning hand. This can be annoying if you have the third-best hand and bluff the best hand out only to lose to stubborn Duke. But he regularly calls your good hands, too, and makes you a winner and himself a steady loser. Duke regards bluffers as close to criminals, and doesn't accept the notion that folding the winning hand some of the time is to be accepted and expected. Even Bill is learning not to bluff when Duke is in the hand.

David ("Doc") Wright: Professor Wright has a Ph.D. in math from Cornell and teaches probability and statistics at the local college. He regards poker as the science of applied probability. (If you call his house on poker night, his wife and kids are asked to say that he is attending a probability seminar.) He neither seeks risk nor is averse to it—he is *risk-neutral.* Doc has studied seven books by acknowledged experts, knows the right way to play any given set of cards, and does so almost without variation. In 7-card stud he always drops unless he has a high pair in the first four cards; in draw he never opens under the gun without at least two pair, and he never keeps a kicker. If there are two raisers in a hand, he will drop out unless he has a lock. Since his rigid rules are based on sensible principles, he doesn't do badly, because most of his opponents don't notice, don't believe, or don't remember; if they did, his predictability would do him in. He knows the odds of everything, but rarely goes beyond them. A mathematical genius, he'll gladly tell you that you were lucky to win that big pot because the chances of hitting the winning card were only one in seven. "Is that so?" you say as you stack your newly won chips. He'll tend to play a given hand the same way whether it's against Bill, Ty, or Duke. He believes that it's the probabilities, not the pot odds or the opponents, that require his energies.

A regular if small winner in your game, Doc takes his vacations in Las Vegas and doesn't understand why he usually seems to lose in the poker games there. He wonders if the games are honest.

Louis ("Lucky Lou") Lang: Lou is a sportswriter for the local paper and a stringer for *Sports Illustrated*. He is no longer married and believes that the old saying that begins "Lucky in love . . ." means he should win at poker. He is superstitious, frequently refers to his horoscope, which is usually quite positive (hence his nickname), and has been known to drive his car around the block a dozen times if he can thereby improve the poker hand on his odometer before parking at the site of the game. Lou always has the feeling that "this time" things are going to work out for him. He knows that drawing to a pair of 8's or two to a flush isn't usually a good idea, but he remembers one time when he did so and won a big pot, and now he feels he's "due" again. After all, only last month he won a set of golf clubs in a charity drawing when the odds were at least 200 to 1 against him. Lou hangs in there on high hopes and is enough of an optimist to remember his triumphs and forget the hands that didn't work out. In fact, however, Lou is a regular loser, but he can't help it because he's just been having more than his share of bad luck lately. While other players have hit their flushes, straights, or full houses, he seldom seems to. But by the law of averages, that's bound to turn around, right? A little more knowledge of probability would help him a lot, and Doc reminds him of this regularly.

("Hardluck") Harry Hansen: Harry is Lou's opposite number and his best friend since high school. He is called "Hardluck Harry" because, though he's a successful real estate agent, he always seems to be talking about a big deal that got away. He keeps it up until you say to him, "Hard luck, Harry." So far in his poker-playing life he has also been unlucky: he never seems to get the cards that will turn a promising hand into a winning one even when it seems he can hardly miss. But he doesn't believe in fate and keeps trying, confident that his luck will change. He kids Lou about his superstitions. Harry doesn't believe in superstitions because, he says, "They're unlucky." He too could benefit from a bit more knowledge about probability.

Kenneth ("Knott") Wah Chin: Wah is a third-generation Chinese-American whose grandfather made it out of the laundry by opening a Chinese restaurant that gradually achieved gourmet acclaim. His father named him Kenneth to make it easier for him in school, but he prefers to be called by the family name Wah. Wah manages his family's far-flung investments, including a restaurant chain and an import-export business. His special pride, his own creation, is a vegetarian health-food restaurant called Sweeney's.

Wah professes to take his poker seriously but always seems to be thinking about something else. He often has to be told when it's his turn to bet or call, and Doc's nickname for him, Not (as in "Watchin' . . . *not!*"), has caught on. Wah loves it, pretends it's spelled Knott, and has even changed his business cards to read: K. W. Chin. At his worst, he'll sit with a 5, 6, 8, 9, looking for a straight even though an opponent is showing a pair of 7's and the other two 7's have been folded.

Counting cards is hard in games like blackjack, and Knott doesn't want to work hard; after all, this is recreation. Anyway, he reasons, things average out. (Actually, counting is pretty easy in poker, because the only cards you have to remember are the ones that have been folded in the course of one hand.) Most of the time Knott does watch for the cards he needs for his own hand and only forgets about the rest. In the end, when he has his Aces and 5's, he won't have a clue about whether your pair of 8's showing is likely to have a third 8 behind it. Eights weren't important to him when all those other guys dropped out. This matters a lot if you make a big bet into him and he has to decide whether you are bluffing or have him beat.

Imagine yourself now as a regular in the group with these seven, one of whom is usually out of town. If they behaved the way I have characterized them all the time, playing against them would be easy. Indeed, any consistent behavior or strategy, if thoroughly understood, can be advantageously exploited.[16]

But don't forget that these are caricatures, not real people. What makes poker fascinating, fun, and sometimes frustrating is that it is played against human beings. Unlike chess, poker is a game of dissimulation; every poker player tries to sell you a bill of goods—either that his hand is better than it is so that you will drop out, or that it is worse, so that you will call or raise. He does so intentionally (and there is no stigma attached to either his lying or his trying to mislead) by conversation, by mannerisms, and by the size and pattern of his bets. But he is also likely to give you information unintentionally that lets you penetrate his disguises. While a good deal has been written about *tells*— habits that give away a player's hand—the most common and most reliable clues often come in the *patterns of play* observable not in a given hand but over many sessions. Many poker players fall into one of the styles sketched here 80 or more percent of the time. That is far more than enough to justify remembering and playing against the style as well as against the cards. Unlike Doc, *you* are able to vary your play depending on who your opponent is in a given hand.

---

16. This is the weakness of most of the computer poker games I have seen: you can learn the rules that govern your computer opponents, while they do not learn about and adapt to you.

The really good poker player, whom I'll call Hugh, but who may be you, is none of these guys, or, more accurately, he is each of them some of the time. It is possible for a poker player, like an actor, to invent and reinvent himself, and to play many roles and thus be unpredictable.

GAMES

Anaconda, Baseball, Cincinnati, Draw; Hi-Lo, Holdem,
Mississippi, Razz; Rembrandt, Monte, Lowball, Stud;
Jackpots, Utah, Kankakee . . .

These are just some of the 133 names for varieties of poker
listed in a book published in 1971,[1] and there are even more
that are regularly played today. All of them, however, may
be divided into three main categories: draw, stud, and
widow (or common-card) poker, which vary from one another in a few key ways. Fortunately it is possible to illustrate all the important aspects of poker by considering only
a few variations of the games.

BASIC RULES OF THE GAMES

Draw Poker

In draw poker, after an ante each player is dealt five cards.
The player to the left of the dealer acts first and either
checks or opens the betting. Play proceeds clockwise, with
each player acting in turn. Once a bet has been made, the
next player has the option of folding, calling the previous

1. A. D. Livingston, *Advanced Poker: Strategy and Smart Winning Play*
(N. Hollywood: Wilshire Book Co., 1971).

bet, or raising. If no bet has been made, the player may check or open the betting. There may or may not be minimum initial requirements to open the hand. If not, the game is called *guts*. If a pair of Jacks or better is required to open, the game is called *Jackpots,* or *Jacks-or-better,* or, more simply, *Jacks*. If the hand is not opened, players re-ante and the deal is repeated. As soon as the hand is opened, a round of betting occurs, and those calling the opening-round bets may then in sequence discard from their hands and *draw* up to three replacement cards from the undealt deck to form their final hand.[2] After the draw there is a second round of betting, with the opener betting or checking first, and the best hand among those who call the second-round bets is the winner.

Stud Poker

5-card.   After an ante, each player is dealt two cards: one down (the *closed,* or *hole,* card), one up (the *open,* or *up,* card); then a round of betting ensues. It is followed, sequentially, by three more up cards, after each of which there is a betting round, and the best remaining hand wins.[3]

6-card.   The same as 5-card, except there is one more card, dealt down, after the round of betting on the fifth card. A player's hand consists of the best five of the six cards dealt.

7-card.   The same as 6-card, except that the initial deal consists of two down cards and one up card, before the first betting round. The fourth, fifth, and sixth cards are dealt

---

2. If there are insufficient cards to permit all players to complete their draws, the practice is to shuffle the discards of previous players and complete the draw from them.
3. In one variation it is possible to have the last card dealt down.

up, one at a time, and the seventh card is dealt down. A player's hand consists of the best five of the seven cards available to him.

Widow Games

The key feature of *widow* games is that the open cards (or, common cards) are not the exclusive property of a particular player but are part of each player's hand.

In *Holdem* (also known as *Hold'em*, *Hold-me*, and *Texas Holdem*), each player is dealt two down cards, followed by a round of betting. The first three common cards (the *flop*) are then dealt face up, followed by a second betting round. Subsequently two more common cards are exposed (on the *turn*, and on the *river*), each one followed by a betting round.[4] The player's hand may be taken from *any five* of the seven cards available to him—his two down cards and the five cards in the widow.

In *Omaha* the common cards are dealt in the same manner as in Holdem. The differences are, first, that the initial deal is four cards to each player, and, second, that the player's hand, though based on the nine cards available to him, is constrained: *it must consist of exactly two from his down cards and three from the widow.*

Table 4.1 summarizes the characteristics of these different types of games in a few key dimensions that will be discussed in this chapter. The differences are important in judging the suitability of specific varieties of games for specific poker groups.

---

4. Among professionals, who proliferate jargon, the turn and the river are sometimes called Fourth Street and Fifth Street, respectively. Indeed, in any game the use of "Street" to indicate the round of betting is common, preceded by a number that refers to the number of cards each player has available. Thus, for example, the next-to-last round in 7-card stud is referred to as Sixth Street.

Table 4.1 Characteristics of Different Varieties of Poker

GAME	Winning Hand Chosen from This Number of Cards	Open/ Closed Cards	Common Cards	Betting Rounds	Restrictions That May Apply
DRAW	5 (+ up to 3 replaced)	0/5	0	2	opening requirements to be met
STUD					
5-card	5	4/1	0	4	none
6-card	6	4/2	0	5	none
7-card	7	4/3	0	5	none
WIDOW					
Holdem	7	5/2	5	4	none
Omaha	9	5/4	5	4	must use two from closed, three from open, cards

REASONS FOR VARIETY

A first reason for variety is simply that people have different tastes and find one or another game more fun—or easier to play or win at—than another.[5] Casinos offer choices of games as well as stake levels because it serves their purposes to cater to a broad range of tastes. A similar variety of tastes

5. There are two different sorts of variety, that among tables and that from deal to deal at a given table. A casino will offer several different varieties of poker by having tables devoted to each of them, but at a specific table a single game (e.g., 7-card stud) is played for a prespecified set of stakes. Most amateur (home) games allow the dealer to choose any one of a number of games.

among a group of regulars who play together may well
exist, and is easier to accommodate by compromise than by
being restricted to a single game. Thus, allowing *dealer's
choice*—that is, giving the dealer the right to choose—seems
both fair and democratic. (In such games it is common to
put some constraints on what the dealer may choose—for
example, outlawing wild cards or certain varieties of poker
that a majority of the players dislike.)

More fundamentally, many varieties of poker see regular
play because different games are better suited to different
sets of stakes. What makes poker interesting to play is *action:* the presence of more than occasional confrontations
and of more than occasional big pots relative to the stakes of
the game. In pot-limit or high-limit games, this action may
come by way of a single large bet or raise, and thus even two
legitimate betting interests may suffice. In low-limit games,
big pots require multiple bets and raises, and this is best
achieved by having a lot of players believing that they have
a reasonable chance of winning a given hand. Certain games
produce and sustain multiple legitimate betting interests,
and thus work well even with modest betting limits.[6]

Beyond these explanations of the value of diversity are
others that are no less real. Skill and familiarity with the special features of a game play a role, and better players may
choose to exploit poorer ones by giving full rein to their
knowledge of probability, and of how probabilities change
as the game chosen changes. Shifting back and forth between games where the relative value of, say, a straight
varies from being a very good hand to a mediocre one can
set a trap for the less-experienced player. Those who introduce a new or unfamiliar game under the guise of dealer's
choice often have a big advantage over their opponents, at
least for a while. Beware of the player who *regularly* intro-

---

6. To define what constitutes a "legitimate betting interest" requires the concept of expected value. This is discussed in Chapter 6 (see p. 99).

duces "new and interesting" variations on familiar games. He is often attempting to exploit the other players' mistaken illusions about what constitutes a good hand.

An avoidable source of variety in dealer's-choice games arises when there is a big advantage to the position of the dealer relative to the other players in some varieties but not in others.[7] Players who seek every advantage may elect regularly to deal such a game while their opponents exercise their preferences for games where position confers no such advantage. This advantage can and should be neutralized by having some means of rotating the position of the person *under the gun,* independent of the position of the dealer. One way is to have a token (*button*) of some sort that passes around the table every time a hand is dealt where initial position is important.[8]

HOW GAMES DIFFER FROM ONE ANOTHER

The poker games that people play differ from one another in a limited number of dimensions, of which the following five are particularly important:

1. the number of cards from which the hand is chosen;
2. the amount and timing of information available about opponents' hands;
3. the number and structure of betting rounds;

---

7. Being in the dealer's position is particularly advantageous in draw poker and in Holdem, where the privilege of acting after all the others have done so is an enormous advantage, but it is also true to some extent in all games where position in the betting sequence is determined by position at the table rather than by the showing cards.

8. A final reason affecting the choice of game is, sad to report, that not all games are honest, and it is much easier to cheat in some games than in others. This is the case, for example, if there is one or a small number of critical, or key, cards. It is a lot easier to deal one or two cards "off the bottom" than to control the whole deal.

4. the extent to which common cards may or must be used;
5. the definition of the winning hand.

These dimensions affect the play and are important determinants of why particular games are well suited to particular purposes.[9]

1. Number of Cards

Most poker games define the winning hand in terms of five cards.[10] Indeed, the rank order of hands and the conventional view of the value of hands is based on the distribution of the roughly 2.6 million *different* five-card hands that can be dealt from a normal fifty-two-card deck, as shown in Table 4.2.[11] Don't bother to memorize this table. The fact is that in virtually every kind of poker game except the rarely played 5-card stud, the five cards that are used to define the winning hand are selected from among a larger number.

The availability of more than five cards with which to fashion a five-card poker hand is important because it critically changes the value (measured by its relative scarcity) of

9. Among other dimensions that are not discussed here is the use of wild cards. Because they so distort the odds, wild cards are not popular among serious players, nor in games where the stakes are big enough that there is plenty of action. (If players in such games wish more action they generally prefer increasing the number of cards, allowing replacement, or playing Hi-Lo games to the use of wild cards.) Wild cards greatly increase the element of chance and likewise reduce the skill required to play and have fun. This makes the game popular in nickel-dime and other low-stakes games and thus highly suitable for family or couples' poker, where some of the players are bound to be less experienced and skillful than others but where there is no desire to exploit this fact. Wild-card poker is also a nice way for children to play at poker even with no stakes other than chips.
10. The major exception to this statement is 3-card monte, a once-famous form of poker on the carnival circuit that had its appeal in the speed with which each hand could be played.
11. Mathematically we are looking at all combinations of fifty-two things taken five at a time. Some poker games are played with a fifty-three-card deck, using a joker as a limited wild card. This does not change the basic probabilities drastically and is discussed in Chapter 12.

Table 4.2　Distribution of Poker Hands

(taking 5 cards from a 52-card deck)

HAND	Number	Odds (1 chance in:)	Percentage of All Hands	Percentage of Hands Worse
Straight flush	40	64,974	0.0015%	99.9985%
4 of a kind	624	4,165	0.024	99.97
Full house	3,744	694	0.144	99.83
Flush	5,108	509	0.197	99.63
Straight	10,200	255	0.392	99.24
3 of a kind	54,912	47	2.11	97.13
2 pair	123,552	21	4.75	92.37
1 pair	1,098,240	2.4	42.26	50.12
No pair	1,302,540	2.0	50.12	—
ALL HANDS	2,598,960		100.00	

a particular hand. As Table 4.2 shows, a full house is a rare event in a five-card deal: it occurs in only 1 in 694 hands. If you are one of seven players in a draw poker game, each deal will consist of seven hands dealt, so the chances of someone around the table being dealt a full house is about 1 in 100. Since a typical evening's poker game usually covers about one hundred deals, you would expect to see a *pat* full house—that is, one present on the deal—about once an evening if you played nothing but 5-card draw.[12]

Additional cards.　When poker hands are selected from among more than five cards, the chances of getting any particular five-card combination increases, as shown in Table 4.3. *This one is worth memorizing.*

12. Full houses would be less frequent in an evening of 5-card stud, because many of what might become full houses after five cards would have folded before that. If a player's first two cards were a 2 and a 6, and there was an Ace betting, this player would most likely have folded long before he received the 2, 6, 2, if he had stayed in to see all five cards.

Table 4.3   Number of Different 5-Card Poker Hands

Number of Cards	Number of Hands
5	1
6	6
7	21
8	56
9	126

If you are playing with six cards instead of five, you have the equivalent of *six* different five-card hands to choose from, so you have six chances instead of one to get that full house.[13] If you are playing six-card poker and three of the players stay in to the end of the deal, there are 18 different five-card hands present; 694 divided by 18 is 38.5, which suggests that you should expect to witness a full house in about one deal of every forty of this game. In other words, if it is played all evening, you would expect a full house two or three times during the evening.

If you are playing with seven cards, as in 7-card stud, there are *twenty-one* different five-card hands among your seven cards.[14] If three players stick around to see all seven

13. There are six combinations of five cards each; in other words, you can leave out each one of the six cards in turn, and be left with a different five-card hand.
14. Mathematically we are calculating the combinations of seven things taken five at a time. This is the same number as you get taking seven things two at a time, since every five-card combination in effect leaves out a two-card combination. Consider a specific seven-card hand: you can leave out any two cards and still have a five-card hand. The first card left out can be any one of the original seven—say, the five of hearts (5♥), so there are seven different six-card hands. The second card can be any one of the remaining six, say the Queen of clubs (Q♣). At first glance this seems to suggest forty-two different two-card exclusions ($7 \times 6 = 42$), and thus forty-two different five-card hands in each seven-card hand. But the forty-two exclusions include both the 5♥, Q♣ combination and the Q♣, 5♥ combination. Since the remaining five cards are not different, we have to eliminate the double counting. There are only twenty-one *different* two-card exclusions, and thus only twenty-one different five-card hands among seven cards.

cards, there will be sixty-three different five-card hands, which means that you should see a full house about once in every ten deals. (Don't forget that *you* will get this hand much less often.) A full house, a very scarce event as a pat hand in draw poker, occurs on average about twice an hour in a 7-card stud game. As a general rule, "good hands"— say, better than a straight—occur about five times as often in a six-card game, and fourteen times as often in a seven-card game as they do in five cards.[15]

Table 4.4   How the Winning Hand Changes

(percentage of deals, seven-player showdown)

Best hand is better than:	in 5 cards	in 6 cards	in 7 cards
Pair of Aces	42.6%	78.5%	96.8%
Aces-up	18.4	41.1	68.6
Three Aces	5.2	23.1	53.8
Straight	2.5	12.6	34.3
Flush	1.2	6.1	18.0

Table 4.4 shows that while a pair of Aces is going to win more often than not in 5-card stud—it is beaten only 42.6 percent of the time—it is a distinct long shot in 7-card stud, where it is beaten nearly 97 percent of the time.[16] Similarly,

15. Poorer hands, such as a pair of Aces or two pair, apparently paradoxically, will occur less frequently in seven cards than in five. But the paradox is easily resolved. It's not that a pair of Aces is harder to get in seven cards than in five; it is, instead, that although there are more pairs of Aces, they are much more frequently improved to a better hand. Thus, a pair of Aces after five cards will often become two pair, three of a kind, or better with two additional cards.
16. Table 4.4 assumes that all seven hands receive all their cards. This makes it overstate the quality of the winning hand for the reasons suggested in note 12 (above): the winning hand will be selected from the hands that have stayed in to receive all seven cards, and many hands that might ultimately have proved to be winners will be folded before they reach their full potential.

three Aces, which is a superb holding in five cards, is the best hand among seven 7-card stud hands only about half the time.

An experienced poker player quickly develops an empirical or intuitive sense of the relative frequency of particular hands. Thus, in 7-card stud, a straight, though still a good hand, is hardly what you want to bet the farm on. **You must learn to adjust the five-card odds by the number of card combinations from which a five-card hand is chosen.** Novices repeatedly overvalue their hands by forgetting this adjustment.[17]

In short, choosing one's five-card hand from among a greater number of cards not only gives the psychological advantages of having higher-ranked hands to play with, but also of preserving probabilities for improving hands that are not currently good enough to win. This means that more players can legitimately stay in the hand in the early rounds to see the cards in later rounds, and this will increase the size of the pot and lead to a larger number of contested hands.

Replacement. Similar to adding to the number of cards chosen, but not as dramatic in increasing the number of choices, is the hopeful option of replacing some of the original cards with new ones. Draw poker is the most familiar example of permitting replacement, and its name comes from that feature. **The effect of replacement is to increase**

---

17. An inexpensive way to add to your experience is to deal out a number of hands and observe the relative frequencies. For example, deal out a block of forty-nine cards, seven across and seven down. This contains sixteen easily readable seven-card hands—seven vertically, seven horizontally, and the two diagonals. Not only will you quickly develop a sense of the relative frequency of, say, three of a kind or better, but you will also, by examining groups of seven hands at one time, get some sense of what is likely to be the winning hand in a given deal. It will, however, overstate the relative quality of the of the winning hand, for the reasons suggested in notes 12 and 16.

somewhat the number of cards from which one may make a hand, but not to the same extent that extra cards would do.

In draw poker, where you are dealt five cards and may replace up to three of them, you are better off than if you had to play with only the initial five, but not nearly as fortunate as if you were dealt eight cards from among which to pick any five. If this is not obvious, a simple example will suffice. Suppose in Jackpots (Jacks-or-better) you hold Q, Q, J, 10, 9, of assorted suits. After the initial bet you have the opportunity to draw up to three cards. Your practical alternatives are to draw three cards to your Queens *or* to draw one card to the straight. You cannot do both. If you choose to draw three to the pair of Queens you must give up the J, 10, 9; if you draw to the straight you must give up your good pair. It would be very different if you could draw three cards and *then* decide which five to use. In that situation you would be able to choose the best one among the fifty-six different five-card hands in the eight cards. In that case, not only might you have your straight—and, unlike a normal draw to a straight, you would have three chances to get it, not one—but you could end up with a flush, any one of many different full houses, or even four of a kind.

Replacement is designed to give hope, and thus to motivate a willingness to stay in with *drawing* hands—potentially good hands that are not quite there—but without devaluing certain hands by nearly as much as adding the same number of cards would do (as can happen with *additional* cards). This has the attraction of keeping the five-card probabilities a moderately reliable guide to the relative frequency of hands, though of course it does modify them.

While draw poker is the classic example of replacement, permission to replace one or more cards may be added to almost any other game. For example, in 5- or 6-card stud, it is possible to provide for a round of replacement after the last card has been dealt and a betting round has ensued.

This has several features that encourage more betting in the game. First, by retaining the potential for improvement it will increase the value of some hands that would otherwise have been folded. Second, the replacement round adds another round of betting and thus increases the size of the ultimate pot. Third, it adds to the information available about the different hands.

2. Information Available

Varieties of poker games differ from one another in *how much* information about opponents' hands is revealed, and *when*.

Open cards. The most unambiguous source of information about the hands of your opponents is in the up cards that have been dealt. Stud poker and widow poker tend to reveal a great deal of information this way, draw poker none.

Either too much or too little information about opponents' hands is likely to lead to infrequently contested pots. With a great deal of information revealed, one hand is likely to be clearly dominant, and to find itself taking a small pot when the other players fold. This is often the case in 5-card stud. With only one closed card there is only limited uncertainty. After the fifth card, one of the players will frequently know that he has a lock. While this may seem like an attractive feature—it is, of course, to him—it is likely to eliminate most other betting interests and certainly contributes to the limited appeal that 5-card stud holds today. When your opponent is in a position to *know* that he has a sure winner against you, you will be reluctant to call, will never raise, and dare not attempt to bluff. Further, he will be able to bluff, and you will find it expensive to keep him honest. This would be totally disabling if all of the information were available at once, but it is mitigated since the open cards are dealt one at a time. What saves 5-card stud from being a totally unsatisfactory form of poker is its multiple rounds, each of which adds incrementally to the information revealed.

At the other extreme, with little information, is draw poker, where you are forced to fall back on the pure probabilities that your hand will prove a winner, and where large contested pots only occur when two or more players think they hold very strong hands. Too little information has one advantage over too much: it makes successful bluffing a realistic possibility, and probably explains why draw poker was one of the classic games of the old-style, inscrutable, poker-faced poker players of fiction.

Because of the drawbacks of either too much or too little information, the most popular games seek a middle ground and combine some open cards, which are revealed gradually, and some hidden ones. The open cards provide clues to a hand's quality that can be combined with inferences from the betting, while the hidden ones provide elements of surprise or deception that can be used to increase uncertainty, to nourish hopes, and to encourage bluffing and the possibility of bluffing.

Six- and 7-card stud move in this direction. Six-card stud is played with both the first and last cards dealt down. The presence of two hidden cards to go with the four up cards doubles the number of uncertainties present in 5-card stud and thus makes locks less likely and increases the number of contested hands. Seven-card stud has three down cards and four up cards. Here the large number of five-card combinations, in many of which up to three cards may be hidden, eliminates most of the situations in which one player can be sure he has the winning hand but still provides a lot of information with which you can form judgments about your chances of prevailing. This is a major reason why 7-card stud has become an especially popular form of poker.

The widow games of Holdem and Omaha have even more open cards (five) to combine with closed cards (two in

Holdem and four in Omaha). If all of this information were revealed at once it would destroy most of the action, but the revelation is designed to progress from an initial situation of no information in the first round of betting (before the flop), to a major infusion by way of three open cards on the flop, and then the addition of two more open cards, one by one. It is this progression that gives the widow games their essential character, for it requires players to become adept at processing the changes in information available to them as the hand progresses.

Replacement as an information source.   Replacement gives information as well as increasing choices. In draw poker the number of cards drawn is directly revealing. In stud, if you replace a down card, it leaves you stuck with the up cards; if you replace an up card, it reveals which of those cards you valued the least, and thus sharpens the plausible inferences that others can make about your hole cards. If a player doesn't replace—that is, if he *stands pat*—this too tells a lot about his hand.

In games other than draw poker in which replacement is permitted, the right to do so is sometimes accompanied by a fee. This has several functions if the fee is not trivial.[18] First, it increases the size of the pot. Second, it gives the person with a hand that is already very good the opportunity to stand pat while others build the pot through the replacement fee. And third, it creates some significant bluffing opportunities.

Anytime a player's action may reveal information about his hand, it provides an opportunity for deliberately falsifying the information. For example, a player may stand pat on a mediocre hand in order to convey the impression that it is

18. As a rule of thumb, the fee should be around 10 percent of the typical pot at the time of the replacement round. This is not prohibitive, but neither is it negligible.

a very strong one. A bluff may be his only chance of winning the pot and is an alternative to folding. Here is an example from 6-card stud with a replacement permitted after the sixth-card round. Your open cards are J♥, 10♥, 9♠, and 2♥, threatening either a straight or a heart flush. But your hole cards are A♠, and 3♠, giving you a worthless holding since no single replacement will improve it enough to give you a winner. If, however, you bet or raise with this hand before the replacement round and then stand pat, it will be difficult for an opponent to call a bet on the final round unless he can beat a straight.

While there is, from one source or another, often lots of information available about who holds what cards, such information is not always used. **The information available has to be noticed and interpreted to be useful.** Here is a place where skill and concentration decidedly enter into the playing of poker.

3. Number of Betting Rounds

One important effect of the number of betting rounds, as noted above, is to permit the gradual increase in the amount of information you have about your own hand and those of your opponents. A betting round occurs with each change in the number of cards that are available. Because of the betting the acquisition of additional information costs money, and this fact forces players to confront the question of whether they wish to pay the price.

Putting an incremental cost on additional cards and their associated reduction of uncertainty affects also the nature of what in fact wins, and becomes an element of strategy. By raising the cost of getting an additional card, say by making a big bet or raise, a player can try to induce opponents to fold their hands. They must balance the worth of the increased information against the cost of getting it. In a multiround game these opportunities are repeated round by round.

The other major impact of multiple betting rounds is the effect they have on the ultimate size of the pot. Even in a limit game, a single enthusiastic bettor, whose ability to build a pot in any single round is strictly limited, can build a bigger pot if he has several opportunities to initiate betting. A somewhat different impact occurs in pot-limit poker. Bets in the early rounds are a device to lay the foundation for big bets later—bets that may be either strategic attempts to force opponents out or to extract revenue from them if they call.

There is no unambiguous answer to the question of what the optimal number of betting rounds is, but the most popular games seem to have four or five, and there is a certain logic to numbers in that range. At the first betting round there is typically little information available about opponents' hands, and not much about your own. Typically you are operating on the basis of what are abstractly better or worse starting hands, and doing so in the face of pots whose size, as determined by the antes or their equivalents, is small. While there may be several players, the betting is typically restrained. By the last betting round, there is so much information, and no uncertainty about your own hand, that there are usually few players—often only one—interested in betting heavily, and a last-round bet is frequently uncalled. It is in the intermediate rounds that the action is likely to be heavy, with multiple legitimate betting interests. At every betting round your status is likely to have changed from the previous round, and it remains contingent on what will happen on the next rounds. These changes motivate and lead to changed betting scenarios. Players must rethink, round by round, the inferences they can make based upon the information available to them, as well as the resulting probabilities of their hands becoming or remaining the winner. Here experience and skill are demanded and rewarded.

The absence of those intermediate rounds prevents draw poker from being a popular game in limit poker. Since having intermediate rounds is beneficial to the action of the game, would more be better? For example, in 7-card stud why not bet after each of the first three cards is dealt, instead of only after all three, thus creating seven rounds instead of five? One answer is that beyond a certain point additional rounds will simply add to the time a hand takes to play without supplying the changed circumstances that motivate a new betting round.[19] In the case of any of these games there is a certain critical minimum number of cards you need to see before you can make a sensible stay/fold decision. Seeing only the first widow card, or your first down card, provides some information, but rarely enough to determine behavior.[20] If there were separate rounds one could anticipate either everyone checking, or else a nominal bet with virtually everyone calling.[21] Extra rounds of this sort bring no gains and waste time.

A second major disadvantage of more betting rounds is that an extra round usually adds to the cost of seeing a hand through to the end, and thus has the effect of increasing the effective stakes of the game. If this object is desired, it can be more easily accomplished directly; if it is undesired, it suggests limiting the number of betting rounds.

In any case, the most popular games seldom have less than three betting rounds nor more than five. What survives and thrives is market-tested.

---

19. Particularly for the players who fold early and must sit through the remainder of the hand, any increase in the time it takes to wait for the next deal is undesirable.

20. As I will argue in Chapters 13 and 14, it may be the case in 7-card stud games as played in Thursday-night poker that the distinction between the first and second betting rounds is pretty small and they might well be merged.

21. Where the critical minimum number of cards occurs depends in part on the stakes and structure of the game. There are differences (discussed in Chapter 13) between restrained and aggressive versions of 7-card stud, as well as differences between Holdem and Omaha (discussed in Chapter 16).

4. Common Cards

Several features of widow games such as Omaha and Holdem deserve special attention since they help to account for the rise in popularity of those games. First, once all the common cards have been exposed, it is always possible to define the best possible hand, and it is often possible to predict the winning hand. Second, since all players share the common cards, their final hands will often be highly similar, and may even be identical. Thus the value of a given hand is different than it would be in non-widow games. For example, in Omaha, if the widow contains a pair, it is likely that more than one player will have three of a kind or a full house. Or to take another example, if the widow shows four cards to a straight, it is quite likely that three or more players may each have a straight, and relying on your knowledge that "on average" straights are powerful hands is of virtually no interest. Instead, the relevant question is: Given this particular widow, how likely is my straight to be the best straight? In widow games, apparently minor differences in players' closed cards are often decisive. Suppose the widow shows **A, K, K, 5, 2,** with no flush possibilities.[22] If no one holds a King, two or more players may each hold an Ace and thus have the identical high two pair. If so, the winner will be determined by whether the fifth card is, say, a 10 or a 9. **The use of common cards puts a great premium on evaluating your chances in the specific circumstances of the deal, rather than on general probabilities.** This adds an important skill dimension to playing poker and explains the popularity of widow games among the top professionals.[23]

---

22. In examples from widow games, I will use boldface to designate common cards.
23. Despite identical use of common cards and the number and structure of betting rounds, Holdem and Omaha exhibit important differences. These matters are explored in Chapters 15 and 16.

5. Definition of Winning Hand

A further source of variety in poker games is the definition of what constitutes the best hand. The three main varieties of poker games are high-only, low-only, and high-low.

In high-only poker the rank of hands is the familiar one based on the distribution shown in Table 4.2, with a straight flush the highest hand, four of a kind the next highest, and so on down to one pair, and finally no pair but with the highest card determining the better of two hands.

In low-only poker, usually called *lowball,* this table of values is inverted, and a good hand will not have a pair and will be judged by how low its highest card is.[24] In lowball the Ace is usually construed as a low card, and thus the best low hand possible is the 6, 4, 3, 2, A, provided the cards are not all of the same suit. Because the rank of the highest card determines the merit of the hand, an 8, 7, 6, 3, 2, is better than a 9, 4, 3, 2, A. Plainly, too, a hand with no pair is better than a hand with any pair, and a pair of Aces is better (lower) than any other pair.

In high-low poker, which I call *Hi-Lo,* both sets of values apply, and the pot is divided between the best high hand and the best low hand. In Hi-Lo the Ace is always permitted to be counted either as a high card or as a low card, and thus it is possible for the same five cards to constitute both the highest and the lowest hand: For example, the hand A, 8, 6, 3, 2, is both higher *and* lower than the hand K, J, 9, 7, 2 (the Ace counting in the former case as the highest card and in the latter case as the lowest). Similarly, two Aces might be alternatively construed as both the highest and the lowest pair.

24. There are various possible definitions of the best low hand (see the discussion in Chapter 14). The version described here, in which both straights and flushes count against a low hand and in which the Ace is considered a low card, is the most common one in amateur poker games.

The traditional form of poker is high poker, but lowball, and especially Hi-Lo, have gained great popularity in Thursday-night poker games. The reason is that each of them increases the number of legitimate betting interests in a given deal, and this leads to more betting and more contested pots. This is important in amateur games, since most players do not enjoy spending a lot of the evening on deals with uncontested or minimal pots. Poker-playing time is too short for that.

To see how lowball and Hi-Lo increase the number of betting interests, consider a 5-card stud game (high-only) in which after three cards a high pair is showing. A pair received in the first three or four cards is valuable no matter what the later cards turn out to be. It may or may not be improved by later cards, but it will not get any worse. Thus, in 5-card stud, a showing high pair usually will induce all other hands to fold if its owner makes a hefty bet. Indeed, even an Ace shown on the first up card will sometimes reduce the number of players to one or two. By contrast, lowball requires *all five* cards to be counted, and thus even a superb three-card start in 5-card lowball—say, 6, 2, A—will not induce someone holding a less promising hand—say, 8, 7, 3—to despair: the present low hand has two chances to be ruined, or *counterfeited*, as the pros say, by either a high card such as a King, or by a low card that pairs one of the existing cards. Even with four low cards—say, 6, 4, 2, A, a perfect four-card start—this hand will prove to be able to beat the worst 8-low only about 30 percent of the time.[25] The possibility of a good-looking low hand being counterfeited increases the chances that someone holding mediocre cards will win. As a result there are likely to be multiple callers in games that have moderate limits on early-round betting.

---

25. Ace, King, Queen, Jack, 10, 9, 6, 4, or 2—nine of the thirteen ranks—all lead to hands worse than an 8, 7, 6, 5, 3, the worst 8-low.

While lowball can be played in any form of poker, it is usually found in games with more than five cards. For low hands the effect of having more cards to choose among means that hands are counterfeited much less early, and thus the number of persons who can legitimately stay in the hand is increased.

Hi-Lo poker increases the betting interests even more than lowball. By definition there are always *at least two* legitimate betting interests, the most promising high hand and the most promising low hand. A person who has a good chance in either direction is likely to want to stick around to see if the promise is realized. Hi-Lo poker is particularly well suited to games with relatively low limits. In such a game big pots will usually come about only as a result of multiple raises and reraises of the kind that Hi-Lo makes likely.

Hi-Lo poker can also keep several players in the pot for several rounds because a low start that is counterfeited may turn into a good high hand once all the cards are dealt. Further, even if two players are each betting heavily, they may both be going in the same direction, and so someone else may sneak off with half the pot with only a mediocre hand in the other direction. Finally there is always the appealing possibility that you will end up with a hand that wins both the high and low halves of the pot.[26]

The virtues of Hi-Lo for low-limit poker games can become liabilities in a high-limit or pot-limit game. A promising drawing high hand such as four to a high straight, that might, in high-only poker, willingly call even a pot-size bet by the presently best high hand, is likely to be unable to call if someone with the low hand is in a position to raise behind

26. This possibility is greater the larger the number of cards available to a player. This accounts for the great popularity of 7-card Hi-Lo (discussed in Chapter 14), since a player can use one combination of five cards for his high and another for his low.

him. In a pot-limit game there will often be more action if two or three players are fighting over the whole pot than if two are going to split a pot to which their own contributions have been the dominant part.

II

♠ ♣ ♥ ♦

BASICS

5

♠ ♣ ♥ ♦

PROBABILITY AND HOW TO ESTIMATE IT

You are one of twenty-three people at a birthday party, and someone discovers that two of the twenty-three have the same birthday. What a coincidence!

Guildenstern is flipping coins with Rosencrantz and it comes up heads eighty-nine times in a row. Pretty good luck if, like Rosencrantz, you are betting on heads.

Hardluck Harry is playing 7-card stud and at long last has a good hand: he has four spades to the Ace in the first four cards. He looks around the table and sees there are only two other spades showing. Virtually certain now that he will catch a flush, he bets and raises repeatedly against a measly pair of 10's, confident that he will end up the winner, especially since he has the 10 of spades. When, after seven cards, he still hasn't gotten a fifth spade, he leaves the table broke and disgusted. Can there be better proof that the fates are against him?

Each of these situations relates to chance events, and to evaluate them you need to know the likelihood that the event really did occur by chance.

In the first example, it is not a great coincidence after all. Anytime you have twenty-three people together, the chances are about even that two of them will have the same birthday! That's far from obvious, but it is true.[1] I became interested in this phenomenon in 1944 when I was teaching navigation to numerous sections of thirty-five students in the Navy, and for some reason the grade sheets also included the students' birth dates. I noticed that in most sections there was at least one pair of common birthdays. For a long time I wondered what biological oddity or Navy recruiting practice accounted for this but could discover none that seemed credible. Long before I understood the phenomenon as simply the expected result of chance, I accepted it as a fact and regularly made money betting—at no worse than even money—that it would be the case![2] One lesson in this story is that you often develop empirically the sense of how probable an outcome is.

In the second example, the probability of an honest coin producing eighty-nine consecutive heads is so infinitesimal that no rational person would believe it to be true. While it is possible, it is far more likely the result of a two-headed coin—or a writer's imagination.

In the third example, Harry didn't know the probabilities. Four spades is a very good start for a hand of 7-card stud, but the fact is that his chances of getting the fifth spade were only 46 in 100, even though seven spades were unaccounted for. His hand is certainly worth a bet, but it is far from the sure thing you would bet the condominium on. This, too, is not obvious—until you know it.

Propositions in probability sometimes seem like black magic, or at least highly esoteric mathematics, but this need not be the case. This chapter seeks to provide a certain minimum understanding of probabilities and how to approxi-

---

1. In the Appendix to this chapter, I show, for those who are interested, how to calculate the probabilities of each of these examples.
2. With thirty-five people there will be at least one pair of common birthdays 81.44 percent of the time. See the Appendix to this chapter.

mate them. You must be able to compare pot odds (discussed in Chapter 6) with probability odds (discussed in this chapter) to know when, or whether, it makes sense to call a bet. **That much, but no more, probability is required to play poker well.** Much of what you need to know can be acquired though playing experience. But it is not hard (and surely less expensive) to learn what you need to know by some investment of time and energy. That is the aim of this chapter.

WHAT IS PROBABILITY?

The probability of occurrence of a repeated event is the fraction of the trials in which it may be expected to occur. There are several different, but equivalent, ways of expressing this. If there is 1 chance in 5 of an event occurring, the probability of this event is said to be .20. Or we may say it is 20 percent. Or we may say that the *probability odds* of this event occurring are 1 in 5 (20 in 100). Or, still equivalently, the *probability odds against* this event occurring are 4 to 1 (80 to 20). Sometimes it's convenient to talk about probability odds, sometimes about probability expressed as a fraction or a percent. In the poker context, it is often convenient to think about the odds *against* an event, for that, specifically, is what one compares to the pot odds facing a player. This chapter will talk about probabilities, and how to estimate them in the context of playing poker.

The probabilities of many kinds of events are unknown and unknowable—for example, the probability that Venus Williams (now fifteen) will win the United States Open Tennis Championship when she is twenty-three years old. There certainly is a chance that she will, but there is no way of predicting the likelihood of the many elements that go into achieving or preventing this outcome. That is because it is a single event produced by a mechanism that is not fully understood. **But other probabilities, those that are determined by chance from well-understood mechanisms, can be predicted and calculated with accuracy.** You can either conduct repeated trials of an experiment, or you can completely enumerate every possible outcome and then calculate the fraction of those outcomes that constitutes the event in question. Flips of a coin, rolls of dice, and selection of cards from a well-shuffled deck are familiar examples.

Since any given poker hand comes from a chance selection from a fifty-two-card deck, the occurrence of any particular combination, while never certain, can be accurately described in probability terms. For this reason probability calculation does play a role in poker, but its role is less than it might appear at first, and Doc, our Thursday-night probability expert, is not someone you need fear or emulate.

Most standard books about poker will tell you, usually by including a table such as Table 4.2 (shown on page 50), that your chance of having a full house dealt to you in five cards is 1 in 694. This number comes about because, as the table enumerates, there are 2,598,960 possible different five-card hands from a 52-card pack, of which only 3,744 are full houses; and 3,744 in 2,598,960 is the same as 1 in 694.16. (This is also the same as a probability of .00144.) Thus, one will expect to see a full house in only 1/694th of all the possible different five-card poker hands. Table 4.2 is useful in showing the relative scarcity of particular poker hands, and is in fact the basis of the ranking of hands: for example, a flush beats a straight *because* it is scarcer.

Don't bother to memorize these and similar numbers. In the unlikely event that you happen to be playing straight five-card poker and get a full house, you should assume you are going to win the pot, and you should play the hand for all it's worth—at least until something happens to change your mind. This is also what you should do if you get a flush (1 chance in 509), a straight (1 in 255), or even three of a kind (1 in 47). (The combined probability of getting three of a kind or better in five cards is less than .03—less than 1 chance in 33. Thus, even if you have six opponents, your hand is likely to be the best one around.) Of course you may be wrong in any one of these situations, and the chance of being wrong is greater the lower the odds are in your favor. But even 32 to 1, the probability odds against someone beating trips, makes holding three of a kind a very good hand in five cards.

We have already suggested why these five-card probabilities are not very important. First, you are not likely to be playing five-card poker with no extra information. In 5-card draw, you get to replace cards; in 5-card stud, you see a lot of the cards; and in games like 6- or 7-card stud, Omaha, or Holdem, you not only have more than five cards but will also have information from the cards that you see. Second, you are not playing your cards against a card-dealing machine but against other players, and their behavior gives you information about how good they think their hands are relative to yours.[3] Third, the relevant probabilities concern your chances of having the best hand after all the cards have been dealt and the last bet called. These probabilities change with every new card dealt and seen. The table that is going to tell you most about this is the poker table at which you are sitting.

There *are* probabilities you do have to estimate, but they are relatively few and relatively easy to estimate with sufficient accuracy to guide your behavior. **As a general rule, you need to know only how many cards are left that can help you to get or keep the winning hand, how many you have not seen (and thus are potentially avail-**

---

3. Contrast this with blackjack as it is played in casinos, where the dealer has no discretion at all. The dealer *is*, in effect, a card-dealing machine, and there is an unambiguous best strategy for every card holding, given the dealer's showing card and the other cards that have been seen from the deck.

able), and how many opportunities you have to get the cards you need.

If the answers are 6, 30, and 1, respectively, the probability of getting one of these cards is 6 in 30, or .2, or 20 percent, and the probability odds against you are 4 to 1 (24 to 6). What is hard here is not the arithmetic (if it is, then you *are* in trouble) but, first, knowing which cards will make you a winner, and, second, remembering what cards have been shown and turned over.

SOME RULES OF PROBABILITY

Three rules of probability are important enough for the poker player to learn.

RULE 1: The probability of an event occurring *plus* the probability of the event not occurring *equals* 1. If, for example, the chance of getting a heart on the next card is 1 in 5 (probability .2), the probability of not getting a heart is .8. The practical importance of this obvious and seemingly trivial rule is that you can calculate (or estimate) the likelihood of an event either directly or by calculating its opposite, whichever is easier in a particular instance. Sometimes one way is much easier than the other.

RULE 2: The probability of two events *both* occurring is the probability of the first occurring *multiplied by* the probability of the second occurring, given that the first has occurred. The practical importance of this is that since probabilities are all less than one, the probability of a sequence of events all happening is smaller than the probability of any single one of them. For example, the probability of getting a six on the roll of a die is $1/6$. To get boxcars (two sixes) requires getting two successive sixes, and thus is: $1/6 \times 1/6 = 1/36$. The probability of getting three sixes in a row is: $1/36 \times 1/6 = 1/216$; and so on.[4] In this example the probability of the second event did not change when the first occurred.[5] But the probability of getting two hearts in two straight draws from a single deck is: $13/52 \times 12/51 = .059$. The second fraction gives the probability of getting a heart, *given that the first card was a heart*.

RULE 3: The probability of *either* of two events occurring is the probability of the first occurring *plus* the probability of the second occurring *minus* the probability of both occurring.   The subtraction at the end is to avoid double counting. For example, if you are asking about the probability of getting *either* a straight *or* a flush in five cards, you have to recognize that some hands (namely, straight flushes) are both and thus would be counted twice. Sometimes, as with straight flushes, the amount of double counting is very small and can be ignored, and we shall take advantage of this fact, but sometimes there is so much double counting that it cannot be ignored. For example, if you could win by getting a club or an Ace or a 9, the double counting of the Ace of clubs and the 9 of clubs would have to be avoided.

ESTIMATING PROBABILITIES
AT THE POKER TABLE

The kinds of situations in playing poker where you need to apply these rules are limited to a few basic types, for most of which either the calculations are easy or adequate approximations are both easy and available.

---

4. Does it matter if the three dice are thrown in sequence or simultaneously? No. Any simultaneous process can be conceived of as a sequential process with nominal time intervals separating them.
5. Superstitious craps players do not seem to believe this, but the fact is that dice have no memory.

At the poker table you don't have a computer or calculator at your elbow, and even if you did you wouldn't have the time to calculate the exact probability in the fashion illustrated in the Appendix to this chapter. Maybe Doc can do this in his head in a few seconds, but most of us cannot, and in any case the probability is only one of the factors you have to consider. Indeed, if you pause for a long time to calculate the probability odds, as many poker players do on occasion, you give information to a watching opponent, who may be able to figure out what the question must be, and thus gain an advantage. **It is better to be roughly right in a timely fashion than to be precisely right too late to do you any good.**

Fortunately this is usually possible. You need only to estimate and reestimate the situation-specific probabilities as they arise in a poker hand, and these depend on the cards you see or have seen.

One steadily gains from playing experience, at least roughly, a sense of the relative likelihood of what a winning hand is, and the probabilities of attaining it from different starting positions. It is adapting to the situations as they change, card by card, in a particular hand that is necessary, and here some rough-and-ready probability estimates are of more use than a dozen probability tables.

GETTING ONE CARD IN ONE TRY

Needing to catch a key card in one try is a situation that arises repeatedly: when there is one card to go in stud poker or widow games, and with every one-card draw in draw poker. It also arises every time you ask the question: How likely am I in the next round to get a card that strongly improves (or worsens) my prospects?

Take an easy example. Suppose you hold two pairs, Jacks and 10's, after six cards have been dealt in 7-card stud, and your other cards give you no chance of a straight or flush. And let's say that 22 other cards are either showing on the board, or have been turned over as players folded. This means you have seen 28 cards, and that there are 24 hidden ones, some in the closed hands dealt to your opponents, some in the deck. (From your point of view it doesn't matter which, unless the betting has indicated the presence of specific cards in opponents' hands). Only four cards can improve your hand significantly: the two remaining Jacks, or the two remaining 10's. If none has shown, your chances of getting a full house (and being very likely to win) are 4 in 24 (1 in 6); if one has shown, 3 in 24 (1 in 8); if three have shown, your chances of improving are only 1 in 24, which is usually small enough to forget about. And if all four of the helpful cards have been shown, you'd do well to remember it![6]

If your hand above also had four cards to a straight—if, for example, you had a Queen and King to go with your two pair—your odds of improving would have been greater. Suppose any of six cards will improve your hand, which would be the case, for example, if two Jacks, one 10, one 9, and two Aces have not been seen by you. Your 6 cards in 24 give you a 1 in 4 chance of improving.

Of course the question is only partly whether you will improve. A hand better than Jacks and 10's occurs in a random deal of seven cards to seven players about one time in four. Maybe you have the best hand already, and will still have it after seven cards even if you don't improve. Or maybe you'll improve, but still lose. **Be careful to distinguish between the probability of improving your hand and the probability of having the winning hand.** Con-

6. If you had been drawing one card to these two pair in draw poker, your chances of getting one of the cards you needed to improve would have been 4 in 47, or slightly better than 1 in 12. This nicely illustrates the extra information that is available in stud poker and how it changes your estimate of probability—if, unlike our inattentive friend Knott, you take the trouble to notice it.

sider improving from two pairs to a straight, as in the example just discussed. Getting the straight will be an advantage if your opponent ends up with two higher pair or a
low straight, but will not help if he is drawing to a flush and
catches it; if he improves, you'll need your full house, and
you only have three cards that will do this. Hence, your
chance of having a full house is only 1 in 8—that is, the
probability odds against your *winning* if your opponent
improves are 7 to 1, not 3 to 1.[7]

**The most crucial factor in estimating probabilities for
poker hands is to have a good sense of which cards you
need to get to keep a winning hand.** Once you decide this
question, it is relatively easy to estimate the approximate
odds of getting a card you need.

GETTING ONE CARD IN MULTIPLE TRIES

This problem arises in two different situations. The first is
where, as in draw poker, you get multiple cards at one time
and need to call only one round of bets to get them. The
second situation is where, as in 7-card stud, you have successive betting rounds for each additional card. The probability calculations are the same in the two cases, *but their
relevance is not.* Suppose you hold a pair of Jacks either in
draw poker or after the fourth card in 7-card stud and you
are looking for a third Jack. In each case you have three
cards to come to improve your hand.[8] In draw, where the
additional cards are received simultaneously, you do not
care whether the desired card is received as the first, second,

7. In this situation the probability of your winning depends on two events:
your improving and your opponent not improving, as covered by Rule 2 (see
p. 74).
8. You have more chances to improve in stud since you are adding the cards
rather than replacing them and thus can catch hands that use *both* the new
cards and those that would have been replaced.

or third card. In stud it is critical: if you have a pair in four cards at 7-card stud and you don't get a third one on the fifth card, you will have to reconsider whether you want to pay the price required to get a sixth card. And if you don't get any improvement on the sixth card, you are unlikely even to try for a seventh-card hit.[9]

In draw poker.   Here there is no information to be learned from showing cards, so you need to be guided by the ultimate probabilities. Thus a table that gives the probabilities of improving on the draw (of the kind shown in Chapter 12) may be useful. But even if you don't have such a table, it is usually not difficult to estimate quickly how likely you are to improve. Suppose you hold three deuces, and have become convinced by the first-round betting that you will need to improve on the draw to have a real chance of winning. What are the probabilities? You can improve in two ways: by catching the fourth deuce or by catching a pair to go with them. Since either scenario will give you the hand you want, you need to estimate the probability of each and then add them together (see Rule 3, on page 75).

First, suppose that you draw two cards. You have 1 chance in 47 of catching a deuce on the first card drawn, and 1 in 46 of doing so on the second, assuming that you didn't on the first. Either will do. For easy calculation round these off to be 1 chance in 50 on each draw, or, when added together, 2 in 50. This translates as 1 chance in 25, or a probability of .04 (4 percent), of getting four of a kind. How about getting a pair? Whatever card you draw first, you have 3 chances in 46 that the second card will match it; 3 in 50 is a probability of .06 (6 percent). Getting either quads or a full house is thus approximately .04 + .06 = .10

9. This is why the average winning hand in a game of 7-card stud poker is not as strong as the average hand you would get if every player was dealt seven cards at the outset.

(10 percent): 1 chance in 10. This underestimates your chances a tiny bit: .106 is the true probability.[10]

Suppose you only drew one to your trips, keeping a King kicker. Your chance of improving would be 4 cards (any of three Kings or the fourth deuce) out of 47 cards, or a little better than 1 chance in 12, for a probability of .085 (8.5 percent). Your chances are a bit worse than for drawing two cards, but not so much worse as to deter you from doing so for purposes of deception.

In stud or widow poker. The situation where you have multiple opportunities to get the card you need occurs in Holdem or Omaha after the flop, and it occurs in stud poker with two rounds to go, which is usually the time when the betting and raising will get heavy. It is also the situation in stud poker after the first or second round, when the relevant question must be asked: What cards do I need to get soon in order to stay in for the subsequent round or two?

One Card in Two Tries. Suppose you have two pair or a four flush in the first five cards of a seven-card game. Each of these is a pretty good holding, because if you improve it you are likely to have the winning hand. To compute the probability of catching the card you want *precisely* would call for the application of Rule 3, but that would require a hand calculator, and in any case would take time. Fortunately there is a short cut that is approximately right and can be done in your head almost instantly.

Suppose in 7-card stud you've gotten four diamonds in the first five cards and have seen fifteen other cards, only one of which is a diamond. Altogether you have seen 20 cards, and thus there are 32 hidden cards, of which 8 are diamonds. What is your chance of getting one of those 8 on *either* the sixth or seventh card? (We'll calculate the answer

---

10. This is worked out in the Appendix to this chapter as Example 1.

exactly below[11]—it turns out to be .44—but for now let's approximate.) Your chances of getting a diamond on the sixth card are 1 in 4 (8 in 32). You will be approximately correct if your reasoning goes like this: "One chance in 4 on the sixth card plus about 1 chance in 4 on the seventh card adds up to 2 chances in 4—about even money." You will always overestimate your chances this way because you are double-counting the chances of getting a diamond on each card, but under circumstances that will be defined in a moment, you'll be in the right ballpark: .5 is greater than the true probability of .44, but not by much. Notice once again how important the showing cards are: if 4 diamonds had shown in the 15 other cards, your chance of getting the flush would have been much less: about .29 when you calculate it. Indeed, because there will be new information after the sixth-round cards have been dealt, you'll surely want to recalculate your chances before calling—or making—a sixth-round bet.

The approximation we suggested above (rounding off and then adding the simple probabilities, which involves neglecting the subtraction term present in Rule 3) will work when you are dealing with a small number of draws from a significantly larger group of cards where each individual probability is small. The following rule of thumb is usable: **You can use the shortcut of simply adding the probabilities where your chance of success on each of two draws is .25 or less.**

Take another example. Consider a situation in which you have two pairs plus an unmatched 6 in five cards and want to calculate the probability of getting a full house in two tries, when 3 of your cards are still available in the 32 hidden-to-you cards. You have about 1 chance in 10 (3 in 32) of getting one on the sixth card, and about 1 chance in 10 on the seventh. That's roughly 2 in 10, or 1 in 5. This is

11. See Example 2 in the Appendix to this chapter.

doubly crude—it also ignores the small possibility of getting two more 6's—but it comes close to the precisely calculated probability, which says your chances are 1 in 5.33.[12]

One Card in Three or More Tries. As you multiply the number of tries, your probability of success increases. If you have 1 chance in 10 of getting the card you want on the first try, you will have roughly 3 chances in 10 of doing so in three tries. This application of the shortcut rule of thumb works when the probability of success on each try is small. For more than two draws, the rule should be modified to say that the chance of success on each draw times the number of draws is no more than .5. To see why you cannot simply add, suppose you had four draws for one diamond when the chance of getting one on the first draw was .25. Obviously you would not be able to say, "Four times .25 is 1.0—a sure thing." For here the condition is violated: the number of draws (4) times the initial probability of success (.25) is greater than .5. Your chances of getting one diamond in four draws is very good—about .70—but it is not certain.[13]

NEEDING TWO CARDS TO MAKE YOUR HAND

Early in a poker hand you often require a lot of help even after a promising start. Here the distinction between possibilities and probabilities looms large, and distinguishing between them is often what separates the good player from the pigeon. Suppose you have three clubs, headed by the Ace, and think that an Ace-high club flush would be a winner in this 7-card stud game. If you have received 5 cards and seen 16 cards in total, of which 5 (including your 3) are

12. See Example 3 in the Appendix to this chapter.
13. The exact calculation is shown as Example 4 in the Appendix to this chapter.

clubs, what are your chances? Well, you need to get a club on the sixth card (8 chances in 36) *and* a club on the seventh (7 in 35). That's roughly 1 in 5 each time. But you must do *both*: $1/5 \times 1/5 = 1/25$. Of course this is *possible*, but it's not very likely.[14] Only someone like Lucky Lou expects to pull it off.

But suppose you have your three clubs in the first four cards. You still need two more clubs, but now you have three chances to get two cards. You still have roughly 1 chance in 25 of getting them in any two cards, but now there are *three* different ways you might succeed: on the fifth and sixth cards, on the fifth and seventh cards, or on the sixth and seventh cards.

Here is a useful trick to remember in estimating probabilities: if there are several different paths to success, you can estimate the probability of each and then add them up. Thus your chances in this example are about three times as good as when there was only one sequence available— roughly 1 chance in 8. There are times when this may be good enough—for example, when the cost of seeing another card is not very large.

What about holding 3 clubs in the first 3 cards? Hardluck Harry is forever complaining about how he didn't hit this sure thing, even though only one other club was showing. Actually his chances of success here are still less than 1 in 4.[15] You can approximate it quickly. Suppose there are nine clubs available in 45 unseen cards. Getting a club on any one try is still about 1 in 5 and getting two clubs in any two cards is still very unlikely, about 1 in 25. But now there are *six* ways of getting two clubs in four tries: on the first and second, first and third, first and fourth, second and third, second and fourth, and third and fourth rounds. Six times

---

14. Calculated precisely, the chance is 1 in 22.5. See the Appendix, Example 5.
15. See the Appendix, Example 6.

1/25 is 6/25, a little less than 1 chance in 4. It's not bad luck but simple probability that leads Harry to fail to hit his three-card flushes most of the time.

Knowing the number of different routes to achieve a given result is often the key to quick, shortcut estimation of the relevant probabilities of getting particular poker hands. The accompanying table is worth looking at closely, and perhaps even memorizing. It shows how to use the multipliers as the number of paths to success increase.

Table 5.1   Number of Routes to Particular Results

	You Have 2 Chances	You Have 3 Chances	You Have 4 Chances
You need:			
1 card	2	3	4
2 cards	1	3	6
3 cards	0	1	4

Reading and using Table 5.1 requires a bit of practice. If you need to get two cards and have four chances to get them, you enter the row where it says "2 cards" and read the answer "6" under the column labeled "4 chances." If you have 1 chance in 20 of getting both cards you need on each path, the probability is about .3 (6 in 20) that you will have success on at least one of the six paths available to you.

APPENDIX TO CHAPTER 5:
CALCULATING PROBABILITIES

While the calculation of probabilities beyond the rough approximations discussed above is not required for playing poker, some readers may be curious to see how probabilities are calculated precisely. That is the only purpose of this Appendix. Reading it will not improve your ability to play poker, nor is it necessary to read it in order to understand the rest of the book.

OPENING EXAMPLES ANALYZED

Birthday "Coincidence"

Assume that birthdays are chosen at random from among 365 possible dates.[16] In a group of 23 people any one of the 23 might have the same birthday as any of the other 22. In this group, there are in fact 253 different pairs of people.[17] All we want to know is the probability that *at least* one of these pairs share a birthday. (We assume none of them are twins or other multiple births.) While it is possible that two or more pairs have a common birthday, or even that three or more people do, this possibility need not concern us since in each of these cases there will be one pair with a common birthday (our minimum condition).

The easiest way to answer the key question is to ask its reverse: "How likely is it that no two people have the same birthday?" and then use Rule 1 to answer the question we really care about. Suppose we approach each person in turn and record his or her birthday. The first person has 365/365 chances (that is, certainty) of having a birthday different from people who have gone before, since no one has gone before. The second person has 364/365

16. I disregard February 29 in these calculations. If birthdays are not all equally likely, but are concentrated in some parts of the year, we will end up underestimating the likelihood of some two people having the same birthday.
17. When we multiply 23 by 22 and divide by 2, we get 253 combinations of 23 things taken two at a time. The first person can be any one of 23 (call him Jim), the second person any one of the remaining 22 (call her Sally). We divide by 2 because the pair Jim and Sally is the same pair as Sally and Jim.

chances (probability = .9973) of having a different birthday than the one who has gone before. If the first two are different, the third person has 363/365 chances (= .9945) of having a birthday different from the first two. Every additional person must have a birthday different from all who have gone before if no two are to have the same birthday. Using Rule 2, we must multiply the two probabilities to get the probability that none of the first three have a common birthday. The fourth person has 362/365 chances (= .9918) to be different than the first three, and this too must happen; thus we must multiply this still very high probability by the product of the other two. And so on for the 5th through 23rd persons. If the first 22 all have different birthdays, the 23rd person has 343/365 (= .9397) of being different from the rest. While each of these individual probabilities is high, each, except for the first, is less than one, and multiplying them successively by one another makes the product progressively smaller.[18] To repeat: for there to be no pair with a common birthday requires that each person have a different birthday than all who have gone before. Using Rule 2 over and over again, we see that the probability of *no two* having the same birthday is:

$$365/365 \times 364/365 \times 363/365 \times \ldots 343/365,$$

where the dots indicate that we have left out the terms in between. Doing all this arithmetic (luckily we have computers!) gives us .4927, a number a bit less than .5. Thus we see that the chance of the reverse happening—that is, of some two having the same birthday is, following Rule 1, slightly greater than .5, or slightly better than an even bet.

Each additional person in the group will add another term to the multiplying series shown above, thus decreasing the probability that no two people have the same birthday, and thereby *in-*

18. To see quickly how the joint occurrence of a series of individually probable events is much smaller, consider an easier example. Suppose one baseball team is much better than another—say, four times as likely to win a game between them. Its probability of winning is .8. If these two teams meet in a best-of-seven series, how likely is the better team to win in four straight games? The answer is: .8 × .8 × .8 × .8 = .4096. Thus, it is less than an even-money chance.

creasing the probability that some two do. By the 30th person, the probability that at least one pair have a birthday in common is .6; by the 35th, .81; by the 40th, .89. One can't be absolutely certain that any two have a common birthday until the group contains 366 people, but it is *virtually* certain long before that; indeed, it reaches the level of 99-percent certainty by the 57th person.

Rosencrantz's Good Luck

The chance of a head on a flip of an honest coin is .5. The chance of two heads in a row is: $.5 \times .5 = .5^2 = .25$. The chance of three heads is: $.5^3 = .125$. The chance of 89 heads in a row is $.5^{89}$, which is infinitesimal.[19] It is so small a chance that it is prudent to look for something else to explain the outcome.

Harry's Bad Luck

We calculate Harry's chances of getting a spade by first asking how likely he is *not* to get a spade. Suppose after the fourth card he has seen 14 cards, his own 4 plus 10 others. There are thus 38 cards left, of which 31 are not spades. In this situation the probability of not getting a spade on each of the next three tries is

$$31/38 \times 30/37 \times 29/36 = .54.$$

Thus, Harry's probability of getting his flush if he stayed to the end was: $1 - .54 = .46$, or slightly less than even money.

TEXT EXAMPLES EXPLAINED

Example 1: Improving Three Deuces in Draw Poker

The precise calculation that is the basis for the probability shown in Table 12.1 (on page 207, and roughly estimated in the chapter) would be as follows:

There is only one deuce unaccounted for; thus the chance of *not* getting a deuce on the first card is 46/47. The chance, on the

---

19. We have no vocabulary in ordinary discourse to describe a number so small. In mathematical terms it is $(1/6.2) \times 10^{-26}$. The last term means that there are 25 zeros after the decimal point in the resulting probability.

second card, of not getting either a deuce or a card that matched the first card is 42/46. The chance of neither of these things occurring is:

$$46/47 \times 42/46 = .894.$$

This is the probability of failing to improve the hand. Thus the probability of improving it is $1 - .894 = .106$, a little better than 10 percent.

Example 2: Catching One Card to a Flush in Two Tries

Once again the indirect calculation is easiest. Following the assumptions stated in the chapter, the probability of *not* getting a diamond on the sixth card is 24/32. If this happens, the probability of *not* getting one on the seventh card is 23/31. The probability of both of those things happening is their product (that is, multiply them), which equals .556. Thus the probability of getting at least one diamond is $1 - .556 = .444$. (Of course, once the sixth card is dealt you will have more information based upon the number of diamonds that show up in the new cards that you see.)

If four diamonds had shown up in the cards you had seen outside your own hand, your chances of catching a diamond would decrease. Under these assumptions the probability of failing both times is:

$$27/32 \times 26/31 = .708,$$

and thus the probability of succeeding would be .292, or 29.2 percent.

Example 3: Improving Two Pair to a Full House in Two Tries

Suppose after the fifth card in 7-card stud you hold two Jacks, two 10's, and a 6. Among the 15 other cards you have seen, one Jack but no 6's or 10's have shown. The probability of not getting a Jack or a 10 is $29/32 \times 28/31$. This is 812/992. The probability of getting a full house headed by a Jack or 10 is, thus, 180/992. But there is also the small chance of getting two more 6's. This is $3/32 \times 2/31$, or 6/992. Together the probability of a full house is thus $186/992 = .1875$ (18.75 percent), or 1 chance in 5.33. Notice that this calculation mixes direct and indirect methods of calculating probability. It is easier to figure the chance of getting either a Jack or a 10 by first figuring the chance of not doing so. It is easier to figure the chance of getting two 6's directly. (See Rule 1 on page 74.)

Example 4: Getting One to a Flush in Four Tries

The artificial problem posed here is to find the probability of getting one to a flush in four tries when 8 out of 32 cards will do the job. The exact calculation, using the indirect method, is:

$$1 - (24/32 \times 23/31 \times 22/30 \times 21/29) = .705.$$

Example 5: Getting Two Cards to a Flush

The probability of getting two clubs in two tries in this example is:

$$8/36 \times 7/35 = 56/1265 = .044.$$

This is one chance in 22.5.

Example 6: Getting Two to a Flush in Four Tries

If there are 43 unseen cards, 9 of them clubs, the chance of getting two clubs in four tries can be calculated by finding the probability of getting them on the first two cards, and then recognizing this as one of six equally probable routes. Thus the probability is:

$$6 \times (9/43 \times 8/42) = 432/1806 = .24.$$

6

♠ ♣ ♥ ♦

EXPECTED VALUE, POT ODDS, AND RISK

*The game is pot-limit Jackpots, and you as dealer hold
four spades headed by the Jack. There is $14 in the pot as a
result of the antes, and the third hand opens for $14. Ev-
eryone else folds and it's up to you to call, raise, or fold.
You . . .*

In one respect, poker strategy is similar to chess strategy.
Except in draw poker it is usually impossible to form a com-
prehensive strategy at the outset that will carry you through
to the end, as there are simply too many forks in the road.
You need intermediate signposts to help you take the best
path toward your final destination. Conceptually, though
not actually, you work backwards. Where do you need to be
before the last moves? How do you get to this next-to-last
position? How do you get to the next-to-next-to-last position? And so on, all the way back to the best opening moves
for your overall plan. At each stage you try to pick a strategy
that will improve your position to one you are comfortable
using as a basis for the next decision. In chess it is common
to distinguish between the opening, the middle game, and
the endgame, and one can approach poker strategy in much
the same way.

In poker these stages are the successive betting rounds,
and the question is not how best to get there (since the
cards define where you end up), but whether it pays to keep
trying. You benefit in making this decision by getting addi-

tional information with every new card, but you have to pay to get it. Is the possible improvement in your position going to be worth the cost? The answer to this question in the early rounds derives ultimately from your final position. At that point, after seeing all you are going to see, you are going to answer the final question: "Should I pay to see the showdown?"

Both at this final stage and leading up to it you need a measure that compares the incremental benefit (ultimately derived from the amount you will win *if* you win) to the cost of each increment of improvement. The related concepts of *expected value* and of *pot odds* are the tools—the signposts—that help you do this. They answer the question at the endgame, and they help you decide along the way whether to attempt to get to the next position.

Since early-round strategies derive from the final positions, it is with the endgame that we start. For relatively simple games such as draw poker, with only two betting rounds and one set of incremental information, the endgame analysis may embrace everything all the way back to a starting strategy, but for most multiround games this is not the case. When you cannot evaluate the alternative scenarios because there are too many of them or they are too conjectural, you need to calculate whether the expected benefit of seeing the next card is greater than the cost of getting it.

Starting strategies attempt to do this for games with multiple rounds of betting, but the applications are specific to particular games and stake levels and so are discussed at length below, in the chapters of Part IV. Endgame strategy is virtually identical in every game and is the major focus of this chapter.

The concept of *pot odds*, which is essential to endgame strategy, guides behavior from the point at which it is first possible to visualize all credible alternative betting scenarios right up to the end of the hand. It is the situation that a poker player faces after all the cards have been dealt and he must decide whether to pay to see the showdown. It is also often the situation of a round earlier, when the end is coming into focus. As you go further back, the view becomes more obscure and you need intermediate signposts, but decisions in these rounds are also governed by considerations related to pot odds and expected values.

The central endgame operating principle of a risk-neutral,[1] skillful poker player is that he ought to stay in a hand if, *but only if,* the pot odds of winning are as good as, or better than, the probability odds against doing so. This is precisely equivalent to saying that the *expected value* of the action must be positive. To understand this principle and to apply it correctly requires some definitions, some investment of time in understanding the basic concepts, and some facility in estimating the odds of each kind. What follows is not always easy, but it is basic and worth the effort.

THE CONCEPT OF EXPECTED VALUE (EV)

Expected value is a mathematical concept, but it is not difficult to understand. It is the long-run *value* of the outcome of a course of action after the effect of chance (luck) has been averaged out. Take a familiar example. If you flip an honest coin a large number of times you can expect to get heads about as often as tails—about one-half the time. (That's what we mean by an honest coin.) The "expected" number of heads in a hundred flips is fifty. You are unlikely to get exactly fifty heads in a hundred trials, but this is not what mathematicians mean by *expected*. Rather, they mean

1. Just what is meant by *risk-neutrality* and the role of a player's attitude toward risk is discussed later in this chapter.

that you will get more than fifty heads as often as you get fewer, and that the numbers will tend to average out to fifty-fifty in the long run.

Suppose now that every time you flip a coin and get a head someone pays you $10, and you are allowed to play the game ten times. You might be very lucky and get 10 heads, collecting $100, or you might be very unlucky and get no heads, collecting nothing. But most of the time you will get some result in between. Your expected number of heads in ten flips is: the probability of a head on each flip (.5) × the number of flips (10) = 5.

The expected value (which is short for *expected value of winnings*) of each flip in this game is: .5 × $10 = $5. Somewhat more generally:

$$\text{expected value} =$$
$$(\text{the probability of winning}) \times (\text{the payoff if you win})$$

Invitations to play this sort of game, sad to say, are not likely to come your way very often. More realistically, suppose that you have to pay a fee (X) for each flip in this game. The expected value of each flip of this game is: $5 *minus* X.

If X = $5, this is a *fair game* and has an expected value of zero; if X = $4, the expected value is $1, and is said to be positive; if X = $6, the expected value is *minus* $1, and is said to be negative.

The expected value of a game in which you must pay to play is:

$$\text{expected value} =$$
$$[(\text{the probability of winning}) \times (\text{the payoff if you win})]$$
$$- (\text{the cost of playing})$$

This formula has three terms. As applied to poker, the first is the probability that a particular hand will become the best hand. The ratio of the second term to the third term determines the pot odds. If you can win $50 for an investment of $10, the pot odds are 5 to 1 in your favor.

If a player is risk-neutral, as is Doc Wright, he should play in situations where the expected value is positive, avoid situations where it is negative, and be indifferent about situations in which it is zero. The assumption of risk-neutrality makes a useful starting point for analyzing behavior.

Notice that each part of the EV equation is important. You can get the same EV by having a small probability of a big net gain or by having a large probability of a small net gain. Notice too that the net gain is dependent both on the payoff and on the cost of playing. Because all three elements are present in virtually every poker decision, the calculation of the expected value of calling a bet is seldom as easy as deciding whether to flip a coin. **You need to anticipate likely scenarios and estimate the probability, the payoff, and the cost of each scenario.**

EXPECTED VALUES OF POKER PLAYS

Consider the example at the head of this chapter. You hold four spades, headed by the Jack. Unless you get a spade you will surely not have the best hand. Assume that if you get a spade you will have the winning hand. If you are the only caller, *and if there is not going to be any bet after the draw,* the calculation is easy: There are 9 spades left in the 47 cards you don't see, so the probability of winning is 9 in 47, or a little less than 1 in 5. Call it 1 in 5, or .2. The probability odds are thus 4 to 1 against you. What are the pot odds? The pot odds facing you *at this point* are 2 to 1: the $28 that is there for you to win against the $14 that you will have to spend to have any chance of collecting that $28. These are called the *immediate pot odds*, those that apply only to getting the next card. At first glance this does not look promising, but we will soon take a second look.

The same facts can be looked at in the vocabulary of expected value. To call the bet requires an investment now of $14 for a .2 chance of collecting $42. The expected value of this scenario is:

$$EV = -\$14 + (.2 \times \$42) = -\$14 + \$8.40 = -\$5.60$$

Whether you look at the apparently unfavorable pot odds or the negative EV, the message would seem to be that you should not bother to attempt to catch your flush. But this is not necessarily so: the assumption we made two paragraphs above (that *there is not going to be any bet after the draw*) is critical. If you do not get a spade after the draw, you will almost surely fold.[2] But if you do hit, you will be able to call or raise a bet by the opener, or to bet if he checks. Thus, if you hit, your expected winnings may be more than the calculation above suggested. You need to calculate the *implied pot odds,* defined as the ratio of the expected amount you will win (if you win) to the amount you must put in before you are confident that you will win.

Implied Pot Odds

To calculate the implied pot odds (or the implied expected value) you must consider the likely betting scenarios that will affect the size of the pot and the size of your required subsequent contributions to it. Each scenario has both a payoff (either a net profit or a net loss) and a probability of occurrence. If there are two alternative scenarios, one

---

2. The exception being if you choose to bluff.

of which wins and the other loses, the implied expected value would be:

$$\left(\begin{array}{c}\text{probability} \\ \text{of sce-} \\ \text{nario 1}\end{array} \times \begin{array}{c}\text{profit if} \\ \text{scenario} \\ \text{1 occurs}\end{array}\right) - \left(\begin{array}{c}\text{probability} \\ \text{of sce-} \\ \text{nario 2}\end{array} \times \begin{array}{c}\text{cost of} \\ \text{playing}\end{array}\right)$$

A realistic scenario in the example above might be the following: you draw one card, and the opener checks to you. If you do not catch your spade, you fold, lose your $14, and he wins the pot. If you do catch your spade, you bet $40, he calls, and you win; thus you will win $68 for your $14 "investment."[3] Your expected value is:

$$(.2 \times \$68) - (.8 \times \$14) = +\$2.40^4$$

The implied pot odds of $68 for $14—nearly 5 to 1—are better than the 4-to-1 probability odds against your getting a spade.

Anytime the pot odds in your favor are greater than the probability odds against your winning, the expected value will be positive. This is a key proposition. You can compare the pot odds with the probability odds, or approximate the expected value, whichever is easiest at a particular time.

In the example, if you believe this scenario, you may well call the opening bet.[5] But the margin here is small, and a

3. The $28 in the pot when you called his opening bet, plus the $40 that your opponent paid after the draw to see your flush.
4. This calculation is approximate and slightly overstates the EV—since the probability of hitting the flush is really .1915 rather than .2, and the probability of winning if you hit a flush against one other player is .97, not 1.0—but it is good enough for all practical purposes. The important thing is that the EV is clearly positive.
5. But, you may ask, "What if the opener folds when I bet, rather than calling my $40? Then I'll only win the original $28." The quick answer to that is that if you are sure he will fold when you bet, you'll want to bet even if you don't

conservative player like Ty may well choose to fold rather than draw to his four flush against the opener, who will beat him about four out of five times in such a situation.

If a second player had called the opening bet, the pot odds facing the holder of a four flush would have improved. Fortunately, making a precise calculation is seldom necessary. But you can approximate it quickly where you are confident that you'll win *if* you hit. With three players in the hand, you still have nearly a 20-percent chance of winning $82 (the $42 in the pot before you called plus the $40 extra you'll win after the draw if one player calls your $40 bet) and an 80-percent chance of losing $14. This has a positive expected value (+$16.40 − $11.20) of more than $5. Hence, calling the bet and drawing to the flush is now clearly attractive.

Notice, however, that if you call in this situation and catch your flush you must be prepared to bet. If you are timid and merely check, you'll have followed a strategy that has a negative expected value. You will have invested $14 and can win a maximum of $42. These 3-to-1 pot odds do not justify bucking the 4-to-1 probability odds against getting a flush. You called the original bet knowing that the immediate pot odds were against a call, because the possibility of a big gain after the draw led to implied odds that made it worthwhile. If you are too nervous to bet in such a situation, or if you never bluff and this is known to your opponents, you should not draw one card to a flush in the situation described above. In those circumstances you won't win enough after the draw to justify the probability odds against you.

---

hit the extra spade! Bluffing is the subject of Chapter 7, and as you will see there, one purpose of bluffing is to win when you don't have the best hand, and a second is to increase the likelihood of getting called when you *do* have the best hand.

Calculation of the implied pot odds and expected value was fairly simple in this example because there was only one betting round to anticipate. If there are two betting rounds yet to come, as is the case after five cards have been received in 7-card stud, the calculation is harder but sometimes still possible. Often you have to consider up to three alternative scenarios, and estimate the likelihood of each. Suppose it will cost you $80 to play. Under scenario one, which happens 20 percent of the time, you'll collect $200 and thus win $120; under scenario two, which happens 20 percent of the time, you'll collect $150 and thus win $70; but under the most likely scenario, number three, which happens 60 percent of the time, you'll collect nothing and lose your $80. Your expected value is −$10.[6] In pot-odds terms your winnings, if you win, are either going to be $120 or $70. These average to $95, since they are equally likely. But $95 divided by $80, your required investment, leads to pot odds of 1.19, far below the 1.5 (60 to 40) probability odds against you, and are not good enough. If it had only cost $50 (instead of $80) to have the same scenarios, the implied pot odds would have been good enough, and, what is the same thing, the expected value would have been positive.[7]

To estimate the implied pot odds you need to estimate your expected winnings, and to do this accurately you need to know the whole future betting scenario or a limited number of alternative scenarios and the probability of each one. What if you cannot anticipate a small number of alternative scenarios? Multiple betting rounds imply multiple contributions to the pot, and it is usually impossible to anticipate

6. EV = (.2 × $120) + (.2 × $70) + (.6 × −$80) = $24 + $14 − $48 = −$10.
7. EV = (.2 × $150) + (.2 × $100) + (.6 × −$50) = $30 + $20 − $30 = +$20. In this case the average winnings would be $125, and the required investment $50, leading to pot odds of 2.5 to 1, better than the probability odds of 1.5 to 1 against you.

just how big these will be relative to the pot as it grows. The greater the number of betting rounds, the less likely you are to be able to do this with any accuracy.

This is where middle-game strategies come into play and something like a pot-odds calculation plays a role as a player reevaluates his position at each opportunity. For example, suppose you are playing 7-card stud and hold three to a club flush in the first four cards. Your chances of getting the flush are in the neighborhood of 1 in 9.[8] This would be unpromising if there were to be no more betting. There will be more betting, of course, but you don't know how much, nor do you know how many other players will be in the hand. But your immediate concern is only whether to call the current round of betting. If you get a fourth card to your flush on the fifth card you will have about 1 chance in 3 of getting the fifth one in the final two cards. If you can increase your chances from 1 in 9 to 1 in 3, you are then likely to have favorable pot odds facing you. If there is $30 in the pot and you can get the fifth card for $5, the relevant question is whether the 6 to 1 (30 to 5) immediate pot odds in your favor justify trying to get a fourth club. Since there is about 1 chance in 5 of getting a fourth club on the next card, it is worth doing because if you do, the subsequent betting rounds will give you favorable pot odds.

How Many Legitimate Calling Hands?

Define a legitimate calling hand as one that has positive expected value. It might seem that at any given moment, only one player could have a good enough chance to have positive expected value, but this is not the case. Go back to the

---

8. Just what the chances are depends upon the number of cards you have seen and how many of them are clubs. The figure of 1 chance in 9 applies if you have seen no cards except your own four.

original example at the head of the chapter, where you were the only caller in Jackpots with a four flush, and consider the matter from the point of view of the other player as he makes his $14 bet. When you call his opening bet he has about an 80-percent chance of winning $28—which will occur if you don't get your flush and fold. He has about a 20-percent chance that you will catch your flush, bet $40, which he will choose to call, and will end up losing his $54 in bets. His expected value is:

$$EV = (.8 \times \$28) - (.2 \times \$54) = +\$11.60.$$

It too is positive!

How can it be that since only one of you can win, you both had positive EV's and thus legitimate calling hands? The answer is that there was $14 in the pot (as a result of the antes) that one of you was bound to win as soon as everyone else dropped out. It is no coincidence that his EV of $11.60 and yours of $2.40 added up to $14. **Whenever there is money in the pot, the game is a positive-sum game for those who are still in the competition.** The winner's winnings will be greater than the loser's losings by the amount already in the pot.

Conditions Leading to Favorable EV'S

The general question of when there will be two or more legitimate betting interests in a poker hand is an important one, because only then does the game lead to the confrontations that make it exciting to play.

Many of the rules that govern particular poker games are designed to create situations in which there are two or more legitimate betting interests in the early rounds. In general, anything that builds the pot (relative to the size of the bet required to participate in it) tends to increase the pot odds and makes possible multiple legitimate betting interests. This is of particular importance in the early rounds, when the pot is likely to be small.[9]

Larger Antes. The bigger the compulsory antes relative to the size of the subsequent permitted bets, the more likely that a player will have a legitimate reason to call the first-round bet. With a tiny (or no) ante and a big bet, you should usually drop out of the hand unless you have a better-than-even chance of holding the best hand. Objectively, only one person can have that good a chance, and that is why an ante, or its equivalent, is virtually always required.

With a big ante and a low limit on the size of the first-round bet, everything changes. For example, if there is an aggregate ante of $35 and a $5 maximum bet, there will be $35 in the pot before the first bet, resulting in immediate pot odds of 7 to 1. Anyone with probability odds of better than 1 in 7 has a legitimate calling hand if there is one bet to call. This may well be the case for three, four, or even five players. If, by contrast, the aggregate ante is $5, and the first bettor bets $5, the immediate pot odds to the next potential caller are merely 2 to 1.

Specifying the size of required antes is thus an important part of the structure of the game. If most players are tight, conservative players like Ty Tass, the game will need a high ante to achieve much action. If, on the contrary, most players are loose ones, like Lucky Lou and Bluffalo Bill, even a small ante will suffice, since having multiple callers will quickly build up the pot and compensate for the meager ante. A conservative poker player prefers a game with low antes but loose players because he gets good pot odds right from the start on a great many hands.

---

9. By the late rounds there is usually enough money in the pot that any player who has a reasonable chance to end up the winner will have positive expected value for a decision to stay in except against a very large bet.

Increased Number of Betting Rounds.　Games with many betting rounds, such as 7-card stud, promise bigger pots (for the same rules about limits or antes) than a game such as Jackpots, which has only two betting rounds. While this does not change the immediate pot odds, it does increase the *implied* pot odds because the potential winnings are greater for any initial bet, and thus the probability of winning that is required to justify a call can be smaller. The number of players who see the first round of betting in a 7-card stud hand is greater than the number who do so in a hand of draw poker because the several extra betting rounds mean that there will be a bigger pot near the end and thus better pot odds.

Larger Permitted Subsequent Bets.　In much the same manner as increased betting rounds, rules that permit bets in later rounds to be big relative to early bets (such as pot limit, or double-limit bets after the last card has been dealt) raise your expected winnings if you hit your potential best hand, and thus improve the implied pot odds and make calling more attractive.

In pot limit in particular, the potential winnings, if you hit the best hand, may be much larger relative to the cost of getting there, and thus even some low-probability outcomes may have positive expected value.

Increased Number of Callers.　Other things being equal, increasing the number of players who call in the early rounds improves the pot odds facing each of them. Here such things as blind bets, or the requirement that the worst showing hand "bring the hand in" by a compulsory bet increases the number of callers and thus the size of the pot.

Hi-Lo Poker.　It might seem that Hi-Lo poker—which will tend to increase the number of callers by creating more hands that potentially can win in one direction or the other—would increase the pot odds in comparison with either high-only or low-only poker. But if all players correctly evaluate their expected values, this is not necessarily the case. While there are surely more callers and more ultimate winners, the potential winnings are correspondingly reduced because the winners each collect only half the pot, and their own contributions to it are proportionally larger. Thus, a $100 pot split between two players, each of whom has contributed $25 to it, gives each only an even money profit on his investment. Beginners in Hi-Lo games stay in too often because they confuse the increased chances of becoming a winner with the expected value of each winning. Part of the appeal of Hi-Lo, however, comes from the greater action this confusion brings.

However, there is a way in which Hi-Lo poker does legitimately increase the action in limit games. By providing two winners, it creates a situation where two or more legitimate raisers can effectively increase the size of bets in every round, and thus increase the size of pots. The $100 Hi-Lo pot might have been only a $40 pot in high-only.

Double-Edged Swords?

While multiple betting rounds, a larger ratio of late-round to early-round bets, and an increased number of callers all boost the probable size of the final pot relative to the amount a player must pay to stay in the hand in the early rounds, each of them involves risks or complications that may offset the apparent increase in the pot odds.

There is an opposite edge to the sword of more rounds: other players' hands may improve with additional cards, and thus more rounds can lessen your probability odds of ending up with the best hand. You must pay attention to the possibility that even if you improve, you will not have increased your chances of winning; put differently, you must be careful that you are not buying into a second-best situation. To hope to improve to two pair may be foolish if there are straight, flush, or higher two-pair possibilities suggested by your opponents' hands and several chances for them to catch the cards they need. Multiple betting rounds offer traps as well as opportunities that are not present in games where only one round remains after the initial betting round.

A larger ratio of late-round to early-round bets, such as occurs in pot-limit games, is a double-edged sword: you stand to lose more if you improve into a second-best situation where you feel obliged to call. **The player who is willing to stay in early on long-shot hopes of improving his hand enough to collect some big bets later must have the courage to fold his hand if the play of the cards subsequently suggests a second-best situation.** The highly conservative advice usually given to players in "How to Win at Poker" books is surely accounted for, perhaps justifiably, by the suspicion that most players lack this kind of courage. Good professionals play looser than the advice they give in their books because they have the requisite courage to fold later!

Finally, you must consider whether you are better off being one of five callers rather than one of two. The more callers, the bigger the pot relative to your own contributions to it, and thus the better the pot odds. But the more callers, the greater the chances that someone will beat you. The two factors, increased pot odds and decreased probability of winning, must be balanced.

The key element in this balance is the quality of your hand if you get the card you want. With four cards to a low straight, you will be less happy to have several other people each drawing one card against you than if you hold, say, four to a high flush, or hold two low pair. If you hit your flush or your full house, you'll probably win; if you don't, you are very likely to lose anyway. In this situation even if you hit your straight, you may still lose and will, in any case, be unwise to bet, because anyone who will call you is likely to have you beaten.

The Danger of Loose or Marginal Early Calls

One reason why it is important to evaluate the expected values carefully in the early rounds of a multiple-round poker game even when it seems cheap to call is the danger described as being *sucked in*. A foolish bet or call in an early round increases the attractiveness of calling in a later round, since it contributes to a bigger pot (and thus better pot odds) in the next rounds. This is true of other players' bad calls, and it is also true of your own! The bad calls of others are why good players benefit from playing with poor ones. Your own bad calls are why there is a legitimate fear of being sucked into an expensive second-best situation. It is not, as is sometimes believed, that you should call later in order to protect your earlier investment. Bygones are bygones, and once your money is in the pot, it no longer is your money. Rather, the justification is that the extra money in the pot may make it sensible to call a subsequent bet even if it was foolish to call the previous one.

This point is important enough to warrant an example. Suppose in Jackpots with an aggregate ante of $15, the hand is opened for $15 and you, as the next-to-last player, have a pair of Jacks. Feeling lucky, you call, even though you can be reasonably sure you are no better than second-best. You have called despite the fact that the pot odds of 2 to 1 do not justify doing so. (The chance of any improvement when drawing three to a pair is about 2.5 to 1 against, and you must improve to have any chance of holding the best hand—*and,* of course, you might improve and *still* lose.) For this example suppose that you optimistically judge that your chance of beating the opener after the draw is 20 percent. Your expected value of the call, if no one else calls and if there is no bet after the draw, is −$6.[10] Now, however, the last player in line raises the bet by $5 and the opener calls. The pot facing you now has $70 in it—the ante of $15, your $15, and $20 from each of the other two players—and you can draw for only $5. The 14-to-1 pot odds you now face are surely better than the probability odds against you. So you call, and probably lose the $20 you invested in the hand. Once made, the original unsound $15 call makes it foolish not to call the additional $5. You should have thought this through before you called the opening bet, and recognized that once you called the first bet, you would feel obliged to call a subsequent raise as well. What is more, if after the draw you have not caught a third Jack (which would probably be a winner) but merely a second small pair, you may well find that the pot odds motivate you to call the opener's post-draw bet. If he has caught a second pair, he will have you beaten even if the raiser does not.

Lou, feeling lucky, often lets himself get sucked into calling early-round bets in pots that cost him more money than he anticipated when he made his first call. Hugh does not.

ATTITUDE TOWARD RISK

Whether expected value is a sufficient guide to how to play a given poker hand depends upon your attitude toward risk. There is nothing automatic or compelling about being risk-neutral.

Before reading on, answer the following questions:

1. Do you ever voluntarily buy insurance against fire, theft, or liability?
2. Do you ever buy a lottery ticket or bet on a horse race?

10. Under these assumptions, the EV = $(.2 \times \$30) − (.8 \times \$15) = −\$6$.

3. Do you believe the considerations that determine your answer to question 1 are different than those for question 2?

If the answers to *any* of these questions is yes, you are not being risk-neutral, probably for very good reasons. Many perfectly rational people would answer yes to all three of the questions.

Risk

Risk is a word that has both a technical and an everyday meaning. As used here it does not mean mere uncertainty; rather, it is concerned with the range of outcomes of uncertain events.[11]

Consider a number of games each of which has exactly the same expected value of +$50:

1. A probability of 1.0 (certainty) to receive...... $50.
2. A probability of .5 (1 chance in 2) to receive .. $100.
3. A probability of .1
   (1 chance in 10) to receive................ $500.
4. A probability of .01
   (1 chance in 100) to receive .... $5,000.
5. A probability of .001
   (1 chance in 1,000) to receive........... $50,000.
6. A probability of .00001
   (1 chance in 100,000) to receive ...... $5,000,000.

---

11. Technically, risk has to do with variance of particular results from known mechanisms: the greater the variance, the greater the risk. (There is a technical definition of *variance* that gives it a quantitative measure, but that need not concern us here.) Risk—or more properly, the degree of risk—as defined here is a variable, not an attribute. But there is a contrary view. Consider: "That taught me a valuable lesson about risk-taking—either you do or you don't; there is no middle ground, for you cannot compromise risk any more than you can compromise pregnancy." A. E. Hotchner, *Choice People* (New York: William Morrow, 1984), p. 176.

In the first game the best and worst outcomes are the same: a gain of $50, and playing involves no risk. In the second game the worst outcome is zero, the best a gain of $100. In the third game the worst outcome is still zero, but the best outcome is a gain of $500. *Variance* in the possible outcomes is zero in the first situation, but is present in all the others. It is greater in the third game than in the second. As one moves down the list the variance—that is, the degree of risk—grows.

Risk Aversion

Which one of these games would you choose to play if you had the choice of playing any one of them once, free of charge? Your answer depends on your evaluation of the merits of smaller probabilities of larger gains versus larger probabilities of smaller gains. Different people would answer the question in different ways. If you are truly indifferent about which one you would choose you are risk-neutral. To many people taking the sure $50 would be the most appealing option. They are risk-averse: they don't want to trade a sure gain for a fair-game possibility of either a bigger gain or nothing at all. Indeed, some of them would be glad to take $45 rather than play any of the other games (two through six), which have expected values of $50. In other words, they would give up—implicitly, pay—$5 to be relieved of risk. Other people might prefer the small chance of a big gain, on the grounds that $50 doesn't do much for them but a big win would let them fly free.

Now change the rules. In order to play in any one of these games you must pay a fee of $55. Each game now has an expected value of −$5. Surely you won't now pay $55 to be certain of collecting $50, so the first game is unattractive no matter what your attitude toward risk is. The expected value is negative and is certain to be received. But many people *do* pay $55 to bet on a horse race where the horse bet on has no better than 1 chance in 10 to win and pay $500.[12] This is equivalent to choosing to play the third game, and is explained in good part by enjoyment of gambling. Gamblers are risk-seeking by definition. Many people buy $55 worth of lottery tickets for a payoff with less expected value than those in the fifth or sixth games. The extraordinary appeal of lottery tickets is not explained in the same way as horse-race betting. It is the stuff of dreams and of hope. Lottery tickets give a chance, albeit a disproportionately small one, to jump to a level of wealth beyond the dreams of avarice, and thus to a lifestyle wholly outside the practical possibilities of an ordinary person. Who is to say that dreams and hope are not worth the cost of having them?

Now consider another change in the example. Instead of receiving the amounts listed, you must pay them out, with the probability shown. Suppose you do not have the option of simply saying you won't play. In each case, however, you are permitted to get out of playing the game by paying $55. Your choice, no longer pleasant, is between buying your way out and thus incurring a certain loss of $55, or taking the chance (in all but game one) of bigger loss, whose expected value is −$50. Buying out of risk is what you do when you buy insurance. You might be willing to risk losing $100, but what about $50,000? Most of us are risk-averse here, and gladly pay much more than $55 whenever we buy fire, theft, or liability insurance to avoid a 1-in-1,000 chance of an unexpected $50,000 loss. This is like paying to avoid playing in the fifth game.

What about the person who buys both insurance and lottery tickets? Is he risk-seeking or risk-averse? Is he either

---

12. The negative expected value of pari-mutuel betting arises from the taxes and the track "take." While some horse players may actually have positive expected values if they are sufficiently shrewd about how and when they bet, the average bettor surely has negative expected values.

crazy or stupid? The answer to the first question is that he is both, but in different contexts. The answer to the second question may well be no. Either a huge windfall or a disastrous loss may fundamentally alter his life, and he'll gladly pay to keep the hope of the windfall alive as well as to be sure that the disaster is avoided. Thus, one's attitude toward risk usually depends on the context: one may enjoy taking small risks and be in dread of taking large ones; one may value big sums of money (either won or lost) proportionately more seriously than small ones; one may have unequal feelings about the risk of losing and the risk of not winning large amounts of money.

Since risk-neutrality can hardly be said to be a demonstrable attribute of human beings in their everyday life, it may not be a good assumption when talking about how people do or should play poker. Sensible people try to play poker under rules assuring that the level of possible (and expected) winnings and losings is not greater than they are willing to accept. A player who relishes taking the risks inherent in playing in a poker game with a $10 limit on any bet might be paralyzed with fear if he found himself in a game with a $100 limit and a $50 minimum bet. **By choosing the games they play in, players also choose a risk level.**

Within a given poker group, individuals may choose to take more risk, or less, by the way they play, and there are poker players of numerous persuasions. Ty is risk-averse, Bill is risk-seeking. A friend of mine, Andy, is extremely risk-averse and folds his cards in many situations where the expected value of calling is positive but where he might end up with a big enough loss to go home a loser if he loses the hand.[13] Andy doesn't mind not maximizing his winnings

13. Andy's counterpart is easy to recognize in every poker game: he regularly shows the cards he has folded to a neighbor and says, "I'd have won if I'd stayed in." He does so without regret, as if to say, "You guys are lucky that I'm not taking more of your money."

since he rarely goes home a loser, and he accepts a much smaller-than-average expected value in order to avoid the possibilities of ever being a big loser. Another friend, Jim (now deceased), so loved the excitement of a "really big hand" that he regularly drew two cards to a flush in draw poker (the chance of hitting a winning hand on such a draw is about 1 in 30) even though he knew the expected value of so doing was negative. He was risk-seeking and didn't mind losing on average because his joy when he made the big, unexpected killing was unbounded.[14]

The more risk-averse you are, the more conservatively you should play. While you maximize your expected winnings if you bet anytime the expected value is positive, this strategy is bound to produce some big losses as well as big winnings.

Your attitude toward risk affects how you play, but it does not affect your need to evaluate expected values. A risk-averse player may demand that the pot odds be somewhat better than the probability odds before he will call, while a risk-seeker may call even if the pot odds are somewhat unfavorable. Each of them pays some price, in terms of long-run winnings, relative to the risk-neutral player. But keep in mind that making as much money as possible is not the objective of most amateur poker players.

14. Even fifteen years after he drew two cards and caught a straight flush that beat my full house, he talked about it often, and glowed when he did.

III
♠ ♣ ♥ ♦

SKILLS

♠ ♣ ♥ ♦

7

BLUFFING

The game is Jackpots and you have four cards to a flush in clubs. After the pot is opened by Harry, and Duke calls, you raise, so that the others will have to guess about what you have when you draw one card. Both the others call. Harry draws three cards. Duke draws one, as do you. After the draw Harry looks at his cards, seems disappointed, and checks "to the one-card draws." Duke throws away his cards. You squeeze your cards and find a stranger, the nine of spades. You bet the maximum allowed, and Harry hardly hesitates as he throws his cards away, showing a pair of queens and saying, "I never improve," while you reach for the pot.

There are few pleasures in playing poker as great as making a big bet when you know you're outgunned and watching everyone fold. As you rake in the pot, you may even want to show your hand or let a self-satisfied smile do it for you. Of course your enjoyment of these situations may be offset by your chagrin when you are called by someone with a pretty minimal hand and you have to show your busted flush. He gets the pot, including your last big bet, and the acclaim. The others will tell him, "Nice call," but don't bank on them giving you a "Good try." You seldom get praised for trying a bluff that fails.

If all poker players only called or bet when the probability of their holding the winning hand exceeded the pot

odds in their favor, poker would be a much more predictable and less enjoyable game than it is, for you could
correctly infer just how good others' hands were from the
size of their bets. Of course you could still take pleasure
from being better than the others in the inferences you
drew, or in taking advantage of others' mistakes, or in the
purely chance aspects of the game. The fact is, however,
that all players, good and bad alike, often bet when they
have poor prospects, and sometimes fail to do so when they
have strong hands, as part of the deception that is an inte-
gral part of the game. Bluffing—betting heavily when you
know that you do not hold the best hand—is a key aspect
of this deception.

HOW OFTEN TO BLUFF

What is the right amount of bluffing? Neglecting the purely
psychological matter of the pleasure you may get from
being clever, or the pain you may suffer from being caught,
there *is* a right amount of bluffing, and it is neither "never"
nor "always." What this frequency is depends crucially on
the size of the bets that the rules permit and on the styles of
your opponents.

**As a general observation, most poker players bluff
too little in pot-limit games and too much in low-limit
games.** This is because a small bet relative to the size of the
pot is much more likely to be called than a large one, and a
bluff depends on a bet not being called.

How often to bluff is a complex question, more so than
is commonly appreciated even by pretty good poker players,
for it depends not only on the outcome of the individual
hand but on the dynamics of the game. Bill loses many of
his bluffs because he is usually called as a result of his reputation, but he also gets called frequently on hands where he
is the winner. Ty, who seldom bluffs, and almost never with-

out success, finds that only the poorer players call his big bets on his monster hands.

Consider an analogy from baseball. During a recent World Series the play-by-play announcer admiringly summarized a particular player's season-long performance as follows: "He stole 17 bases in 17 tries! That's as good as you can do." But is it? Would the player have contributed more to his team if he had stolen 28 bases in 30 tries? The answer is almost surely yes: 11 successful steals in an additional 13 attempts would lower his success ratio, but it would put a lot more runners in scoring position. In his prime, the premier base stealer of all time, Rickey Henderson, was successful about 80 to 85 percent of the time, and succeeded 70 to 90 times in a good year.

How should one compare, say, 75 steals in 90 attempts with 17 out of 17? One has to know something about the game to answer this kind of question, but there is little doubt that in baseball (where winning 60 percent of your games is the path to winning your division) an 83-percent success rate in steals pays off. Would 80 out of 100 be better than 75 out of 90? Most of us don't know, and managers are paid to decide if the extra 5 successes in 10 extra tries would help the team. (Of course, whether to go for an extra steal depends not only on the chance of success but on the game situation, on who the next batter is, and so on.)

The central lesson here, to which I will return in the final section of this chapter, is that some failure is not only to be expected but is desirable, since to refuse to risk failure means refusing to risk success. The same is true in any situation where the outcome of any single trial is uncertain.

To stay with the analogy, the advantage of having a Rickey Henderson on base is not merely the extra bases he steals, and thus the extra runs that are scored. The *threat* to steal has benefits in addition to the steals themselves. Distracted by the presence of a noted base stealer on first base, the pitcher may fail to concentrate on the next batter, or he may pass up the slow curve or knuckleball in favor of a fastball to give his catcher a better chance at throwing out the runner if he goes. Any of these will cause the batter at the plate to have a better chance of getting a hit or a walk.

The roles of bluffing when playing poker are similar. **Bluffing is designed to help you win some pots that you would otherwise lose, but also to enhance your payoffs on some pots that you would win in any case.**

Neglect the second of these advantages for the moment and simply ask how often a bluff has to succeed to make it worthwhile merely in its own context. Here the payoff is readily calculated. Suppose you are playing 7-card stud and after the seventh card you have not improved the pair of Aces you have showing. The high hand on the board shows two low pairs and has checked to you, the sole remaining player. There is $150 in the pot, and you are convinced from the previous betting and the cards you have seen that your rival does not have a full house. This is a pot-limit game, and you know that if you also check you are a sure loser since you can't beat the showing hand. Suppose, however, that you bet $100, a sizable but not unheard-of bet in your game. This is a bluff designed to make your opponent think you have at least a second pair. If he calls, you'll lose $100; if he folds you'll win the $150 that was in the pot when you bet. Notice here that the relevant probability is not that you have the best hand (you don't), but that your opponent will think you do and thus fold. To break even in such situations you'll have to succeed on your bluff only two times in every five tries.[1] Even if you are caught bluffing half the time in such situations, you end up a winner. If your bluffs never fail to work, you are bluffing too seldom.[2]

---

1. Two wins will net you $300, the same amount you'll lose in three failed bluffs.
2. Herbert Yardley tells of using a particular bluff forty-one times in a row without being called (*The Education of a Poker Player*, p. 14). If true, he should have tried it more often.

Notice that in poker games where the maximum bet is not allowed to be larger than the size of the pot—which is always the case in Thursday-night games—your bluffs never have to succeed more than half of the time. As the size of the bet required to bluff successfully goes down relative to the size of the pot, the success ratio you need to break even decreases. For example, if there is $100 in the pot and a $50 bluff will give your opponent real pause, you only have to succeed 1 time in 3 to break even. The psychologically fascinating fact here is that most poker players hate to be caught bluffing anywhere near half of the time, and thus bluff too infrequently in terms of their expected winnings.

Of course breaking even on your bluffs isn't really your objective. But even so limited a goal may well be a sensible one when you also consider the benefits of having a reputation as someone who bluffs a lot. Some of the time in what appears to be a bluffing situation you actually will have the cards that give you the best hand. Behind that pair of Aces *is* a second pair or a third Ace. Behind some possible straights, flushes, or full houses are *made* straights, flushes, or full houses. In those situations you will want to make a big bet and have it called because you expect to win the pot, and the bigger the pot the greater your gain. The chance of your big bets being called increases the more often you have been caught bluffing in the past. The rival who pushes his money in and says, "I wouldn't call this if it were anyone but you" thinks he's putting you down, but in fact he's playing into your game.

It doesn't hurt for you to be thought to bluff more than you actually do. Many good poker players tend to bluff early in a poker game and then ease off as the session wears on. This is called *advertising*. In any case, there is a natural tendency to overestimate how often someone bluffs if that player is caught bluffing fairly often. Every time a bluffer loses he is exposed as a bluffer; every time he is not called after a big bet, in many of which cases he has the best hand, people will suspect that he may have been bluffing, a reputation that will benefit him in the long run, particularly if it is exaggerated by his opponents.

Bluffing is a key element in the subtle art of *pot management*—the art of seeing that the pots you win are, on average, greater than the pots you lose.

You may argue that this is all well and good as a matter of abstract theory but that in actual experience the heavy bluffers, such as Bill, tend to be the losers, while the rocks, such as Ty, who bluffs only about once a month, are the winners. The observation is correct, but the explanation is not based on the amount of bluffing. Ty is the base stealer who goes 5 for 5 in his attempts. He is frequently a winner in your poker game not because he doesn't bluff but because he avoids all kinds of loose and foolish situations that a poor player walks into, such as obliviousness to the hazard of being second-best, or trailing along on long-shot hopes even when the pot odds are against him. But while he wins regularly, Ty misses many opportunities both to steal pots and to increase the size of pots that he does win. Bill loses not because he bluffs too much but because he plays too loosely and doesn't think ahead. **Getting caught bluffing is not in itself a sign of loose or foolish poker playing, although many loose and foolish poker players also bluff a lot.**

Of course you have to know your opponent. You play poker against people, and people have their patterns of habitual response. Duke follows what has come to be called "Duke's Rule" and always calls in a 7-card stud game if he has two pairs or better unless there is a better hand showing.[3] Hugh quickly learned never to bluff against Duke's

3. In fairness to Duke, he developed his rule in a game that had a fixed, relatively low limit to any bet. His mistake was in sticking with the rule after the betting limits increased.

two pair but to sympathize with his bad luck in being second-best so often when he had two good pairs. Knott, who
seems aware of little except how *he* is doing, plays cautiously
when behind, but expansively when well ahead. If near the
end of the evening he is losing for the session, he can be
bluffed out on hands he would readily have called earlier in
the evening.

BLUFFS AND THE SIZE OF THE BET

A bluff depends upon how large a bet it will take to deter
an opponent from calling even though he suspects he may
well have the best hand. A big bet is designed to make the
target reluctant to risk that much more money. The bigger
the bet the greater the reluctance, especially since a big bet
may also persuade him that you must have a pretty good
hand on which you are risking your hard-won money. A
big bet both worsens his pot odds and tends to diminish his
estimate of the probability that he will be the winner. Both
the absolute amount of the bet and its size relative to the
pot are important. **In low-limit games you usually can't
bet enough to overcome the pot odds in favor of being
called.**

A successful bluff is usually only possible if the size of the
bet is both significant in itself *and* a significant fraction of
the pot. With $50 in the pot and a $2 bet you'll almost always be called because your rival will only have to think he
has 1 chance in 25 to win to make it a sensible call, and also
because $2 doesn't seem like much money.

Does the same analysis apply to a situation where there is
$500 in the pot and $20 is bet? To many amateurs the two
situations are not the same: calling a $2 bet is easier than
calling a $20 bet, even if the pot odds are equivalent. This
difference has to be taken into account even if it is not

wholly rational.[4] If this is the case for you, and if you would fold because $20 is "real money" even though the pot odds are greatly in your favor, then you are probably playing in too steep a game. There is nothing shameful in knowing what level of game you can afford or enjoy. (A good rule of thumb is that if you are not having fun in your regular game, the stakes are either too high or too low.) But you cannot play poker well unless you can distance yourself from the inherent value of your money in deciding whether to bet, raise, or call. The other side of the coin is that the money involved has to be big enough for you to take it seriously.

Varying the Size of Bet

A bluff bet is designed to make your opponent doubt that the pot odds really are in his favor. Consider the matter from the point of view of the target of a bluff. Suppose you—the target—have four spades showing in 7-card stud, and have actually made your flush by getting a spade in the hole on the seventh card. Your opponent, Hugh, an excellent poker player, is showing two pairs, Jacks and 7's. There is $100 in the pot, Hugh has the bet, and somewhat to your surprise he bets into you. With nothing more than two pairs he would normally check, since he knows that if you can't beat two pair you won't call him, but that if you do call he'll surely lose his bet. Thus his bet either signifies that he has his full house and wants you to call or that he believes you have your flush and will be induced to fold your winning hand by reasoning that he wouldn't have bet unless he had a full house. Suppose you think there is only about 1 chance

---

4. As discussed in Chapter 6, it may be rational to view big and small amounts of money differently. A classical economist would argue that the "diminishing marginal utility of money" explains the reluctance to risk a large amount on the same probability of winning as was accepted for a small amount.

in 5 that he is bluffing. A pot-odds calculation tells you that if his bet is under $20 you should call. If he bets $100, you should fold.

But the player who always plays the same way will become predictable. An unimaginative player may reason as follows: "The more confident I am, the bigger the bet I should make." A slightly more sophisticated one may reason: "A small bet is apt to be called, thus it should be made when I have a good hand, whereas a large bet may well cause you to fold, which I want you to do when I'm weak." Following this logic, he reserves his big bets for his bluffs. It will not take long for opponents to fathom both of these strategies if they are followed consistently, and to be able to judge the strength or weakness of the bettor's hand from the size of the bet. When an opponent mixes his tactics, however, you will be unable to infer his hand confidently merely from the size of his bet. Here psychology enters. Does a small bet this time mean he really wants me to call, and a large one that he can't afford to have me call? Or does he figure I'll think that way and he really has a good hand when he makes a big bet?

There are two messages here as you consider the size of a bluff bet. First, never make a bluff bet so small that it can be called painlessly in order to "keep you honest," nor so small as to make calling an irresistible pot-odds bet. You are unlikely to gain the benefits of bluffing without risking a significant amount of money. Second, vary the size of your bets, whether bluffing or not, so that the size of your bet does not reveal your tactics. In the situation above, in a pot-limit game where the maximum bet is $100, you might bet $40, $70, and $100 each a third of the time *whether you are bluffing or whether you have the hand made.* One way to randomize this is to use the second hand on your watch, the first twenty seconds telling you to bet $40, the second $70, and the third $100. It is useful to use a truly random device, like a second hand, rather than to rely on haphazard mixing so that you don't fall into predictable patterns. (But beware of using something like a watch to randomize. Don't look at the watch *only* when you are thinking of bluffing; use it in bluffing situations when you have the cards, too.)

WHEN NOT TO BLUFF

Bluffing makes sense when it is your only chance to win a pot, but it has to have a reasonable chance of success. Plainly the bluff must constitute a credible threat both in terms of the bluffer's behavior as well as in terms of his showing cards and the other cards that have been seen. Bluffing with a pair of 7's showing in stud poker is much more credible if no other sevens have shown than if one or both of the others have been seen. Similarly, showing three or four cards to a straight or flush will be much more threatening to an opponent if the key cards to complete the hand are not already unavailable to you. It is not only what you hold but what is showing that matters in bluffing, or in setting up a bluff. *Scare cards* are those showing combinations that look so powerful that they may induce an opponent to fold. While scare cards are not strictly necessary to bluffing, they certainly help to establish credibility.

A bluff becomes tempting whenever you suspect weakness on the part of your opponents. This is often the case when the high hand checks and no one else is anxious to bet. A bet by you in such a situation may well win the pot, or at the very least reveal which of the other hands is a relatively strong one. Indeed, when suspecting weakness in pot-limit poker, you may well try to set up a bluff by betting moderately heavily before the final card has been dealt, both to suggest your own (nonexistent) strength and to build up the pot to the point where a sizable bluffing bet is permitted. Once again, however, you must be aware of who your opponents are; is one of them likely to have checked with a strong hand in order to sandbag?

It is usually easier to bluff good players like Hugh or Ty than poorer ones like Lou or Duke. But especially against good players, you must be prepared for an occasional subsequent raise by the target of your bluff. It is usually a good idea to cut your losses by folding when this happens rather than being tempted to reraise on the chance that his raise was a counterbluff. For reasons that are not entirely clear, the phenomenon of two bluffers raising each other in the same hand is extraordinarily rare in amateur games.[5]

There is one important situation in which one should virtually never bluff, and a surprising number of pretty good players neglect it. This is when an opponent can know with certainty that he has you beaten. This happens frequently in games such as Holdem or Omaha. As an example, take the following hand from an Omaha game:

> The widow shows, in the order received: **4♦, 10♦, 7♣, 9♠, K♦**. You hold: **8♠, J♠, 10♣**, and a card I'll call X. You had a good chance to win with your straight until the diamond King was added to the widow. Now, however, a diamond flush is almost surely present. Despite your high bet on the previous round, which was designed to eliminate competitors and thus protect your straight, three other players remain in the game. The first two check, but Hugh makes a moderate-size bet and it's up to you. You are confident he has a flush, and thus

---

5. It is not, however, uncommon in high-stakes games among the top pros. When it occurs in a game that has both amateurs and pros, it raises at least the suspicion that the pros may be colluding to drive out the amateur.

you may be well advised to fold. But perhaps he
can be bluffed out.

If, *but only if,* your X card is the Ace of diamonds do you
have an excellent opportunity for a credible bluff; the best
possible hand will hold the Ace and another diamond, but
only you know that this hand does not exist. Even if Hugh
holds the Queen and Jack of diamonds (a holding with
which he would surely have stayed in up until this point,
and have bet when he did), he may well fold in view of your
raise. He realizes that his hand, though good, may be second-best. Thus a bluff by you is possible. But suppose your
X card is not the Ace of diamonds; let it be anything else. A
person with the Ace-high flush has an unbeatable hand and
will surely not only call your bluff raise but reraise the maximum. If he does so, you can hardly afford to call.

To be sure, a bluff by you into a potential sure thing
might still succeed if no one has a lock (such as the Ace-high
flush in this example), but this would be a pretty big risk to
take. In this example, three opponents have stayed in the
hand despite your earlier bet, and this strongly suggests that
at least one of them is there because of the two diamonds
that showed on the flop.

You should always try to avoid the disaster of having a
hand that is *known* by one of your opponents to be second-
best. The next chapter will have more to say on the subject
of avoiding second-best, but a good general rule is never to
bluff (or bet) into a potential sure thing if that holding is
reasonably likely. This possibility often occurs after the last
card in games with a widow (and in 5-card stud with only
one down card), and this fact explains why, if bluffing occurs in those games, it is likely to be done before the last
showing card is exposed, in the hope of causing hands that
might end up with a sure thing to fold before they are
achieved.

CALLING THE LAST BET

> The game is 7-card stud, pot limit, and you have been sitting quietly with two pair, Kings and 5's, since the fifth card, facing a showing pair of Aces. Your cards are all alive, and you have high hopes. You show K, 5, 5, J, and have K, A, in the hole. The high hand on the board shows A, A, 9, 3, and has been making more or less standard bets. Two others have called through six cards, probably looking for straights or flushes. There is about $80 in the pot as the seventh (down) card is dealt, and you find you have not improved. Duke, with the Aces, bets $40, and the other two players fold. It's your turn, and you . . .

Particularly in pot-limit games, but to some extent in all games, the decision about whether to call the last bet after all the cards have been dealt is one of the most crucial. Obviously if you could see all the cards, you would call only if your hand was better than that of the bettor and of other likely callers. But in an honest game you do not see all the cards, and thus the decision you make may be right or wrong. Is this last bet, to which you must now respond, made from strength or is it a bluff?

The probability in the above example is that Duke has you beaten: if his three hole cards were chosen randomly from the deck they would improve the showing pair of Aces about 55 percent of the time. But the pot odds are $120 to $40, or 3 to 1, better than these probability odds.[6]

In the last analysis, the most important part of all of this consists in forming a necessarily somewhat subjective guess

---

6. Remember, however, that two of Duke's hole cards were received *before* his Aces, and may have been the reason he has stayed in this long.

about how good your chances are of winning. This will depend on the quality of your hand, the other showing cards that help you to define your opponents' possible and probable holdings, the cards that may already have been folded, and of course the previous betting, as well as the habits of the other players.

By the time of the last bet many—in fact, most—hands do not require a difficult decision; you are either clearly beaten or probably a winner. It is the deals where you have a chance to win, though not the *best* chance, that test your skill. The biggest difference between good and mediocre players is the ability to judge their chances in the questionable hands, and then to take the appropriate action. The art of poker comes in making this judgment accurately most of the time. Indeed, you sometimes feel that a particular decision is correct based on factors no more tangible than the body language of your opponent. But there is no escaping the fact that however expert you may be, you often cannot be sure.

Folding Errors and Calling Errors

It is useful to distinguish three possibilities: you can make the correct decision (folding hands that would lose and calling with hands that will win), you can make what I will call a *folding error* (that is, folding a winner), or you can make a *calling error* (calling with a loser). You hope you make the right decision often, but you must expect to make errors some of the time.

Errors of either kind are costly, but not in the same way. A folding error means you are forgoing winnings (the amount in the pot that you might otherwise have won), but it costs you nothing out of pocket. A calling error costs you the money you put in the pot to call the bet. The first is a virtual (or unrealized) loss, the second an actual (or realized) one.

While making errors is inevitable given uncertainty, you can always avoid, control, or limit the possibility of making one kind of error, but only at the cost of increasing the likelihood of making the other kind of error. The ultraconservative player who never calls unless he is sure of winning avoids calling errors, but frequently makes folding errors; the ultraloose player who calls everything unless he is beaten on the board does the reverse—he avoids folding errors but frequently makes calling errors.

Since the conservative player usually comes out a winner and the loose one a loser, it may seem that the second kind of error is the more serious. (At the extreme, this is surely so because you get so many more chances to make calling errors.) But an intermediate strategy is better than either extreme. You need to make each kind of error some of the time in order not to *always* make the other kind of error. **You must risk failure to achieve success.** But to what extent? That depends on your objectives.

Maximizing Winnings

If your objective is to maximize your winnings in the long run, then, ignoring the psychological overtones of the decision, there is a best strategy for calling the final bet.

You should incur calling losses up to the point where you equal the virtual folding losses you avoid, but not beyond. This will occur if you call whenever the pot odds are greater than the probability odds. In other words, **call if (but only if) the expected value of doing so is positive.**[7] I call this the "optimal strategy."

For example, if there is $100 in the pot, which you can call (as the last caller) for $20, you should call if there is anything better than 1 chance in 5 of winning. On the other

---

7. If the expected value is zero, it doesn't matter whether you call or fold, you'll end up in the same position in the long run.

hand, if the last bet was $50 (the maximum possible if there was $50 in the pot before the bet was made), your chances of winning must be at least 1 in 3 to make it a sound call.

Notice here that our old friend "pot odds" applies not to the chance of getting a given card, which can often be accurately calculated, but to the probability (as you evaluate it) that the cards you have will beat those of your opponent, which is *not* readily calculated. There's the rub! One seldom knows for sure what the relevant probability is. But here is a useful guide to your behavior: keep rough track of your last-card errors as they occur in those cases where you can tell. How much did you lose by each calling error? How much did you forgo in winnings by folding when you would have won? If the cost of your calling errors is greater than the cost of your folding errors you are calling too much; that is, you are calling where the probability odds against you are greater than the pot odds in your favor. If you find big folding errors relative to calling errors, you are failing to call when the odds are in your favor. This is an aspect of learning by doing, which is treated in Chapter 10.

As the example above shows, you ought to be more reluctant to call a big final bet (big, that is, relative to the size of the pot) than a small one. This is why bluffing is possible, and why it is more likely to succeed in pot-limit games or in games with large limits rather than low limits. Returning to the example on page 127:

> . . . you call the $40, knowing that Duke may well have Aces up. But the pot is giving you 3-to-1 odds ($120 to $40), and you believe there is at least 1 chance in 4 that Duke does not have more than his showing pair of Aces. This judgment is based on the cards you've seen, including the Ace you hold—every other Ace, 9, or 3 improves your odds—but it is also based on the fact that the bettor is Duke, who you think would tend to bet

Aces rather than check them even if he didn't improve. (After all, he's bet them before into possible straights with impunity.) Now, if it had been Ty, who seldom bluffs, you would certainly think twice and probably fold.

Other Considerations

The optimal strategy for when to call the last bet is mathematically correct if maximizing money winnings over time is your objective. Yet many—probably most—good players play more conservatively than this, and fold more often than this rule suggests. That is, they make too few calling errors relative to folding errors. Why?

Minimizing regret. One answer is psychological: the regret of having been beaten in a showdown ("when I should have known better") may be greater than the regret at knowing you'd have won if only you'd had more courage ("Okay, so I would have won that time, but the odds were against it"). But this psychological attitude varies among players; some people, like Duke, hate the thought of being bluffed out or beaten by a rash bet on the part of another player. In any case, minimizing regret (which is different from maximizing winnings) may lead to a departure from the optimal strategy in either direction.

Coming out a winner. A second possible reason for folding more often than the optimal strategy would dictate is that for a better-than-average player the probability of ending up a winner in a given session is greater with a strategy that folds more often. Virtual losses from not calling may limit your winnings, but they do not deplete your stack of chips. Maximizing the number of winning sessions in a regular game with friends is a different objective than maximizing the number of dollars won. In your poker game,

Hugh may prefer to have people say, "Hugh always seems to end up a winner," than to have them say, "Hugh sure makes a lot of money playing poker." A strategy that folds "too often" will reduce the average size of one's winnings, but the swings will be smaller.[8] For example, a player may choose a strategy that has an average win of $50 per session, with swings of up to plus or minus $60, in preference to a strategy with average winnings of $75, but with swings of up to plus or minus $150. Thus, in sessions where he is in fact unlucky (holding worse-than-average cards), his chances of coming out a loser are reduced. The more a player cares about coming out a winner in a given session, the more unwilling he should be to make calling errors.

Fleecing sheep.   A third situation where it may make sense to employ a strategy that is more conservative than the optimal one occurs when you feel your opponent will quit playing after he loses a certain amount. (This is often the behavior of tourists in casino poker games, and explains the conservative calling strategy of many professional poker players.) If Joe Pigeon is going to play foolishly, but only until he loses $200, you might as well wait until the odds are greatly in your favor rather than just slightly so. After all, you don't want to build up his stack temporarily only to have someone else relieve him of it.

Enjoying action.   All of the above may explain playing more conservatively than the optimal strategy suggests. But not all considerations work in this direction. You may choose to play more loosely because the amount of money won or lost may not be as important to you as being in on the action. Playing extremely conservatively

8. Technically, the conservative strategy has lower *variance* than the optimal one, and thus the chance of the better-than-average player (who wins on average) losing in a given session is reduced.

can be boring, and certainly gives you less action per hour than a looser strategy.

This matter of valuation of time deserves a bit more comment. Generally, amateur poker players have a strictly limited amount of time that they are able to devote to playing poker, and thus a strategy that tells them that they should do such and such but which neglects the time involved (implicitly assuming that its value is unaffected by how they play) is unlikely to be attractive. If it is not too expensive to play loosely, the winnings forgone may be justified as a good buy of pleasure per hour.

A personal example: on a one-day stopover in Las Vegas I used the opportunity to play moderately low-stakes poker at a casino. Having just read a very conservative "How to Win at Poker" book—there are many of them—that gave what seemed to me to be excessively rigid rules for when to drop out of the particular game I was playing (Omaha, Hi-Lo), I kept track of the number of hands I was dealt that met the prescribed standard for staying in to see the flop. In six hours, I had only eight such hands. Had I played only those hands, I might have gone home a modest winner. Five of the eight proved to be winners, one of them a very big winner. I did not keep track, but those winnings were probably greater than the blind bets I was forced to make to stay at the table. But if I had followed the book's advice, I would surely have been a pretty unhappy camper. My time and the extra costs of the trip would have made playing eight hands in six hours a pretty dreary way of having a poker diversion. (During those six hours I actually played about eighty hands, called the final bet in about thirty out of roughly two hundred dealt, and just about broke even, but I'd had a good time, with plenty of action.)

Keeping opponents honest. At the poker table you often hear a just-beaten player show his hand and say, "I had to call," or grumble, "Someone had to keep him honest." Or as he throws away his cards you'll hear another say, "I'd be ashamed to call with these cards even though I may have the winning hand." This may merely be small talk, but if it is more than that, it is foolish.

You never have to call, neither to honor the cards you hold nor to keep someone honest. Indeed, you never need explain why you did what you did. One of the enjoyments of playing poker (in contrast to serious bridge playing) is that it is not necessary to be consistent in what you do, nor to justify your actions to anyone. When you call an opponent where you have only 1 chance in 4 or 5 of winning (because the pot odds are in your favor), your opponent will have you beat more often than not, but you only have to win 1 time in 4 or 5 in such a situation to break even. *That's* why you called him, not to keep him honest.

8

♠ ♣ ♥ ♦

AVOIDING SECOND-BEST

The game is 7-card stud, pot-limit, and after six cards you hold four cards to an open-ended straight, needing only a Jack or a 6, neither of which has shown up in the cards you have seen. On the sixth card, Knott, who had shown a pair of Queens, now catches a third Queen, which surprises you since a Queen is one of your hole cards. He bets, and you . . .

Every poker player knows that the thrill of getting a good hand is tempered by the fear that while ordinarily it would be a winner, this time it may not be good enough because someone else is making a large bet or raise just when you thought you had the pot counted. Sometimes this misfortune cannot be avoided, but more often than not you will have walked into a second-best trap, beguiled by the beauty of a particular hand.

THE DANGERS OF SECOND-BEST

Consider the example. While a straight is ordinarily a good hand in 7-card stud, and you have about 1 chance in 5 of hitting it this time, calling Knott's bet would be a poor gamble. The reason is not in the immediate pot odds facing you, but rather that your subsequent betting opportunities are unpromising because of the possibility of being second-best even if you improve.

Suppose you make your straight. You will not dare to make a bet if Knott checks, nor raise if he bets, but you will probably feel obliged to call his bet. In a pot-limit game, where the biggest bet is likely to occur on the last round, you'll find that the expected value of buying that seventh card is almost surely negative.[1] It is really not necessary to calculate this expected value, since your poker experience should tell you that hanging in and making reluctant calls is not the way either to have a good time or to come out ahead. If you do hit your straight, but end up losing to a full house, you'll feel bruised by your bad luck in having a straight at the wrong time. But in this case you were warned. Knott's chances of improving his three of a kind (if that's all he had after six cards) are about as good as yours of getting your straight, but if he hits, it puts him in the driver's seat *whether you hit or not.* Nor could a bet or a raise by you change his strategy. He would pay to get a seventh card to his trips even if he suspects you already have your straight—and he would be right to do so, since if he hits he will have a sure winner.

Anticipating future scenarios, both favorable and unfavorable, is a vital component in good poker playing. It is the poker equivalent of a chess player thinking ahead a few moves. It is surprising how many fairly good poker players, such as Doc, don't bother to do this, concentrating only on the probability of getting the hand they seek. The lesson is this:

You can afford to take risks to reach situations where, if you hit, you are virtually sure to win, but you should avoid situations where, even if you hit, you will still have a significant chance of being second-best.

1. In other words, the implied pot odds will be less than the probability odds of winning.

This lesson is obvious in the present example, and most poker players have little difficulty in folding a *potential* straight or flush when facing a showing set of trips. But what if you already have the straight after six cards? Should you grit your teeth and brace yourself for a reluctant call on both this round and the next one? Here the answer will depend crucially on the betting rules. In a limit game the answer is usually yes; in a pot-limit game, it is almost surely no. Folding is what the holder of trips wants you to do if that is all he has; nevertheless, it is still your best response, because you will be at his mercy after the seventh card. If he checks, you would be foolish to bet into his potential sandbag; if he bets, the pot odds at that stage will make it sensible for you to call even a big bet. You thus risk losing a big additional bet, but have no opportunity for a big bet or raise on your own initiative. Of course if his bet is very small you may decide to call and hope for the best. But you will have no one but yourself to blame if you end up with a big loss on a second-best hand—a loss big enough to make your possible sacrifice of the pot before the seventh card seem not so great. Here it is more important to anticipate the betting opportunities that will emerge under different scenarios than to try and figure out whether you are already beaten. Even if you are not, you are in jeopardy.

Another Example

Avoiding big second-best losses depends critically not on the absolute value of a given holding but on your hand in the specific context of a poker deal. Here is another example, this one from pot-limit Jackpots.

> You are sitting in the fourth position (of seven) and you squeeze your dealt cards and discover a full house: three 4's and two 10's. To add to your sense of well-being, Doc, the player to the left of

the dealer, opens under the gun for $14, matching the total of the antes. The next two players fold, and you merely call, hoping that one or more of the remaining players also calls or even raises. (You might raise instead, but this would almost surely prevent any further calls and might even lead the opener to fold if he has only a modest hand. You are content to lie low and hope for a chance to show your strength when the pot is bigger). In the hand as played, one more player, Duke, does call, so there is $56 in the pot at the time of the draw.

Doc draws one card, you stand pat, and Duke draws one. You expect Doc to check to you, and intend then to bet $40, hoping for a call, or, if you're lucky, for a raise from Duke if he hits a flush or a high straight. (In his position he would prob-ably have raised with two pair before the draw.) But like life, poker is full of surprises. Doc, the opener, bets $50, right into your pat hand and that of the one-card draw. What should you do in this situation?

You should call but not raise. Doc, you reason, either had two pair or trips for his openers. If he has improved in any way, he will almost surely have a better full house than yours, and if you raise him he'll surely raise back. If he did not improve his openers, but is bluffing by betting into your pat hand, he won't call your raise. Your hand is good enough to call, and you surely don't want people to think you can be induced into dropping a pat hand by a big bet.[2] You call nervously because the original overwhelming odds in favor of your winning no longer apply. Suddenly you face

2. There are always exceptions: if the bettor never bluffs and is too careful to bet trips into a pat hand and a one-card draw, you might fold your full house, but that takes enormous confidence in your card-reading ability.

the risk of being second-best, and while you cannot avoid it, you can limit the cost if it turns out that you are.

When this hand was dealt, Harry, in "your" seat, raised, was promptly reraised by Doc, and lost a bundle to the fourth Ace that Doc had hit on the draw. Harry is still muttering about how unlucky he was to have a full house against four Aces, a very rare hand indeed, and so improbable that, he said, asking for agreement, "I had to call!" (Of course any improvement by Doc would have done as well.) Harry *did* have bad luck; however, the consequence was much more expensive for him than it need have been.

SMALL DIFFERENCES CAN BE CRITICAL

In some games, particularly lowball and widow games, the difference between a safe hand and a potentially second-best one can be small and subtle. The following example happened to me in a hand of 6-card stud lowball, where the first and last cards are dealt down and the best hand is defined as 6, 4, 3, 2, A. An 8-low is usually good enough to win, and a 7-low is a very good hand indeed.

As it was played, after the last up card (the fifth card) had been dealt, the cards were as follows:

ME: [2], 7, K, 3, 6 (of assorted suits)
OPPONENT: [X], 10, 3, 7, 5

From my opponent's play—he stayed in with a 10 showing after two cards—I believed that X must be an Ace, and the reader should assume the same for this exercise.

At this point in the game my opponent bet, and everyone else folded. Plainly, unless I improved I would not have the best hand, but my chances seemed pretty good. If I caught an Ace, 4, 5, 8, or 9, I would have the best hand if my opponent caught a King, Queen, Jack, 10, 7, 5, 3, or Ace.

That is, if I improved, there was a better-than-even chance that my opponent would not.[3]

After getting his fifth card my opponent bet the amount in the pot, $50, and I had to decide whether to call or fold. The immediate pot odds, $100 to my $50, weren't bad, so I called. Should I have?

The answer here is no, because the anticipated last-round betting scenarios, and thus the implied pot odds, were not in my favor. Notice that if my opponent catches a 2 or a 4 he will have a *sure thing* no matter how good my final card is. Thus, if he bets, I dare not raise, but probably will feel obliged to call if I can beat a 10-low. If he checks, I dare not bet, again because he can be sure that I don't have the nuts and I can't be sure that he doesn't. To see the danger, suppose he checks, I bet, and he then comes back with a maximum raise. Do I call, in the hope that he is bluffing, or do I now fold without even finding out? This is precisely the kind of situation you want to avoid. Even though the probabilities of having the best hand would be in my favor if I improved, there was no money to be made by me after the last card. Making reasonable assumptions about my rival's behavior, I would be likely to call if he bet $100 after the last card, and to check if he checked. The expected value of my calling the $50 bet to get that sixth card turns out to have been about *minus* $14.[4]

The mathematics merely documents common sense: it doesn't pay to spend money to put yourself in a

3. The actual probabilities here are not important, but my probability of having the best hand *after the last card* was approximately 30 percent. This is a measure of how often I would improve and my opponent would not.

4. Again, the calculation isn't important, but here it is. The probabilities depend on the cards that have been seen. Neglecting all but the ten cards listed above, I will fail to improve 61 percent of the time and lose $50. I will improve and my rival will not be able to beat me about 30 percent of the time, and thus I'll win $100. We will both improve about 9 percent of the time and I will lose $150. EV = $-(.61 \times \$50) + (.30 \times \$100) - (.09 \times \$150) = -\$14$.

situation where even the best hand you can get may well be facing a sure thing on the part of your opponent. **It is the other player's sure things that produce your big losses.**

So I was wrong to call.[5] But now let's change the cards a little bit by changing the spots on that fifth card that improved each of our hands. Suppose after five cards the hands look like this:

ME: [2], 7, K, 3, 5
OPPONENT: [X], 10, 3, 7, 6

As before, we'll assume X is an Ace. Here too I will not have the best hand unless I improve, and more than half of the remaining cards will not improve my hand (any Queen or Jack, or any of the five ranks of cards that would pair me). My overall chance of ending up with the best hand works out to be about 35 percent, a little, but not much, better than before, largely because this time if I get a 10 and my opponent doesn't improve, I will have the best hand. The crucial difference is that now I *can achieve a lock* if I catch a 4 or an Ace, and there is nothing my opponent can catch that will put him in a sure-thing position. This changes totally the last-round betting scenarios. Even if my opponent improves his hand, he will not sensibly bet for fear I will raise. If he checks, I can bet whether I have improved or not, without fear that he will raise. The threat that I will bet, bluffing some of the time, probably means I will get called much of the time when I improve and bet. If my opponent checks, but calls my $100 bet when I make it, the expected

5. In the event, I was lucky: I improved, he did not, and I won the pot. He, of course, was unlucky, and he let me know what a dumb play I had made. He was right.

value of this hand to me is approximately *plus* $4![6] That's a significant contrast to the −$14 of the previous hand.[7]

Notice that in each of these situations, both the actual and the hypothetical, I had the second-best hand after five cards. Indeed, in each of them, more often than not, I would expect to have the second-best hand after six cards. But in the first situation my opponent could *know* I was second-best, whereas I could never be sure; in the second situation, I could *know* I was now best and my opponent could never be sure. **This knowledge doesn't change the odds of my winning; what it does is transform the plausible betting scenarios, and thus the implied pot odds and the expected value of the hand.[8]**

These examples may have been difficult to follow, but the general lesson should be clear. Everyone has his share of losing on second-best hands; in the long run, good players avoid the unnecessarily big losses that can accompany expected cases of bad luck. This is all part of pot management.

6. Subject to the same assumptions as in the previous example, I'll fail to improve about 54 percent of the time and lose $50. Further assumptions are now needed. Suppose that after the last card, my opponent checks, and I bet $100 if I improve, and he calls if—but only if—he has improved. These are the outcomes: 28 percent of the time, I'll bet, he'll fold, and I'll win $100; 8 percent of the time I'll bet, be called, and win $200; 10 percent of the time I'll bet, be called, and lose $150. EV = −(.54 × $50) + (.28 × $100) + (.08 × $200) − (.10 × $150) = $4.

7. Does it seem that the difference of $18 between the expected values in the two situations is not much in a game where $100 bets occur? You play about a hundred hands in a session, and to make an $18 expected-value error even ten times would add up to a $180 difference in the outcome of the session.

8. Is the payoff in the second situation so good that I might want to raise before the last card is dealt? No, because with the probability odds in his favor after five cards, my opponent would be well advised to make a maximum reraise and then would very likely not have any chips left on the table for a final-round bet. My advantage in just calling was that I could take my 35-percent chance of getting the best hand relatively cheaply, with the possibility of a big final bet if—but only if—I succeeded.

9

♠ ♣ ♥ ♦

POT MANAGEMENT

The game is Jackpots, pot-limit, with seven players each an-
teing $2. On the deal Duke opens for $14 in third position
with two pairs, Jacks and 5's. (This is about the median
two-pair hand). Hugh, in fifth position calls with four
cards to an Ace-high flush, Ty in sixth position calls with
three deuces, as does Lou, the dealer, with a pair of Queens.
Thus there is $70 in the pot at the time of the draw and an
opportunity for big bets in the next round. Duke draws one
card; so do Hugh and Ty. Lou draws three. Duke intends
to check after the draw to the other two one-card draws,
but when he squeezes his cards he sees he has caught a third
Jack. Virtually sure he now has the winner, and wishing to
maximize the size of the pot, he . . .

If you play poker regularly with six other players, you will be
dealt the best hand about one-seventh of the time. If all the
pots are the same size, and if everybody stays in to the end
of every hand, you'll tend to win about one hand per round
and break even. There will be variations in the winning and
losing, but who wins and who loses, and the amounts won
and lost, will be strictly matters of luck. But while showdown and poker games played for pennies by small children
are like this, most are not. The key to doing better than
breaking even in the long run may be described as *pot man-*
agement. There are three rules that are easy to state but
harder to achieve.

1. Minimize your contributions to hands that you have a high probability of ending up losing.   This involves a willingness to drop out of hands when the probability of losing is moderately high, even if the possibility of winning is still there. (Good players pay attention to probabilities, poor players to possibilities.) This also means staying in some other hands only as long as it is inexpensive to do so, and, if you can, use betting tactics to keep it so.

2. Stay in and win some hands that you would have lost if the best hand had not dropped out.   This can sometimes occur because you actually bluffed out a better hand; more often it will occur because your betting tactics made it sensible for opponents who might have outdrawn you to fold.

3. See to it that the pots you stay in and win are bigger than the pots you stay in and lose.   This involves *pot building,* perhaps the least discussed, but not the least important, of the tactics that distinguish good players from average ones.

THE EXAMPLE ANALYZED

In the example above, Duke wanted to get as much money in the pot as he could since he had a virtually sure winner. What he did was to bet $30, hoping for a raise. Hugh, who had caught the King to his Ace-high flush, called, but Ty and Lou folded. As Duke was raking in the chips, he indicated his disappointment that Hugh hadn't raised with his flush. Hugh replied that he felt lucky to have lost only $30, and Ty complimented himself silently for folding his low trips. Lou couldn't wait for the next hand to be dealt and felt lucky that he had resisted the temptation to call.

Duke could have done better. His opening bet and the calls by Hugh and Ty were all sensible; Lou's call on a pair of Queens was loose, based on hope rather than on reasonable expectations, but it was not an outrageously foolish bet given the pot odds at the time he made his call.

The mistake was Duke's. He should have checked after the draw rather than bet. He should have realized that when he bet neither Hugh nor Ty would call unless they had improved, since they surely recognized that his bet into their one-card draws was unusual. Even Lou wouldn't call Duke's bet unless he had caught a second pair, and probably wouldn't call even then unless the bet was relatively small and neither Hugh nor Ty had stayed in ahead of him. Thus Duke's bet will gain him nothing if none of his opponents has improved. Moreover, his bet will discourage a raise if they *have* improved. Suppose, instead of betting, Duke checks. If either Hugh or Ty has improved, one of them will surely bet, thus giving Duke the opportunity to raise. By checking, Duke gives up the possible gain of, at most, one caller in favor of his chance of a much bigger gain.

Why did Hugh not raise Duke's $30 bet, even though he caught the very card he had hoped for when he stayed in, and which he had surely counted on to give him a winner when he called the opening bet? He had read Duke's opening hand and subsequent one-card draw for either two pair or trips. His flush will beat either of those hands, but he correctly wonders why Duke bet instead of checking in deference to the two one-card draws. One possibility is that Duke has him beat, and would reraise if he now raised. (If he were absolutely certain this was the case he would fold his flush, but of course he isn't certain.) Even if Duke couldn't beat him, he might reraise on a bluff, giving Hugh a very tough decision. On these grounds alone he properly decided not to raise.

Should Hugh have even called? Another possibility was that Duke didn't improve his two pair but bet $30 in order to discourage a hand with a higher two pair or even small trips from making a bigger bet—say, $50 or $70—that

Duke would feel obliged to call. Still another possibility was that the bet was designed to cause Ty, a very conservative player, to fold his hand. It was even possible that Duke's bet was designed to discourage any of the others from trying to bluff him out. Because of all these possibilities, Hugh was not going to fold his flush, even though he suspected he might lose, so he was glad merely to call. Moreover, if it turned out that he had the best hand with his flush, he didn't want to discourage Ty or Lou, whom he could beat, from calling as well. After all, Ty might have been drawing to, and hit, a straight or flush (which Hugh would beat); if so, he would surely call, and Lou might catch three of a kind and call, or even raise. So to limit his loss if he is second-best, and as sound pot management if he happens to hold the best hand, Hugh simply called.

Here is an alternative scenario to Duke's $30 bet:

> Duke squeezes his cards, finds his full house, and checks to the one-card draws. Hugh looks at his flush and says, "Well, I'm probably beat by all of you, but let's see what'll happen if I bet." He bets $40, and Ty, after thinking for a few seconds, calls. Lou finds he has caught a pair of 3's to go with his Queens and calls too! Duke pauses and then raises the bet by $100. Hugh decides the chance that Duke is bluffing is large enough that the pot odds favor his call, and he throws in his $100. Ty folds, annoyed that he called Hugh's $40 bet but not prepared to spend more money in a losing effort. Lou thinks too long and finally throws away his two pair.

In this scenario, instead of having one person call a $30 bet, Duke has had one player put $140, and two others $40, into the pot he ends up winning.

In the example as it was actually played, Hugh played his cards correctly but Duke did not, even though Duke's pile of chips grew and Hugh's declined. Duke had not managed the pot to his advantage. One or two pots like this per session make a big difference in the final outcome, even though they don't change the count of hands won and lost.

GENERAL PRINCIPLES

The actions you take, the bets you make, and their timing are tactics by which you seek to achieve the three keys to pot management. Tactics are the servants of your objectives. Do you want to induce opponents to fold or to call? Do you want to forestall a bigger bet, or do you want to induce a raise? The link between your objectives and the appropriate tactics depends upon a number of variables.

The Size of Bets

Important decisions involve the size of the bets or raises that you choose to make. But what is a "big" bet or raise? Usually it's not a question of a specific amount, even in a given game, but of a departure from the expected pattern. Every regular game develops a betting rhythm, a pattern of typical or usual betting round by round. Bets and raises have to be evaluated accordingly. Consider a pot-limit 7-card stud game where the usual betting rhythm is an opening bet of $1, $2 on the fourth card, $5 on the fifth card, and $20 on the sixth card. Any raise, or a $4 bet on the fourth card, will seem big, as will a $10 bet or raise on the fifth card. But a $10 bet or raise on the sixth card will seem small since it is only half as large as the usual bet at that stage. In a limit game, the normal bet is often the minimum required bet in the early rounds and the maximum permitted bet in the later rounds. Here, too, checking one's hand, making an unusually big bet, or raising will signal departures from the norm, and thus send a message about the bettor's hand.

The relevance of this is that if you follow the usual betting patterns, your opponents won't begin to think hard about your hand. If you depart from the patterns, they will, so it is a good idea to do so deliberately, though not in an invariable pattern.[1]

Whenever you do more than passively call or make the standard bet, you have three possible competing objectives in mind. One is to discourage other players from calling; in this way you reduce the number of opponents who might beat you. The second objective is to increase the size of the pot—which you believe you have a good chance of winning—by inducing people to stay in the pot and/or inducing those who do stay in to contribute more than they otherwise would. The third is to keep the pot small by discouraging or preempting some larger bets. Which of these you want to do will depend upon the quality of your hand. Which of them you succeed in doing will depend on a number of variables, of which the most important are the round of betting, your position in the betting sequence, and (as always) the identity of your opponents and their patterns of play.

---

1. It took me almost a year to figure out that Art, a physicist who was widely thought to be a tough, analytical, but unpredictable player, raised the opening bet in 7-card stud every fifth hand in which he stayed, independent of what he held. The only thing wrong with his strategy (which was cheap, since the early-round bets and raises were small relative to the typical size of pot) was its mechanical regularity. Once I found the key I was able to take advantage of it by anticipating that it would happen—if only I could remember to keep track of which hand was the fifth.

Quality of Hand

Proper pot management starts early in a hand with a candid evaluation of the cards you're holding. While weak players passively go with the flow in the early rounds of betting, good players do not. They look at their starting cards and form a strategy that will serve them for several rounds. To illustrate this, consider five (somewhat stylized) levels of hand quality, as viewed after four cards have been dealt in 7-card stud.[2]

Monster hands.   A monster hand is one that is very powerful, and will usually prove a winner. With such a hand—say, high trips after four cards—you surely don't want to drive anyone out who might contribute, at least for a while, but of course you don't want to let people stay in so cheaply that you don't build the base for a big pot. You would prefer to have five people call a $5 bet than to have only one person call a $25 bet. Indeed, you might prefer four callers, or even three, at $5 to one $25 caller. You want lots of callers because you want to keep a number of players in the game, players who may improve enough to call your big bets later on. Your strategy is to lie in the weeds concealing your strength for as long as you can. If it is your bet, your early-round tactic is to make a normal or even below-normal bet, or to check if you are confident that someone else will bet.[3] You should call but not raise another's bet or raise. While you may get called if you raise now, you are more

2. I will argue in Chapter 13 that in most Thursday-night games the critical moment of decision in 7-card stud is at the fourth card. If, however, the game is one in which significant betting or raising occurs after three cards are dealt, this evaluation must occur then.
3. But avoid the disingenuous check. If you show a high pair and check, good players will suspect that you have powerful hole cards and frustrate your strategy by checking too.

likely to cause some or all of the others to fold. With a monster hand it pays to be patient. (This is called *slow-playing* your cards; the term refers to when you show your strength, not to the speed of your response.) In the middle rounds you will want to make normal bets if it is your bet, and merely call again if someone else bets or raises. This is especially the case if your hand has improved, say by becoming a full house instead of three of a kind. Your big betting and raising will come later, when the pot odds will make it likely that some of those who have stayed all this time will call your bet. Indeed, even if they have not achieved their hoped-for hands, one of them may be tempted to bluff into you if you have not shown much strength earlier. At that point either a check by you with the intent to raise or a maximum bet is likely to succeed.

Of course once in a while your monster will turn into a paper tiger. Your three Aces do not improve, and someone hits a straight or flush that beats you. When this happens you'll wish you had driven him out early, but in the long run you can afford an occasional loss of this kind with the extra money you have accumulated from your monsters that are called and are winners.

Vulnerable hands.   All four-card hands are vulnerable, of course, but I here refer to hands that you believe are currently the best but which are eminently beatable by any one of a number of other players if they stay in for the showdown. Your objective is to discourage some or even all of them from doing so. Such a hand after four cards in 7-card stud might be a pair of Queens, or two pairs headed by 10's. Your strategy here is to exaggerate your strength and to make the pot odds facing your opponents less favorable—that is, to make it expensive for them to try to catch the cards that would beat you. If it is your bet in the early rounds, your tactic will be to bet the maximum possible, and if it is not your bet, to raise or even reraise if others bet.

You may even wish to check-raise, but only if you are sure someone else will bet. **You must reduce the opposition.** Your chances of winning the pot are much greater against one opponent than against three or four or five.[4]

If you have not improved after the fifth and sixth cards it is necessary to be flexible. A check is usually the best tactic in limit poker. If bet into, merely call, or even fold. A more aggressive strategy is appropriate only if you read weakness on the part of all of your opponents. Any opponent who has stayed this far is likely to continue to stay if he has improved. A departure from this restrained strategy may be called for if your latest up card is a scare card. It may be worth trying to win the pot right now with a big bet. In limit games, however, maximum bets, which tend to drive people out in the early rounds, are much less likely to do so in the middle rounds unless the pot is relatively small as a result of one or more of the previous rounds having been checked around.

In pot-limit games a maximum bet on the sixth card may work to eliminate some or even all other players. Thus, if you have a vulnerable hand after six cards, have no chance of significant improvement, and you find that several players remain, you may wish to bet as much as possible now in the hope that some of them will fold. In any case, if they stay and don't improve, you want more of their money. You make your move *now* because you will certainly not be in a position to bet after the seventh card, nor will you find it comfortable to call a big bet into you. Here, as in limit poker, a big bet on the sixth card is worth considering if your latest up card is a scare card; if it is, you may win the pot with a big bet now, or set up a bluff for the last round.

---

4. Suppose there are three opponents, each of whom has only one chance in four of outdrawing you. The chance that at least one of the three will do so is 58 percent; if one of them drops out, your probability of being outdrawn decreases to 44 percent; if two drop out, it falls to 25 percent; and of course if all drop out, it falls to zero. In these circumstances, you would be glad to have just one caller.

It goes without saying that if at any point you are convinced you are beaten and cannot bluff out a better hand, you should quietly fold. The vulnerable hand is perhaps the most difficult kind of hand to play. It requires a mix of calls, bluffs, and folds, and which of these you choose depends on who your opponents are and what you believe they are holding.

Drawing hands.   A *drawing hand* is one that is worthless unless it improves, but if it improves is highly likely to be a winner. Good examples are four-card straights and flushes. Your objective on such hands is to stay in as inexpensively as possible until you hit or until you judge that your showing cards make a bluff credible. In the early rounds you have no desire to drive out opponents because if you hit you expect to beat them all, but neither are you afraid to call most bets or raises. However, the longer you stay in without completing your hand, the dimmer your prospects, and a round-by-round reevaluation of the pot odds is essential. Much depends on the other cards showing. Weak players tend to neglect this, and if they have a four flush at the outset grimly stay to see the seventh card, no matter what is showing, who is in the hand, or what they must call.

If your potential hand is well concealed, the appropriate tactics will be different than if it is not. For example, if after six cards in 7-card stud you have four to an Ace-high heart flush, but only the Ace and a small heart show, you will not be likely to bluff anyone out, and if you check, someone else will probably bet. It is possible that you can preempt a bigger bet by making a below-normal bet, but a check is safer. If three of your hearts are showing, a check by you may well lead others to do likewise and give you a chance to get the last card for nothing. If all four of your hearts show, a maximum-size bet is surely indicated and will usually win the pot then and there.

Long-shot hands.   Define these as hands such as three to a flush or straight in four cards. Here the probability of ending up with the winning hand is not large (roughly 1 in 9), but neither is it negligible. Your objective is to keep the betting small so that you can get additional cards and reevaluate your chances. After another card or two you will either have improved, in which case the hand is no longer a long shot, or you will have seen enough to fold. If it is cheap enough, and if the next round's cards will greatly clarify your chances, calling a normal-size bet is justified, but only if you have the discipline to fold if a desired card does not appear. If there are early raises or big bets, it is usually best to give up on long-shot hands before you are sucked into expensive calls later.

Poor hands ("garbage").   With a poor hand, of which there are, regrettably, a great many, the sensible strategy is to fold as soon as it becomes necessary to make a sizable call. What defines a poor hand? That depends on the size of the required antes in limit poker and on the ratio of early-round bets to likely later-round bets in pot-limit poker. The higher the required ante, the more hands it will pay to see in limit poker. Similarly, the smaller the required bet relative to the likely later-round bets in pot-limit poker, the more hands it will pay to stay in for a card or two. What actually defines a poor hand varies from game to game, and is discussed in some detail in Part IV.

The better a player you become, the less risky it will be to stay in on marginal hands, for better players have the courage to fold later. But many good players resist the temptation to stay on such hands. Their motto might well be: "When in doubt, don't."

The exception to the advice to fold garbage hands early is when the up cards of a poor hand are scare cards. Suppose in 7-card stud you show the K♣ and J♣, but have the 7♦ and 3♥ in the hole. Your chance of winning if others stay is very small. But a big bet or raise may both reduce the field to only one or two others, and set up a winning bluff if the next card is a club or an Ace, King, Queen, Jack, or 10—which is close to an even-money proposition. Be wary, however, of persisting with such a bluff if others call. Someone like Duke will hang in there with two pair and beat you in the end.

Round of Betting

The effect of a given size of bet or raise will vary round by round, as has already been suggested. As a general observation, big bets or raises are more likely to cause players to fold their hands in the early rounds of betting than in the middle ones, and they are more likely to fold opponents after all the cards have been dealt than on the next-to-last round.

A big bet or raise in the early rounds of betting is likely to reduce the number of your opponents because they are not heavily invested in the hand (financially or emotionally), because the size of the pot is relatively small (and thus the pot odds are not clearly favorable), and because there is great uncertainty on their part about how good their hands are going to be. In the face of a big bet, which surely suggests a strong hand, it will often seem prudent to an opponent to throw away an uncertain one. For these reasons, if reducing the number of your competitors is your objective, you will get more bang for your buck by a big bet or raise in an early round.

The reasons for a greater willingness to call in the middle rounds than in the early ones are sometimes sound and sometimes unsound, but you can take advantage of both. An unsound reason is that many players don't like to let go of a hand after they have "invested" heavily in it. (This is unsound because bygones are bygones. Once you have put money in the pot, it is neither your money nor an investment to which you have any claim. Trying to "protect your investment" involves throwing good money after bad.) A sound reason is that in later rounds the nature of both your own hand and those of your opponents is likely to be clearer, which makes it possible for each player to estimate reasonably accurately the pot odds he faces. Uncertainty in the early rounds tends to induce caution in most players, and caution promotes folding. Another reason for being called frequently in the middle rounds is the size of the pot; it is likely to be large enough that the pot odds may be favorable to calling with a drawing hand. For all of these reasons, in the middle rounds there are likely to be two or more callers of even a moderately large bet, and this becomes an important pot-management fact to remember.

These considerations peak in the next-to-last betting round, where a big bet is most likely to be called by a number of players. In the final round, after everyone has seen all of their cards, though the pot will be bigger and many players will have contributed a lot to it, many players with promising hands will have had their hopes deflated. There is likely to be, at most, one caller of a sizable bet. **It is promise, not busted promise, that induces people to call.**

The differences between the last and next-to-last rounds, and how they affect pot-management strategy, are illustrated by the example shown in Figure 9.1:

> It is a Holdem game with a $50 limit on the maximum bet. You hold the 9 and 7 of spades, and your full house is virtually sure of winning the pot.[5] Lou, on your right, is under the gun and bets $30. You want to maximize your winnings

---

5. You can be beaten by a straight flush, or by a higher full house if someone holding a high pair in the hole has those cards matched by the last common card, but these are low-probability outcomes.

FIGURE 9.1

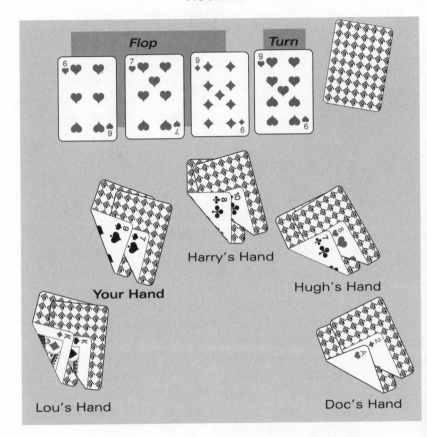

from this hand. Should you raise now, or wait for the last card in order not to discourage others from staying in?

You should raise $50 now, because any of the hands that would be willing to call the original bet will also call your raise if they have good prospects to improve their not-yet-made hands. In the actual situation, Lou, with his K♦, K♠, was hoping for a King on the river but also thinking that his high two pair might well be the best hand; Harry's

10♣, 8♣ gave him a made straight, which is usually a winner in Holdem; Hugh was holding 7♣, 8♥, and thus had
the possibilities of a straight, a full house, and even of a
straight flush; Doc's A♥, 2♦, along with the pot odds,
made him think that it was worth trying to get another
heart. The reason for you to bet the maximum now is that
only four or five cards out of the forty-six you don't see can
beat you (either of two Kings, or the hearts that might
make a straight flush). The probability odds are thus better
than 8 to 1 in your favor, and every call of your raise is welcome. If, however, you wait until the last card is turned and
then bet or raise $50, you are likely to have at most one or
two callers.[6]

Of course, on the next-to-last card you might have simply
called Lou's bet, hoping that one of the other players behind
you would raise and that you could then raise back, but anyone who is likely to have done so—for instance, Harry, with
his straight—is just about as likely to raise you now.

**The general rule is to bet heavily in the early rounds
to fold people; bet heavily in the middle rounds to build
the pot; and bet heavily on the last round only when
you are quite sure you have the winner or if you are
bluffing.**

There are exceptions to the above—there are *always* exceptions!—perhaps the most important of which is that a
large bet on the next-to-last round in pot-limit poker may
discourage risk-averse players from calling with hands that
depend on one more card, even if the pot odds are favorable to their calling. Here, as always, you must know your
opponents.

The interplay between the quality of hand, the betting
round, and betting tactics is summarized in Table 9.1,

6. Harry with the straight is likely to call you, but the chances are that, at
most, one other player will improve enough to call a big final bet and yet have
a hand that you can beat.

which involves a progression from assessing the quality of your hand to forming an immediate objective, to the strategy that best serves that objective, and then to the tactics best suited to implement this strategy. An experienced player does all of this more or less automatically, in a single step, and appears to move effortlessly and instantly in a particular hand in a specific situation to a decision about whether to check, bet, call, raise, or fold.[7]

There is more to pot management than Table 9.1 covers, of course, especially the fact that you must never forget to gear your bets or raises to the specific opponent you face and to what you think he has.

Opponents

Knowing your opponents is crucial, as always. A bet or raise that will fold Ty or Hugh is likely not to drop Lou or Duke, and may induce Bluffalo Bill to reraise just to show his manhood. You learn about your opponents by how they respond to particular bets or raises, and it is necessary to invest some attention—and perhaps some money—in that process when you meet new players. The investment needn't be great if you watch how they react to other people's bets and raises even when you are not playing the hand.

In the early rounds you know less than you will later about who among the other players will prove to be the competition, but even if you have no special insight, you may gather information by the response to an unusual bet or raise. If Ty calls an early-round raise when you expected him to fold, it tells you something, and it pays to see if you can figure out what he might have to make the

---

7. An analogy is to the decision of a driver to pass a car on a two-lane road with oncoming traffic visible in the distance. An experienced driver can do it a lot more quickly than it takes to describe all the variables and calculations that are required to formalize the decision-making process.

Table 9.1 Pot Management

QUALITY OF HAND

	Monster	Vulnerable	Drawing	Long Shot	Poor
OBJECTIVE	Keep opponents; build base.	Discourage opponents.	Get cards inexpensively.	Keep inexpensive.	Minimize contribution.
STRATEGY	Lie in weeds.	Exaggerate strength; make staying expensive.	Keep as inexpensive as possible.	Fold unless inexpensive.	Fold unless free.
TACTICS:					
Early round	Below-normal bet or simply call.	Above-normal bet; raise.	Check; call.	Below-normal bet; call if cheap.	Check; fold.
Middle round	Normal bet; call.	Caution; call unless setting up bluff.	Minimum bet; call.	Reevaluate pot odds.	Observe!
Final round	Maximum bet; or sandbag.	Mix: call, fold, and bluff.	Fold or bluff.	Did long shot come in?	Observe!

call. Doing so explicitly will help you to evaluate how his next card fits in.

Position in the Betting Sequence

The effect of a given bet or raise will be different under the gun than in a later position, and this must be factored into your own behavior and your expectations about others' behavior. Suppose the game is 7-card stud and the high hand shows K, 10, 10, after the fifth card and makes the normal (for this group) $5 bet. You are sitting on his immediate left, with four other players behind you. You show an Ace, 7, and 4 of assorted suits. If you raise $5 in this position you are likely to fold most or all of those sitting behind you, but probably not the original bettor. Among the folders is one who you suspect has four cards to an inside straight and a pair of 9's. He might have called the original bet to see one more card, but will not be willing to buck both you and the high hand. If your object was to reduce the game to a two-man hand, it was a good raise.[8] This might well have been your objective if you had an Ace and Jack in the hole, but with the other showing cards reducing your chances of improving beyond a potential of Aces-up. But if your hole cards were an Ace and 7, or a pair of either 7's or 4's, it would be a poor time to raise, since your chances of ending up with a monster hand are substantial and you want to keep potential victims in the game. After all, even two more callers of the original bet, if unraised, will provide as big a pot going into the next round as your raise if called only by the original bettor, and it is better to have three potential callers of your anticipated later big bet if you make your full house.

---

8. Such a bet does not always achieve what you intended. But even if this happens and you get more callers, or get a reraise by the opening bettor, you have acquired a lot of information for a relatively small price.

Contrast the situation if, with the same cards, you are sitting to the right of the bettor—in the last position—and two of the players in between have called before you. A $5 raise now is likely to be called by at least two and probably all three of the previous contributors to the pot. Given this, the raise would be foolish if you only had the pair of Aces (the situation where it made sense before) since it will not serve its objective of eliminating potentially better hands, and you will only be contributing to what is likely to be someone else's bigger pot. But with Aces-up it would now be a good raise.[9]

In general, a raise before others have called the original bet is likely to fold people, but one after others have already called is likely to be called.

Varying the Size of Bets and Raises

Table 9.1 seems to suggest that the weaker your hand, the more vigorously you should bet. In the early rounds and in early positions, there is a good deal of truth to this seemingly paradoxical advice. But of course, once perceived by your opponents, such a strategy would be fatal, and so it is necessary to mix it up, tending in this direction but betting mediocre hands heavily only often enough that your opponents will call big bets when you want them to, and betting good hands heavily in the early rounds often enough that your opponent can't be confident whether a big bet represents strength or weakness. As a rough guide, if you follow the pattern implicit in the table 75 to 80 percent of the time, and depart from it the rest of the time, you will be in the right neighborhood.

---

9. Whether it would be a good one with three of a kind is harder to say: you will build a pot you expect to win, but you also give a sign of strength that may be to your disadvantage later—for example, if you catch a 4 or a 7 on the next up card. I tend to slow-play trips in this situation.

As to the size of bets and raises, a main requirement toward getting the result you intend is not to let the size of the bet reveal what you are doing. This requires varying the size of bets in some haphazard or, better yet, random fashion. Even small, random variations in the size of bets may cause your opponents to puzzle over what you are conveying. Did your betting $27 instead of $30 mean you were trying to get him to call, or was it a small sign of weakness? An opponent worrying about this is likely to outsmart himself.

10

♠ ♣ ♥ ♦

LEARNING WITHOUT LOSING

You play poker every two weeks with six or seven friends, depending on who is in town, out of a group of nine or ten. You've been playing together for several years. The game has well-defined stakes and is dealer's choice, but most of the time you play two or three games. You tend to break even in the long run, but you don't really keep track.

Recently a couple of new players have joined the game and introduced some variations on familiar games, and one of them tends to bet a little more aggressively than has been the standard pattern. This has added some spice to the game, but you seem to be losing more often than you did before. Maybe it's time to read that poker book your wife gave you for Christmas . . .

Reading a good book is always a good idea, but if that is all you do, it is seldom the best way to improve your performance. This is as true in poker as it is in golf, tennis, or almost anything else. You need to learn by doing, and this is especially true if you have been playing for many years and have fallen into a regular pattern of play. But wouldn't it be nice to learn without having to pay too much tuition?

One of the best and cheapest ways to learn, and also not get bored, is to use the time when you have dropped out of a hand to gather information. Typically you are sitting out as much as you are actually playing, and you can learn a great deal just by watching the cards and the betting. Don't go out for a smoke or chatter with your fellow dropouts while waiting for the next deal; watch what is happening and try to figure out what people must have in their hands. When there is a showdown, you can check out your inferences and, if you were way off the mark, consider whether you should have known better. It is a lot easier to make a dispassionate analysis of a deal when you are a spectator because your inferences are not as likely to be colored by your hopes and fears. But the insights from your watchful waiting will eventually carry over to your play.[1]

This chapter will discuss two kinds of activity that occur away from the poker table—activities that, perhaps surprisingly, most poker players neglect. These are (1) warming up by practicing, and (2) conducting a postmortem on your play after you return home from a poker session. There are others, including reading the myriad poker manuals, watching videos, or playing computer poker.[2]

WARMING UP BY PRACTICING

In all sports, any serious athlete would advise you to warm up so as to get yourself into the proper physical and mental state to play at your best. Concentration on the tasks at hand is essential to peak performance. The same is true in playing poker, yet almost all poker players come to the table straight from dinner, work, or putting the children to bed. If you play poker regularly it may seem unnecessary to

---

1. One opponent of mine is fond of studying the stock-market quotations when not in the hand. While this conveys the intended impression that he has money to invest, it has made him a remarkably slow learner of the habits of the rest of us.

2. The magazine *Card Player* is replete with ads for these things. My opinion is that they are of limited value to the Thursday-night poker player because they are so heavily directed toward play as it occurs in casinos. Still, there are usually some valuable lessons to be learned from each of them.

warm up, but unless you do little but play the game or think about it, this is not the case. To focus on the poker decisions you will have to make, it is always useful to spend half an hour dealing out hands to remind yourself of the patterns of cards that will occur in the games you are about to play.

If, for example, you often play 7-card stud with six other players, deal out seven hands of seven cards each and see what turn out to be the best couple of hands. Then look at just the first three cards dealt to each hand. Was it reasonably clear then? Probably not. How about after four cards? After five cards? Did the winning hand look so bad at the start that you probably would have folded it? If you repeat this exercise five times you'll have a big head start on the evening. When you think you've got the knack of knowing what looks like a promising hand after four cards, deal out seven hands of four cards each and put a chip on each of the hands that meets your test. Then deal three more cards to each hand. Do this six times. If one of the hands with a chip on it is not the best hand at least three quarters of the time, rethink your conclusion. Also ask yourself if an early raise by what you considered a promising hand might have knocked out the hand that turned out to be best.

If your group plays 7-card Hi-Lo frequently, also look at those seven-card hands and ask yourself which starts looked likely to become winners after four cards. Notice how often a low start turns into a high hand. Notice how seldom the reverse is true. Remind yourself that good low starts are more promising than good high ones.

If you play a lot of draw poker, deal out seven five-card hands, then see how often the openers are merely one pair. Then draw and see how often opening hands near the minimum requirements improve on the draw. Identify the nonopening hands you are tempted to call on (for example, a pair of tens with an Ace kicker) and see how seldom they outdraw the opener. While there are tables that can tell you much of this, you won't remember them as well as the cards-on-the-table experience just before you play poker.

These exercises are useful even if your group plays only one kind of poker game over and over. They are even more useful if you play dealer's choice and have to shift from game to game. Reasonably good poker players are much more likely to make a big mistake in valuing a particular hand in the first hour of a poker session than they are later on.[3] This is where warming up may protect you.

This kind of practicing goes from being helpful to being necessary when someone has introduced a new game, or a new variation, or when you are a newcomer in a group where everyone else seems familiar with games that are new to you. Suppose, for example, that as an experienced 7-card stud player, you find that your new friends play 6-card stud. Deal out six-card hands, and then add a seventh card. Notice how much the outcomes change. Until you adapt, you will undervalue your six-card hand and miss some betting and raising opportunities.

If someone adds the opportunity to replace a card, deal out hands and then make the anticipated replacement decision. Notice how much the winning hand improves. Also, as you consider the replacement hand by hand, ask yourself what someone watching would be able to conclude about what the player is holding from what he chooses to discard. Every time you throw a card away (or keep it!) you give information that may be used against you.

If you play a widow game, a different practice scenario is appropriate. Consider Holdem and Omaha, in each of which there are five common cards. The same common cards usually produce the same *possible* best hand in the two

3. Toward the end of an evening different kinds of mistakes occur as players become tired and lose concentration, or as they try to press their good or bad luck because time is running out.

games,[4] but very different *actual winning hands.* If your group plays both of these games you must become familiar with the differences. Deal out five common cards, and then write down what you believe the winning hand will be in Holdem, and then in Omaha. Then deal out seven (if you regularly play with seven players) hands of four cards each, pausing after the first two to see what's best in Holdem before going on to the Omaha hand. You'll quickly learn to improve your predictions, and you'll discover that while a pair of Aces or two small pair often win in Holdem, they are seldom worth much in Omaha. You may have known this already, but you'll also get a feel for how frequently the straights and flushes that the common cards make possible are actually held. In the process you'll get some feel for which starting hands are promising.

Next do something like the exercise suggested above for stud. Deal out seven or eight holdings, and try to see if you can predict which of them are the three or four that are the most likely to end up the winner. When you can do so correctly most of the time, you will have developed a good rule for when to drop at the time of the first bet and when to stay in.[5]

---

4. Because in Omaha (but not in Holdem) you must use two from your down cards, the exceptions occur if the best hand would require using four or five of the cards in the widow.

5. An incidental advantage to this sort of practicing is that you often tend to learn things that you may have failed to notice in the playing of actual games, even if you have played them for years. In looking at widows in practice sessions for an Omaha game, I noticed for the first time how regularly, after the full widow was exposed, there was either a straight potential, a flush potential, or a pair on the board that made a full house possible. After a difficult calculation, I discovered that those situations are indeed very likely—in fact, they *fail* to occur only about 1 time in 50 random deals. The practical significance of this for playing Omaha is huge. It means, for example, that ending up with three of a kind—even three Aces—is unlikely to give you the winning hand. A pair of Aces in your hole cards is a monster holding in Holdem but is worth much less in Omaha.

This sort of warm-up is also extremely helpful in adapting to any significant change in the conditions of play. For one example, if you change the number of players from, say, six to eight (or even nine or ten, as is sometimes the case in groups where Holdem is the dominant game), the quality of the winning hand will improve significantly. The same result can occur if the betting pattern changes so that fewer people drop out early: the effective number of hands increases and so does the *quality* of the likely winning hand. You can learn how much it changes either slowly and expensively by playing, or more quickly and cheaply by practicing. If you are changing from six to eight hands of, say, Holdem, deal out eight two-card holdings, and then the common cards, and notice that one of the last two holdings proves to be best about one-quarter of the time. That's a matter of simple logic. But how much *better* is the winning hand with eight players in the game? That is difficult to calculate, though easy to observe.

Finally, before you head to the poker table, review in your own mind who is playing tonight, and what you ought to remember about each of them. It's cheaper to do so in advance than to rediscover it the first time you try to bluff out Duke when he's holding two pair.

POSTMORTEMS: REVIEWING YOUR PLAY

If you are like me, you come home from a poker session both tired and exhilarated, sometimes glowing about the way you played, sometimes annoyed or puzzled by your failure to do better, sometimes depressed by what in retrospect were clearly mistakes. At that late hour you are unlikely to be able to sort it all out, but your memories will fade by morning. Out of the hundred or so hands that were played, you are likely to have a clear memory of only three or four. Take five minutes to write down the essential features of them for future consideration. My notes (substantially cleaned up) from a recent session looked like this:

How lucky was I in the big Omaha pot when my Jack-high straight stood up?

Paul called my big bluff with only two small pair. Did something tip him off or am I bluffing too frequently?

Sixes-full on the flop in Holdem, and I carefully kept three other players in, only to be counter-feited on the river by an Ace! Bad luck or bad strategy?

The hands you remember are likely to be of three kinds: your triumphs, your disasters, and your missed opportunities. Everyone has all three kinds, and some of them are not avoidable. But some are. Sorting through particular hands in the course of your idle moments between sessions may be painful, but it is often constructive.

Of course, not all hands benefit from rethinking. There are many "no-brainers" where room for discretion is nil, even if the consequences are large. If you are dealt a pat hand in draw poker, you open and hope that you have one or more callers. Or, for another example, you open in Jackpots with two pair, Kings and 7's; two players call, both draw three, and one of them beats you by catching a third Jack. There are many, many times in poker when, with the pot odds in your favor, you bet and are called. Whether you end up winning or losing depends purely on the probabilities and says nothing about the soundness of your strategy. Such hands are the staples of a poker session, are seldom memorable, and don't do much to distinguish the good from the average poker player except in their pot management.

Perhaps only one hand in eight or ten will truly reward good over just average play. Some of these are ones where you didn't bother to think through the consequences, and simply threw money away. One example in Holdem is where you hold an A, 3, both clubs, and the widow shows **A, 10, 4, 2, 7,** but without three clubs. You felt pretty good after the flop, and even after the turn, but you haven't improved on the river. The player under the gun makes a small bet, and the next player raises a modest amount. It seems cheap relative to the pot, so you call, seeing a nice pot and hoping for a miracle. After all, you reason, a pair of Aces wins often enough in Holdem. But realistically there is no chance for you this time. One—and possibly both—of the other two players must hold at least an Ace, and if he does, his other card will surely beat you.

Or, to take another example, you are playing 7-card stud and after all seven cards have been dealt you show three 5's into an opponent who is showing two pair, Queens and 6's. It's your bet, and while you haven't improved, you have been betting heavily and getting good cards all night, so you bet now. But this bet is plainly a mistake: if your opponent has nothing more than his two pair, he will not call; if he does call he is sure to have you beaten.[6] These are obvious mistakes when thought about, but it is surprising how often they are made in the course of a poker session.

Sometimes it is not easy to know in retrospect what the right play was. You need to consider whether the probabilities were in your favor in situations where you had to act on your gut feelings. Some people, such as Doc, can do this mathematically, but most of us can't, or don't want to bother. But if you wonder whether you were lucky or un-

6. Might not your bet prevent him from calling, even if he has caught his full house? Only if he believes you have the fourth 5, and that is so unlikely that few players would fold without calling you. Indeed, if you had the fourth 5, you would surely have been wise to check, hoping against hope that an opponent had caught a full house, in which case he would then surely bet into you.

lucky in a particular situation (since similar scenarios are sure to arise in the future), try to reconstruct the cards that were visible and deal them out up to the point where the key event occurred. For example, if you were beaten on the last card after a very promising flop in Holdem, set up the three common cards that were there and what you came to know about your opponents' hands, and then deal out a fourth and fifth card ten times. This will give you a quick sense of the probabilities, and perhaps next time you'll remember the lesson. If you feel, like our friend Harry, that you are exceptionally unlucky, check your "luck" in the postmortems. How often have you heard a player say, "I can't see how I didn't hit that hand, I had *everything* going for me." "Everything" may turn out to be a lot less than it seems. While evaluating a specific probability is sometimes easy to do in your head, it is often easier to re-create it experimentally, with sufficient accuracy to guide your behavior in the future.

The hardest sort of post-game analysis is to evaluate your missed opportunities: the times you folded with what turned out to be a winning hand, or the occasions you didn't bluff when it turns out that your opponent had so little that he surely would have folded had you bet, but just edged you out when you both checked. You can't evaluate each such hand, but you can rely on three kinds of retrospective memories. First, what was the approximate ratio of known calling errors to folding errors? If the dollar consequences of the two kinds of errors seem about equal, you are on the right track. If your memories are dominated by "If only I'd called . . ." you're being too conservative. But if your evening was dominated by second-best hands that cost you a bundle, try to decide if it was just one of those nights (they do happen!), or whether you are getting too suspicious of the other guys' tendencies to bluff. Remind yourself that among good players a big bet into you will be made from strength most of the time.

A second question to ask is: What was my success ratio in bluffing? If it is low, either you are bluffing too much or you are tipping something off either by your manner or by your betting pattern. If your success in bluffing is almost perfect you are probably bluffing too little, and this may be indicated by your answer to a third question: When I bet unbeatable hands, how frequently did everyone fold? Honest answers to these questions will greatly increase your subsequent successes.

As to the bluffs that would have worked, ask yourself if in a hand you remember, your opponent's early betting indicated the weakness of his final hand. Here trying to figure out what he was doing in the hand in the first place may be critical. Should you have suspected that he was going for a straight or flush and failed? If so, his possible weakness may have been predictable. But if he started with a high pair, it would have been risky to have assumed that he did not improve enough to call you. A bluffing situation depends both on what *he* thinks *you* are doing and on what *you* think *he* is doing. It's only when you *should have known* that you were facing a mediocre hand that you should regret not having bluffed.

Finally, in reviewing the night's session, ask yourself whether you learned anything new about your opponents' strategies or tactics. Further, did you make any mistakes by failing to remember what you really always knew about them?

Once you understand its source, you can sometimes turn last night's disaster into a future triumph by relying on an opponent's memory of how you play. I lost a big-bet bluff one night to my friend Paul, who called with a mediocre hand. As he gathered in the pot he said, "Your bet was too big. If you'd wanted me to call you'd have bet less." He was right, but it rankled. Two sessions later, with a hand that was unbeatable, I paused for a short while, then made an unusually large bet into him, and was called. When I said, "If I'd wanted you to fold, I would have bet less," Paul gave me a wry look. (Next time in that situation I'll have to use some random method to decide how large the bet should be!)

Lying in wait for a particular opponent in a particular situation is one of the pleasures of a regular game with the same players, a pleasure that is never there in a game with a fluctuating crew. But to do it, you must catalogue and remember the situation and the player—and be patient, because the right combination is unlikely to happen right away. I was the victim of a memorable example of this sort of planning. An occasional player in one of the games in which I play regularly sandbagged me for a big loss with a very powerful hand (a full house against my Ace-high flush). As he raked in the pot he said, "I've been waiting to do this for nearly fifteen years." I didn't think I'd known him that long, and so I looked puzzled. He went on: "That was when you gave me a D in your statistics course, the only grade below a B I ever received."[7]

7. I've planned my revenge for when he returns to the game. The situation I have in mind will occur eventually, and meanwhile I enjoy thinking about it. Planning this sort of thing doesn't happen spontaneously, but it is a good way to keep your interest in poker high between sessions.

11

♠ ♣ ♥ ♦

SEEING THROUGH THE CARDS

The game is Hi-Lo draw poker; you sit in fifth position and find you have a pair of Aces. The players before you all check, so you open for the usual bet. The players behind you both fold, but two of the players who had previously checked now call. Each of them draws three cards. What should you do now?

The only reasonable inference you can reach from the behavior of your opponents is that each of them has a pair and is drawing for the high hand. While your hand is also going the high way, and you intended to draw three cards to your pair of Aces, this is no longer sensible. By the conventions of Hi-Lo poker, a pair of Aces is both the high and the low pair. Based on what you have inferred, do not draw to your Aces, nor split them. Simply stand pat and then bet the limit. If the cards speak for themselves you will either win half of the pot or all of it, and without any risk. If players must declare high or low, you will declare low. You may get lucky and have your opponent(s) also declare low, but you are still assured of at least half of the pot.

It's not hard to play poker well if you can "see through" your opponents' hidden cards. If you knew them all, you would always know with certainty when to raise and when to fold, when to bluff and when not to try. Indeed, the advantage of having this knowledge is irresistible to the mob and others who cheat, and they are not reluctant to use marked cards, stacked decks, or *mechanics* to give them the decisive advantage over their victims.[1]

But even if you know only some of the hidden cards, you have a big advantage, and even if you know only the *probable* identity of a given hidden card, you are on the way to an advantage over those who do not have similar information about you. This sort of information is often available at the table, and is of three main kinds: (1) carelessly revealed information by a player either flashing his cards (often after he has lost interest in them) or talking about them; (2) *tells*, or the mannerisms of a player that inadvertently reveal information about the quality of his holding; (3) betting patterns that enable an alert player to infer what his opponents' unseen cards probably are. While each of the first two kinds occur and can be exploited to advantage on occasion, they are seldom the main advantage of the attentive, skilled poker player. The third—the ability to draw valid inferences about his opponents' hidden cards—is his primary advantage and constitutes an important part of the art of poker.

CAPITALIZING ON OTHERS' CARELESSNESS

The most obvious, and sometimes embarrassing, source of information is when a neighboring player is careless about the way he holds his cards. If he shows them to you, you can hardly not notice, although you may warn him. You will not

1. Unlike legitimate casinos, which are content to take a regular cut out of a gambling pie, and unlike the usual poker professionals, who rely on their skill to separate tourists from their money, cardsharps want to do it all in less time and with less risk. Listen to Vincent Teresa (with Thomas C. Renner, *My Life in the Mafia*): "We set up suckers in our rooms. That's where the real money was. To do this required mechanics who could control the games, broads who would entertain the suckers, and a cool-off man who, after a sucker had been stripped of his money, could calm the sucker down and make him feel like he'd had a good run for his money. The best of the mechanics was Yonkers Joe Salistino. He was a genius with cards . . ." (pp. 217–18).

only know about his hand, but have information about others' hands too. The flasher may let you see a pair of sixes that don't do him much good but that are very helpful to you as you evaluate your chances (say, with two pair) against an opponent across the table who is showing a potential straight but lacks a six. Moreover, if you know that a particular player tends to show his cards to the neighbor on his right, you will do well to watch the neighbor. If he folds what looks to you like a promising hand, it probably means he has seen hidden strength in his neighbor. But if he stays despite the neighbor's apparent flush, it surely means either that he is very strong or that the flasher does not have his flush.

Talking about one's hand is often a source of unintended information. Of players still active in the hand, it is well to tend to disbelieve what they say: if they ask the dealer for an Ace, they probably want a spade! But by far the most useful conversation—useful, that is, to an opponent—is likely to come after a player has given up on his hand. What he tells the assembled world about his disappointment often tells you about some of the unseen cards that may be critically important to those left in the game. Here is a particularly dramatic example in which I was the beneficiary:

> The game was pot-limit Holdem, and the widow showed **K♥, Q♦, 2♠, 5♠, K♦**, received in that order. I held the King and 5 of clubs, and thus had made the second-highest possible full house, a very good hand in Holdem. But an extremely conservative opponent, Ty, had been betting since the flop, and I suspected that he had either a pair of Queens or a King and Queen in the hole. I feared the latter. When he now made a pot-limit bet, I expected the worst.
>
> On the verge of folding, I heard Duke say softly to his neighbor, "God, I'd love to be in this hand! I folded the winner!" Duke's statement almost

surely meant he had folded the missing King. Instead of folding, I called (and actually thought of raising).[2] As Ty turned over his two Queens, he said, almost bitterly, "I don't see how you could call my bet without at least a King and Queen." Raking in the pot, I didn't tell him.

Ty was victimized here by a third party, and had a right to be bitter. A basic rule of poker etiquette is that when you are not playing in a hand, you keep your cards to yourself, your mouth shut, and your folded cards folded. Even after the hand is fully played out, a postmortem by one player can reveal another player's strategy. Such lapses in etiquette do occur, and you can benefit by listening carefully to what is said or shown by the nonparticipants.

TELLS

The romantic literature of big-time poker stresses the virtues of maintaining a poker face, and is replete with examples of fatal giveaways by opponents who inadvertently reveal their hole cards at key moments. But in my experience such episodes are greatly exaggerated. Not only is most poker-table behavior not closely correlated with card holdings, but even when it is, it can so easily be manipulated by the perpetrator that it is dangerous to bet the ranch on Slim's habit of scratching his left ear when he is bluffing.[3] But it is sometimes helpful to notice certain habits of others, and prudent to avoid giveaways of your own.

2. To have done so would, however, have revealed that I had privileged information, since a raise into a hand that on the surface might very well beat me would have been foolhardy. And anyway, Duke may have been lying!
3. There is a book by Mike Caro, *The Body Language of Poker: Mike Caro's Book of Tells* (Secaucus, N.J.: Gambling Times Books, 1994), that includes photographs of purported tells.

Common Sources of Tells

The number of ways in which a player may inadvertently tip off the strength or weakness of his hidden cards is limitless, and include such physical clues as excessive sweating, trembling hands, or a change in voice tone. Here are a few that are less dramatic, but which I have observed so often that I look for them. But several warnings are in order. First, you must know your opponent and have observed his habits over a long enough time that you are confident you are witnessing a regular pattern. Second, you must be wary of a tell that seems too pronounced, for it may well be faked for your consumption. Third, if you do win a hand you would otherwise have lost by spotting a tell, do not feel obliged to brag about it afterward, either to the victim or to another player. If you do, you'll set yourself up for a planned repetition under reverse circumstances, and you'll never know when it might occur. Finally, remember that nothing works all the time, so don't overvalue recognizing a tell on the part of a regular opponent. He may behave inconsistently for no reason at all.

Pauses. Among beginners and poor players, the longer the pause before taking action when it is the player's turn, the greater his uncertainty, and thus the weaker his hand. Among better players long pauses are frequently employed to *suggest* weakness and uncertainty. For such a player, a long pause followed by a maximum bet or raise almost always indicates a very strong, probably unbeatable, hand. A corollary is that a bluff is virtually never made after a long pause, because the bluffer feels that the pause will subtract from the confidence he is trying to show. A quick call, with no raise, suggests a strong hand but not a dominant one.

In the normal course of play, pauses will occur; even good players have to stop and think sometimes. Moderate-length pauses for this purpose are worth taking into account, for they may let you figure out what sort of question the player is considering.

Eye contact.   Watch your fellow players, especially after they have made a big bet in the final betting round. See if they sometimes look hard at the opponent whose turn it is to bet next, and who is considering his options, or if sometimes they avoid his eyes. If this behavior varies, you may well be able to figure out why. A number of players I have observed will sometimes, but not always, avoid eye contact with an opponent into whom they have made a big bet. This is usually because they are afraid their eyes will reveal apprehension and thus lead the opponent to call their bluff. When they stare down the opponent, it is usually an attempt to dare the opponent to call, and thus indicates a strong hand.

Future intentions.   An obvious and not uncommon form of telling behavior is to bet or fold out of turn. Anyone can make a mistake and bet or fold before it is his turn, but some players do so sufficiently frequently to make it revealing. Betting ahead of turn is usually the sign of a strong hand that the player is anxious to push quickly toward its eagerly anticipated conclusion. Some players will induce such behavior by deliberately pausing to let an impatient rival reveal his strength. While folding out of turn may seem harmless, it is not, for it will often provide information that benefits some opponents but not others.

Somewhat less obviously, a surprisingly large number of players who are careful about acting only when it is their turn are not content merely to observe and think about their options before they must act, but instead anticipate them by handling either their cards or their chips well in advance. This is especially likely if there is a slow player in the game and they have become impatient with him. Holding cards loosely in one hand often reveals a player's intention to fold as soon as a bet is made into him; picking up just the amount of chips expected for a standard bet usually indicates an intention to call but not raise; and picking up a whole stack of chips may suggest that the player is anticipating a raise or, more likely, making a conscious effort to dissuade a player ahead of him from raising. A better player, intending to raise, will usually sit back and wait patiently until it is his turn. (The best players will do this no matter what they intend to do.) Here, as elsewhere, you must observe a particular opponent long enough to see if he varies his behavior in these ways, because it is in the variance that the potential tell occurs.

Choice of chips.   Does a player you watch sometimes (say, in a $10 limit game) call a $5 bet by throwing in a chip worth $5, but other times by gathering up a collection of $1 chips? If he does, he is usually revealing confidence that he will win the pot in the first case, but is showing his lack of confidence in the second; the unconscious message is that while he is willing to call, he expects to lose and would prefer to get rid of his small change rather than his big chips.

Pay attention to how players handle whatever is the largest denomination chip being used in the game. Most players like to hoard them, and spending them when lesser chips are available is a sign of strength, or of bravado. A player virtually never bluffs by gathering up all of his small chips and pushing them into the pot. The other side of this coin is that if you are sitting in a pot-limit game with about $40 in smaller-denomination chips in front of you and one or more chips of larger denomination, a player betting a little less than $40 into you wants you to call, and someone betting just a bit more than $40 wants you to fold. Since chips of different denominations are all exchangeable in proportion to their face values, the psychology of all this is for someone else to explain; but in my observation, the fact is that most poker players prefer higher-denomination chips to an equal sum of lower-denomination ones. This harmless preference can be revealing.

Rechecking hole cards.   Some players, like Knott, never seem to remember what their hidden cards are and check them after every new card, as well as every time it's their turn to act. While this is annoying to others, since it slows down the game, it signifies nothing more than lack of attention. It is the rare player who looks once and only once at his hidden cards. Most people who play poker have memories quite capable of looking at their hole cards when they are dealt and remembering them for the few minutes it takes to play the hand. The reason for the repeated looks is that most players tend only to concentrate on the "significant" cards, as they perceive them at the time that they were dealt. Thus in 7-card stud, if a player has a pair of nines in the hole, or the Ace and King of hearts, he will not be tempted to check them if the next up card is a nine in the first instance, or an Ace, King, or heart in the second. But let a player hold what he thinks of as an Ace and an unrelated middle card, and he'll tend to reach for his cards and squeeze them if he is next dealt a 6, to see if it pairs his hole card. Similarly, if after four cards he has a King and a 6 up, and gets a 7 as his fifth card and looks at his hole cards, you can be pretty sure he did not have a 6 in the hole. Or consider a player who is dealt a third spade up, and then checks his hole cards. He surely does not have two spades in the hole—he'd remember that—and probably wonders if he has even one.

Asking who is still in the hand.   A player who asks instead of casually looking to see how many players are still in the hand behind him when it is his turn to call a bet is almost surely thinking about a raise. This may be because he has a strong hand and doesn't want to discourage callers, or because he wants to try to bluff out the original bettor and is worried about a strong hand behind him. You'll need other information to decide which is the case.

All of these are only small clues, but over the course of a hand several little clues can add up to a lot of information. To take advantage of them you must watch and remember from card to card. It is these tells, among others, not ESP, that lets Hugh seem to see through the cards.

Avoiding Tells

The small, revealing habits discussed above are innocent enough, and most of your amateur opponents don't pay much attention to them. But it is to your advantage to be among those who do, and to avoid being a teller yourself. How do you do so? One way is to concentrate hard to be sure to play the same way at the same speed all the time, to be aware of clues such as your eye contact, to always wait until it is your turn before either betting, folding, or picking up chips, and to assiduously remember your hole cards—all of them, including their suits—and so on. Like all good habits, these are easier preached than accomplished.

Alternatively, you can vary your behavior in any of these respects consciously, rather than inadvertently and revealingly. Or you can be sufficiently haphazard in your behavior so that the correlation between your behavior and the strength or weakness of your hand is hard to detect. Haphazard behavior is usually sufficient, but if you find you are being repeatedly outmaneuvered by a particular opponent, give some consideration to tells that you may be displaying.

INFERENCES FROM BETTING AND RELATED BEHAVIOR

"Reading" something about your opponents' cards can vary from being quite easy, almost trivial, to being very subtle. Every player does it to some extent, but the better the player, the more consciously and more successfully he does it. Professionals call it *putting an opponent on his hand.* Here are some familiar examples of easy-to-make inferences:

In Jackpots, a three-card draw virtually always indicates a pair; after failing to open, a one-card draw indicates a potential straight or flush, and a two-card draw suggests a pair with an Ace kicker. A two-card draw by the opener strongly suggests trips; but this move is mostly avoided by better players, who prefer to draw one to trips.

In Hi-Lo draw games, multiple-card draws almost always indicate potential high hands, while standing pat, or drawing one, usually signifies a low hand.

In 7-card stud, a player staying in against a showing pair that has bet almost always has hole cards higher than the rank of the pair.

In Holdem, a player raising before the flop is very likely to hold either an Ace or a King (or both), or a high pair.

In Omaha, if two clubs show on the flop with no pair and two or more players call, you can be reasonably sure that one of the callers has the A, X, or K, X, of clubs, so your potential straight or low flush is worthless. But if the second flush card did not appear until the turn, it is likely that potential high club-flush cards were folded, and thus your straight or low flush may be worth playing.

These kinds of inferences are not difficult, but it is surprising how often players do not think them through while the hand is being played. Instead they wait until the last card has been dealt and then try to reconstruct the earlier behavior of an opponent to decide what he must have had.

Inferences are, of course, only educated guesses and are never guaranteed. But such educated guesses are usually a better guide than the bare probabilities of certain holdings. A player like Doc who neglects inferences and relies only on the relative scarcity of particular hands—who, for example, always calls with Aces-up in games where it is an above-average hand—will make some unnecessary mistakes.

USING YOUR INFERENCES: FIVE EXAMPLES

Drawing correct inferences about your opponents' holdings is an art that can be enhanced by experience and by observing your opponents' patterns of play. Here are five examples of varying subtlety, based on hands I observed in a three-month span of playing pot-limit poker with a regular group of friends.

1. Inferring a Tied Hand

Figure 11.1 shows a hand in pot-limit Omaha after the fourth widow card has been exposed. Several players besides you have seen the flop, it is your bet, and you bet the pot with your made straight in order to make it tougher for those holding potential flushes and higher straights to call. (Your hand cannot be improved and is extremely vulnerable: only eleven of the forty-four unseen cards do not create a widow that makes it possible for another hand to beat you.[4]) To your surprise, the player immediately after you, Duke, raises the maximum amount. The next player,

---

4. Only a 2, 3, Queen, or King, not in spades, will leave you with the lock hand.

FIGURE 11.1

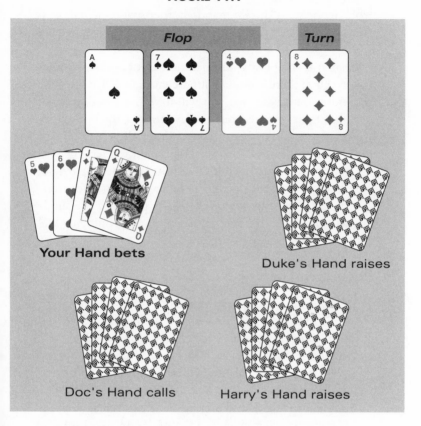

Harry, also raises, and a fourth player, Doc, calls all bets. The pot is now huge, and although you have the best possible hand at the moment, you must call both raises and possibly even anticipate another one to stay in the hand. It is time to think.

Several things can be inferred. As shown by his immediate raise, Duke is evidently as anxious as you to have the others drop, so it is likely that he also has a 5 and 6 among his hole cards, and probably has some possibilities of improvement. Harry may well be in the same position for his raise. And

Doc must have great potential for winning the whole pot, probably holding the King and another spade, or very possibly already having trips, so that any pair will give him a full house.

What you do about your inferences is, of course, another matter. Here there is only about 1 chance in 4 that after the last widow card is turned you will have the winning hand, and even then you are likely to have to split the pot two or even three ways. Further, if you call now there will be bets and possible raises yet to come. Will you then feel that the pot odds make it worthwhile to call the next betting round, even if a better hand is possible? Believing your inferences, you should now fold your hand![5] The pot odds are surely against you once you realize that your best outcome will only give you a fraction of the pot.

2. Exploiting Fear

Figure 11.2 illustrates the final position in a pot-limit Holdem hand in which you stayed for the turn since the betting was light and you were convinced that no one had either an Ace or a 4. The Q♣ on the turn encouraged you: another club or a 10 would have led to a probable winner. After a sizable betting round among the three remaining players, the river produced the 4♦. Your hopes are dashed! There is more than $80 in the pot, and the hand under the gun bets a mere $8. The other player drops, and it's up to you.

There is virtually no chance that you have the better hand at this point, so it would be senseless to call even though the bet is small. Most of the time with a busted hand you would fold, but you are intrigued by the bettor's unusually small bet.

---

5. Of course if you are all-in, or nearly so, you may be able to call and hope for the relatively small chance that you will win part or all of the pot.

FIGURE 11.2

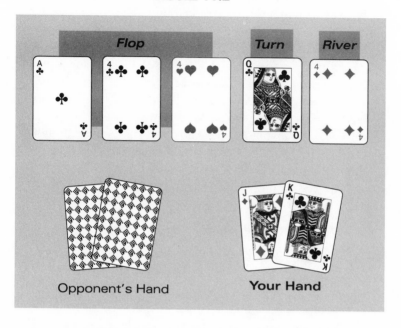

Opponent's Hand   Your Hand

What did it mean? With the fourth 4 (the nut hand) he would probably have checked, hoping someone with an Ace, Queen, or a high pair would bet into him, or else he would have bet close to the maximum. With nothing he would either have checked or made an all-out bluff with a big bet. With a flush he'd be nervous and check, probably planning to call. But why the small bet? There is one likely answer: he has a good hand, but a beatable one, and is making a *probe bet* to see if a nut hand is out there. He's not afraid of a call by someone with a flush, but is afraid of a big full house, or the fourth 4, and doesn't want to spend too much money to find out. He probably holds a small pair in his hand, perhaps as small as 5's, but surely something less than Queens. Alternatively, he might hold a Queen but fear that one of his callers holds an Ace.

Sensing his fear, you now bet the pot, and he folds. Once you figured out what your opponent held, the bluff bet was not hard to make since there was no one else in the hand. He was probing for information, but in the process gave his hand away. You exploited his fears by giving him the answer he was (reluctantly) looking for.

Was this a riskless bluff? Of course not; nothing works every time, and the inference and the bluff both assume your opponent is a competent player. The bluff will not work against Duke, who always calls with a hand as good as this, nor against a novice who may not have thought through his initial bet. But if you can make an opponent think you have the cards he is worried that you have, you will succeed far more often than not.

3. Evaluating a Bluff Possibility

The game is pot-limit Jackpots, with $14 in antes. The third player behind the dealer, Hugh, opens for $14, and you are the second of two callers. You hold a 9, 8, 7, 6, K, of assorted suits. You intend to draw one, expecting that if you hit, the post-draw betting will justify your present call. Hugh, however, stands pat. The other caller, Knott, draws three, and you draw one. You catch a 5, which makes your straight. Hugh bets the amount in the pot, $56, and Knott folds. What do you do?

Everything depends here on your knowledge of Hugh. Would he ever stand pat on less than a straight—say, holding two pair? If not, the chances are about 3 to 1 that his pat hand will beat your straight.[6] Since the pot odds are only 2 to 1, you should fold. But they are not so bad that you shouldn't call if you think there is a reasonable chance that

---

6. Roughly half of all pat hands are straights (see Table 4.2, page 50), and about half of all straights are higher than your 9-high straight. Thus, in only about one-quarter of all situations will your straight beat or tie a pat hand.

he is bluffing.[7] You'll win if he was bluffing or if he had a lower straight, and you may even make a bit of money on the off chance (about 2 percent) that you tie. Here your inference is that he either has two pair and is bluffing, or that he had a pat hand. The inference is easy, but what to do about it is harder. To decide depends entirely on your knowledge of Hugh's past behavior.

4. Considering Earlier Behavior

> The game is pot-limit Omaha, and Knott, who holds J, 5, 4, 3, is ecstatic when the flop shows J, J, 5, since he knows no one can beat him at this stage. The bet is checked to him, and he makes a modest bet, hoping to keep others in, but only Hugh calls. The turn card is a **10.** Hugh checks, but then calls Knott's $50 bet. The river card is a **4.** Knott chooses to sandbag, checks, and is pleased when Hugh bets $50 into him. He pauses for effect, then raises $100. To his surprise, Hugh reraises by pushing his remaining chips, about $220, into the pot. What is Hugh holding?

The answer is unambiguous: Hugh must hold a J, 10, among his four cards, and thus has an unbeatable full house, as Knott discovers when he calls the raise that Hugh had made. When his neighbor, Lou, commiserates on his bad luck, Knott says, "I assumed he had a pair of 10's in the hole." But this was not a valid inference for a simple reason: Hugh would never have stayed in after the flop showed a pair of Jacks without either a pair of fives, a Jack, or a pair higher than the widow's Jacks. To have stayed with an un-

---

7. How good a chance? Making a precise calculation, it turns out that if the probability that he is bluffing is 9 percent or greater, your call is sound—that is, it will have a positive expected value.

derpair, such as 10's, would invite being second-best if the 10's eventually became the basis for a full house.

Knott did everything correctly up until he raised Hugh on the river. A more prudent step would have been to call Hugh's $50 bet and hope that Hugh had 5's-full. His sand-bagging check-raise of $100 is defensible, if risky. Having made it, however, Knott should surely not have called the final reraise. That was giving money away.

But, you may ask, how could Knott be sure that Hugh was not bluffing? The answer is that Hugh would never bluff in a situation where his target might hold the nuts against him, and if Hugh did not hold both a Jack and a 10, Knott might well have them, or even four Jacks.

5. Believing the Improbable

Figure 11.3 shows your holding in an Omaha hand after the full widow has been exposed. The flush and straight possibilities that were present after the flop led you to raise at that point, and both Ty and Duke called. When the turn card did not help your hand, you checked and Ty made a maximum bet, plainly hoping to win the pot right there. But Duke called without hesitation. You were convinced that Ty held a 5 and 7 among his cards, and thus had a straight made. But the pot odds made it worthwhile to call: after all, any spade, 7, or Queen would give you a better hand than an 8-high straight. When the river produced the 9♠, you had the nut flush, and made a moderate bet hoping for at least one caller. Ty, however, came back with a maximum raise. What can he have, and what should you do?

It is now crunch time, and it is essential to review the information you have. What can Ty have had, and what does

FIGURE 11.3

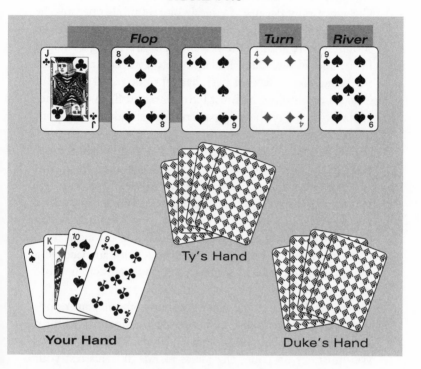

Flop | Turn | River

Ty's Hand

Your Hand

Duke's Hand

he have now? You were confident that Ty's big bet after the **4** appeared on the turn indicated that he had made his straight with a 5 and a 7, and was trying to get rid of opposition that might outdraw him. Even if he improved his straight with the last widow card, the **9**, he must read your bet as indicating that you hit a flush, and he will reason that you would not have called his previous bet without the possibility of having at least a King-high flush. So even if he has a Queen-high flush he would not dare raise you, especially with Duke behind him. It's hard to believe, but the only thing that makes sense out of Ty's betting behavior is that he holds the 5 and 7 *of spades* and has had his straight transformed into the straight flush that gives him a sure winner!

But could he be bluffing? While that is possible, it's un-likely, not only because Ty rarely bluffs but also because he will realize that if he bluffs, you are likely to call even though you recognize the possibility of his having a straight flush, and in any case, Duke, a notorious caller of hands where he may be second-best, has yet to be heard from. But if he is not bluffing, he must have a straight flush. No other explanation fits his betting pattern. You should believe your inference and fold.

Few of us have the courage to fold so good a hand, espe-cially in the face of something as rare as a straight flush. But this kind of courage is worth developing. A second-best hand is expensive, whether it is a pair of Kings beaten by a pair of Aces, or whether it is the best possible flush, which can be beaten only by a straight flush. While a straight flush is a low-probability hand in the abstract, it can become a highly probable one in some circumstances, such as those described above.

You need to combine what you know about your oppo-nent with what you observe in the specific situation to form your best inference about what he holds. Then, of course, you must act on your inferences. Hands like this test your expertise; you need to make your best inference and have the courage to act upon it.

A CAUTIONARY TALE

Whenever inferences can be based on behavior, it is possible to manipulate that behavior in order to mislead. Here is a spectacular example, possibly apocryphal, of which Oswald Jacoby was the reputed victim.[8]

8. I was told this tale in 1945 by a highly reputable person who claimed to have witnessed it. Jacoby, noted as a bridge expert, was also a demon poker player. While the account is unforgettable, the name of his opponent has been forgotten, which is unfortunate, because he was clearly a very imaginative player.

The game was high-stakes 5-card stud low-only, where after the fifth card players could replace any one of their cards. The best possible hand was defined as a 6, 4, 3, 2, A. After the fifth card had been dealt, only two players remained. Jacoby sat with [2], 6, 4, 8, A, facing [X], 5, 4, 3, 2. His opponent, who had to replace first, threw away his 5 and promptly caught another 5. Jacoby stood pat, and when his opponent made a small bet, made a tapping raise, pushing all of his chips into the pot. When his opponent called, Jacoby reached for the pot, saying, "Only a 7 or 8 in the hole will beat me, and I know you don't have that." His reasoning was that with a 7 or 8 in the hole, his opponent would not have replaced his 5, since he could not have improved his hand by doing so. Indeed, the only thing that made sense was that his opponent had either a 6 or an Ace in the hole, and thus had to replace the 5 to avoid a straight. With anything else in the hole, Jacoby reasoned, he would either stand pat or replace the down card.

The reasoning was impeccable, but when his opponent turned over his hole card, the 7 of clubs, he collected the pot and left Jacoby stunned.

Why had Jacoby's opponent replaced a card when he already had the winning hand? He explained as follows: "I wasn't going to win much from Oswald if I stood pat on so good a hand, so I looked for a way to win a very big pot. My chances weren't bad: I'd win if I caught a 6, 5, or Ace, I might well win with an 8, and a 7 would have given me a perfect bluffing opportunity."

IV

APPLICATIONS AND EXERCISES

12

♠ ♣ ♥ ♦

TRADITIONAL POKER: 5-CARD STUD AND DRAW

It's The Kid against The Man, Lancey Howard. Five-card stud, no limit. The Kid is pulling away, slowly, inexorably. It's the decisive hand. After the third card, The Kid has [A♥], 10♣, 10♠, and Lancey has [J♦], 8♦, Q♦. There is $1,000 in the pot. The Kid bets $1,000 and Lancey raises $1,000! Lancey has only about 1 chance in 20 of making either a straight or a flush in the next two cards, and thus the pot odds do not favor even calling The Kid's bet. The Kid, with an Ace in the hole, calls. Even though The Kid ends up with a full house, Lancey beats him with the straight flush he catches on the last card and wins a pot of over $25,000. Broken in spirit, The Kid calls it quits. The winner, and still champion, is Lancey Howard.

It's 1944, and the smooth-cheeked ensign they call "Mr." but think of as "the kid" is playing pot-limit Jackpots with five of the merchant-marine officers of the Liberty ship that is zigzagging from San Francisco to Eniwetok, where the naval officer is to pick up his ship. The kid is cocky and has run the $120 he came aboard with to over $200. Then this: under the gun, he is dealt a full house, Aces full of 8's. His $20 bet is called by two others. He stands pat and then bets $40. The second mate, who drew two, now folds, but the chief engineer, who drew one card, raises $40. After a slight hesitation, the kid taps, pushing all his money into the pot. The chief calls, and takes the pot with the four 6's he had from the start.

This is the stuff of poker fiction, right? Yes, at least it is in the first example, which is from the movie *The Cincinnati Kid*. All the experts agree it could never have happened because no good player would be dumb enough to call, much less raise, with The Man's hand after three cards.[1] The second story, alas, is not fiction: I was that ensign, and had to spend the remaining eighteen days of the trip being taught how to play cribbage by a fellow passenger for twenty-five cents a game. I lost my last $12 learning.[2]

Whether fiction or fact, episodes like these represent the romantic mythology of conventional poker, but they don't happen often enough to make either five-card game a popular one in Thursday-night poker. In any event, tastes in poker games change. This is mirrored in the coverage given to different games in books about poker. In the 1930's, draw poker and 5-card stud were the dominant games. By the 1950's, 7-card stud and some Hi-Lo games had become popular additions. By the late seventies, there are references to Holdem and other widow games, although they are usually mentioned as interesting regional varieties. By the 1990's, one searches almost in vain for any mention of 5-card stud, and the bulk of professional writing is about Holdem, its spawn, and seven-card games.

There are many reasons for these changes, of which the most important is the increased number and changed nature of the people who play poker. In recent decades poker has spread from the smoke-filled back room of the saloon to

1. There *is* a rational explanation. Motives matter. The Man was being outplayed and was on the road to a sure defeat if he played conventional poker. If he cared about his reputation as The Champ, he had to do something desperate, and this may have been his last, best chance, poor as it was. The money didn't matter, and if he was going to lose, doing so sooner rather than later didn't matter either. As he remarks, "This gets down to what it's about, making the wrong move at the right time."
2. For fifty years I've wondered whether that poker hand was an honest deal or a stacked deck. Either way, my serious poker education began that day.

both the country club and the family room. As it became a form of recreation among friends, instead of a way to separate cowboys, traveling salesmen, and sailors from their pay, it turned to forms that were better suited to the new players and their objectives. For these players, who had limited time for playing cards, games that demanded very tight play and great patience were not particularly attractive.[3] Meanwhile, among big-time professionals, new and more complex varieties of poker (most notably Holdem) became popular—varieties that gave ever more scope to individual skill, to possibilities for intimidation, and to imaginative play.

As new forms of poker were invented and tried, evolution occurred at the expense of the old standbys. In Thursday-night poker, the widespread use of dealer's choice provides a device by which new games are introduced, either to flourish or fade. In that particular poker marketplace, the traditional games have been losers. The main reason for the decline of 5-card stud and draw poker is that all serious players quickly learn the conservative playing strategies that are essential to success in those games. This makes for infrequent confrontations and relatively little scope for imaginative play.

5-CARD STUD

Five-card stud developed, historically, to remedy several perceived defects of the older game, draw poker. First, draw was limited to two rounds of betting; second, with all cards concealed there was nothing to go on except the bare probabilities of one's own holdings and the behavior of the

---

3. The desire to gamble, surely part of the original motive for poker playing, did not go away, but it was redirected by the development of readily accessible opportunities to bet on sporting events, participate in lotteries, or play slot machines. The recent spread of legal casinos has led to a boom in blackjack, craps, and other faster-than-poker forms of gambling.

players; third, draw required a high ante to have any pot at all, and this proved unattractive to players who did not like to contribute significant amounts of money before seeing their cards.

Five-card stud provided a clear antidote. Its four rounds of betting provided multiple betting opportunities and made it possible to play with a small (or even no) ante. Its four open cards offered lots of inferences about what a particular opponent held, as well as chances to modify those inferences as further information was revealed by the additional cards dealt to each player. It thus provided increased scope for the skilled player over the inexperienced one.[4]

But the drawbacks of 5-card stud, unless played in a no-limit or high-limit game, are great. Among good players many hands go completely uncontested, and many more are quickly reduced to two players, with little raising. A whole evening, or even an occasional round, of 5-card stud can be dreary. Interspersed into a dealer's-choice game, it usually provides the opportunity to visit the kitchen or bathroom.

Five-card stud is exciting only if the possibilities of bluffing are substantial. This requires rules that permit large bets relative to the size of the pot, as is the case in no-limit poker of the kind reputed to have been played in the old West, and by the legendary inscrutable Chinese gamblers sitting cross-legged and puffing on their opium pipes as they push mountains of money into the pot.

To see the bluffing possibilities, suppose you have a 10 showing and raise the bet made by the holder of a showing Ace. While this will be an invitation to disaster in the unlikely event that the opponent holds another Ace, this early

---

4. Five-card stud also simplified life for the cheating cardsharp, since it is much easier to control the nature of a single hole card than a whole hand. It is not as hard to *deal seconds* (described in Chapter 17) as it is to stack the whole deck, or introduce a stacked one. In 5-card stud, if you know the victim's hole card, you need nothing more.

raise on nothing more than a 10 may cause the Ace to fold, for it suggests either a 10 in the hole or an Ace. But even in the event that you are called, any subsequent improvement of your hand, followed by a massive bet, will win a large percentage of the time. Similarly, merely calling a sizable first-round bet with something as unpromising as a 4 showing, thus violating the first of the rules given below, strongly suggests that you have a 4 in the hole and may well set up a pot-stealing bet or raise before the showdown occurs. Given another 4 in the next couple of cards, a big bet will make even a pair of Aces pause.

Because it is simple to represent and because of its high bluffing potential, 5-card stud survives in movies. It is also played sometimes in some small-stake casino games where tight-lipped small-time pros sit for hours playing the percentages against one another and waiting like spiders for the careless tourist.

Decision Rules for 5-Card Stud

As you know by now, there are exceptions to every supposed rule of poker behavior, but the exceptions in 5-card stud are so infrequent that good players look at their first two or three cards and then fold most of the time. The decision rules that it is sensible to follow are both clear and simple. There are, at most, four:

1. Never call the first significant bet if you cannot beat the board. This usually means having either a pair, an Ace, or a King.[5]

---

5. The chance that with two unpaired cards you will end up with a pair in five cards is less than even money, which means that more than half the time you won't be able to beat even an Ace-high. Further, even if you catch a pair, you may well lose to a higher pair. Yardley (*The Education of a Poker Player,* pp. 40–41) suggests an even stricter standard: both the first two cards must be 10 or higher. This will happen to you in only one deal in seven.

2. Never bet with a *showing pair* beyond the third card if higher cards are showing in your opponents' hands and they have called a bet after seeing your pair. Never stay with a *hidden pair* if a hand with a higher card showing is betting or raising.
3. Never be beguiled into staying with two- or three-card straights or flushes.
4. Never bet into an opponent who can know that he has you beaten at the time of the bet.

As is evident, the "nevers" dominate. In a well-played seven-person game, generally there should not be more than three players who pay to see a third card, and no more than two who see a fourth. Unless the betting rules permit very large bets, which make bluffing possible, the primary virtue required to play the game well is patience. But for high-stakes games Holdem provides more opportunities than 5-card stud for bluffing, more for psychology, and more for clever pot management.

Reasons Behind the Rules

Suppose you have a Queen in the hole and a 5 showing, but there is either an Ace or a King showing in the other players' open cards. Even if a higher card is not showing, the chance that your Queen is the highest card in the hole is only about 1 in 5 in a seven-person game. If you pair the Queen on any of the next three cards, you will probably have a winner, but the odds against your doing so are at least 4 to 1. (They are even worse if another Queen shows up in someone else's hand.) Even if you subsequently pair the Queen, you may lose; the other guys' chances of pairing their Ace or King are as good as yours, after all. Further, if you don't pair the Queen, you are at best a very long shot to emerge the winner.

Next, suppose you start with a pair of 7's after three cards. You may have the best hand *at this point,* but among seven five-card hands there will be at least a pair of 10's or better more than half the time. Thus your pair will probably stand up only if you improve it, or if you can drive out the players who have higher cards showing. If your opponents stay after you bet or raise, it is likely that they have you beat already, especially if they can see your pair.

What about holding an 8, 9, J (or three diamonds), after three cards? Many players find such a hand attractive. But a skilled opponent with a high pair will make it as expensive as he can for you to stay for additional cards, and for you to hit the two cards you need in only two tries is almost always too much of a long-shot to consider, though if you hit you will have a winner. Pot odds dictate, of course, but if your opponents play the hand properly the pot odds will usually be against you.

Finally, since there is only one closed card, you must be careful about someone holding the nuts against you. Suppose you show K, 10, 9, 7, and have a King in the hole, facing an opponent who shows A, Q, 8, 4. You may well have the best hand and be willing to call any bet your opponent makes. You are tempted to try to build the pot, which you expect to win. But you dare not raise, nor should you bet if the hand is checked to you, for your opponent can know whether he has you beaten and raise with impunity, either holding the nuts, or with a bluff that it will be uncomfortable to have to call. Similarly, if you face a four-card straight or flush, a bet is pointless. An opponent without the filling card won't call your bet, but if he has it he will raise.

None of this is subtle or profound, and there's the rub. **Because these rules are so simple and straightforward, all good players learn them in short order.** As a result, 5-card stud becomes either a dull game, or a way to exploit weak or inexperienced players. Neither is much fun for the serious amateur.

Variations Designed to Save 5-Card Stud

If you are playing with people who insist on playing 5-card stud and want to keep from being lulled to sleep (or being lured into playing unsoundly to avoid it), here are three ways to add some dimensionality to the game. The first is to suggest that the last card as well as the first be dealt down. This has the advantage of increasing greatly the bluffing opportunities, and makes scare cards among the up cards valuable. Indeed, it leads to abandoning the third rule stated above, and decreases the applicability of the fourth one. A second way is to provide for a replacement of one card after the last card has been dealt. This will keep people calling in earlier rounds, for reasons both sound and unsound. As more people stay in, the pot odds you face will improve, and you can stay in more often. A third way to breathe life into the game is to raise the antes so that there is enough money in the pot initially to make seeing another card worthwhile, even without the best hand.

If none of these ways appeal to your fellow players, find a different poker game.

DRAW POKER, JACKS-OR-BETTER TO OPEN

Historically, draw poker was played without opening requirements and without limits on the permitted size of bets. As such it gave unparalleled opportunities for bluffing and for intimidation, and was the quintessential gambling game, requiring and rewarding both skill and nerve. It was demanding as well because it required a significant ante by each player, and a stake sufficient to be able to withstand big bets.[6] In this form it was a difficult game to play well, and

---

6. Without a significant ante, a good player would wait for an excellent hand (at least Aces-up) before betting or calling. Yet the likelihood of having even two players with hands of that quality among seven is under 4 percent. This makes for a sucker game, or a dull one.

regularly relieved cowboys and traveling salesmen of their pay. It had little appeal for those who wished to play without putting large amounts of their assets at risk.

Jackpots with fixed limits changed all that. Introducing minimum requirements to open removed much of the mystery caused by the fact that all the cards are concealed. Limiting the maximum size of any bet before the draw permits players to pursue their hopes without risking a large fraction of their stake. These changes tamed draw poker, decreased the opportunities for intimidation, and created a game that was wholly different strategically. But in the process they also made the game too mechanical. Like 5-card stud, Jackpots has a straightforward optimal strategy that can be reduced to a small number of easily remembered rules of behavior. Once players learn the strategy, the game becomes one with much dealing but only infrequent confrontations of the kind that lead to big and exciting pots.

An Exercise

The following exercise is instructive not because it is hard, but because you will find it quite easy.

> You are playing Jackpots where the aggregate ante is $14, bets and raises are limited to $10 before the draw and $20 after. Consider six different hands you may have been dealt, as illustrated in Figure 12.1.
>
> For each hand, suppose you are in each of the five following alternate situations. In each case, do you bet, and, if so, how many cards do you draw?
>
> A. You are sitting under the gun.
> B. You are sitting in second position and the first player has opened for $10.
> C. You are sitting in sixth position and no one has opened.

FIGURE 12.1

D. You are sitting in sixth position and the player in fourth position has opened for $10.

E. You are sitting in seventh position and the hand has been opened in third position and raised by a player in front of you, each time for $10.

My answers to this exercise are given later in the chapter. Most players will agree with them in large part, because the answers depend so heavily on pure probability and so little on whom you are playing against. This is what makes Jacks a dull game.

The Relevant Probabilities

Because there are no open cards to provide information, draw poker is the one poker game where the relevant probabilities can be provided in a simple table. Table 12.1 pro-

Table 12.1   Odds Against Improving Hands in Draw Poker

Draw	Odds Against*
Drawing to one pair	
3-card draw	
any improvement	3 to 1
trips or better	7 to 1
full house or better	76 to 1
2-card draw, Ace kicker	
any improvement	3 to 1
Aces-up or better	4 to 1
trips or better	11 to 1
Drawing to two pair	
full house	11 to 1
Drawing to trips	
2-card draw	
any improvement	9 to 1
1-card draw	
any improvement	11 to 1
Drawing to flushes	
1-card draw	5 to 1
2-card draw	23 to 1
Drawing to straights	
1-card draw	
open-ended	5 to 1
inside	11 to 1
2-card draw to an 8, 9, 10	22 to 1

*These odds are rounded up to the next whole number.

vides the key to the basic questions that arise in draw: when to open, when to call before the draw, and how many cards to draw. A hand must either be good enough to win much of the time without improving, or the odds against its improving on the draw must be small enough to make the pot odds favorable.

Hands that are usually good enough to win in a seven-player game of Jackpots, even with no improvement, are a high two pair or better. A small two pair or a pair of Aces have roughly an even-money chance of standing up. Hands with a pair of Aces or better will be dealt to you only about one deal in nine.

Opening Hands: The Importance of Position

Position at the table relative to the dealer is important in draw poker because the person to the left of the dealer, under the gun, must act first. If there is a hand that meets the opening requirements, more often than not there will be more than one. This makes it risky to open under the gun or in other early positions with minimal opening strength. Table 12.2 shows the frequency with which hands of Jacks or better occur in a seven-person game.

Table 12.2   Number of Hands with Jacks or Better for Seven Players

	Percent of Deals
none	21
1	37
2	28
3	11
4 or more	3
	100

The table shows why it is unwise to open in first or second position with less than a pair of Kings or in a middle position with less than Queens. The odds are better than even that there is a second opening hand out there that is better than yours. Of course if you don't open with such a hand you take a 37-percent chance of a deal being passed in which your holding was the best hand and could well have captured the ante. But the risk of holding what is already an underpair and of having to meet a raise makes such openings in early positions too expensive in the long run. In a late position it is worth opening with a pair of Jacks, expecting to take the ante, but beware of someone who checked and now calls your bet or raises. He is likely to already have you beaten.

With a pair of Aces or Kings, opening is usually sensible even under the gun. You probably have the best hand dealt. However if your opening bet is raised, it usually comes from someone holding two pair, and if so, you will only be comfortable if you improve on the draw.

Three of a kind or pat hands can safely be opened in any position. In pot-limit it may be worth the risk of checking in any of the early positions, hoping for the opportunity to get called on bigger bets later. If you do check with trips and someone else opens, it is often sensible merely to call and draw one, hoping that the opener will read you for a potential straight or two small pair and call the bet you make after the draw. With a pat hand, however, you should raise before the draw whenever you have the chance, since standing pat will reveal your strength and make it unlikely that a big bet by you will be called after the draw.

Holding two pair on the deal provides the hardest challenge to sound play. While any two pair is likely to be the best hand before the draw, you have such a small chance of improving (odds against: 11 to 1) that you are very vulnerable if two or more players call the opener. With a below-average two pair (Jacks and 5's or less), the sound strategy is to try to reduce the field as much as possible before the draw. This is best accomplished by a raise before others have had a chance to call. In an early position, if no one has bet it is best to check and then raise if you think this will reduce the field. If you open in an early position with a small two pair and have callers, you cannot afford to bet after the draw unless you have made your full house, but you may well feel obliged to call if you check and someone else bets. It is this unpleasant possibility that makes opening on two pairs tricky. Against three or more callers, your two pairs are likely to prove worthless after the draw.

Calling the Opener

How good must a hand be in draw poker to be worth a call? For limit games, the implied pot odds before the draw rarely get as high as 5 to 1, and often they are not better than 3 to 1. In pot-limit poker, they can be as high as 7 or 8 to 1 if a pot-size bet after the draw is likely to be called. These facts, combined with the information in Table 12.1, make it immediately clear why drawing to an inside straight (odds against: 11 to 1) or drawing two cards to either a straight or flush (odds against: about 22 to 1) is seldom sensible. Looked at more closely, the table also suggests two more important behavioral rules.

Underpairs are poor drawing hands.   Suppose a deal of Jackpots is opened and you sit in the last position with a pair of 10's, and no one else has called the opener. The odds against your improving are only 3 to 1—not too shabby. But even if the opener has nothing more than a pair of Jacks, he too can improve. If neither of you do so, he will win; if both of you improve equally, he will win. Only if you improve (probability: .3) and he does not (probability: .7) will you have a good chance of being the winner; and the probability of both of these things happening is only about .2. The resulting 4-to-1 odds against you might be good enough if you were sure the opener had only a single pair, but of course he may *already* be better than that, and this makes calling a risky proposition.

If another player had called before you, you would face a bigger pot, and thus better pot odds, but now there would be two players to outdraw. If, as is likely, each of them has you beaten initially, you must improve and have both of them fail to do so. The odds are 6 to 1 against this. More opponents make your 10's even weaker than before. What if you had an Ace kicker and kept it with your pair of 10's? Another Ace would be likely to give you the high two pair, even if the opener has or catches another pair. For you to improve to Aces-up or better (probability: .2) and for the opener not to catch trips or better if he started with only a pair (probability: .9) has a combined probability of only .18—again, not usually good enough against only one player. Here, too, with more players the odds against you typically increase faster than the pot odds improve.[7]

Draw for straights or flushes only with two or more opponents.   The best of these draws has odds against of about 5 to 1. But here is a critical difference from the underpair situation: if the chance is realized, you have a hand that is probably going to win the pot, and so the potential winnings on bets made after the draw must be added in. As mentioned in Chapter 6, these implied odds are seldom good enough against one player, but become steadily more attractive as the number of callers increases. Flush draws are better than straight draws both in the sense of having

---

7. For example, if two others besides you call the opener, one of whom is drawing to a straight, the other to a four flush, the probability that you will improve to Aces-up or better and none of them make trips or better is only .12; the odds against you are 7 to 1.

slightly better probabilities (9 cards can help you, as distinct from 8), and also because a flush outranks a straight.

Even an open-ended four-card straight flush—say, the 7, 8, 9, 10, all of hearts—while appearing irresistible, is far from a sure thing. Only 15 out of the unseen 47 cards will make either a straight or a flush. This has a probability of .32, so the odds are 2 to 1 against you. This is good enough even against only one player, but it is not the heaven-sent hand that Harry believes it to be, and it is never worth a raise. A raise will not be likely to fold the opener, and you do not want to discourage other players from calling.

The best general advice is never to call an opening bet if you will be uncertain after the draw whether to call or fold. This would be the case, for example, if you hold a pair of Queens in a late position and someone opens in front of you. Even if you catch a second pair, you may well be second-best, so it is best to fold. With a pair of Aces, or Kings with an Ace kicker, you will feel comfortable calling an opener, for the number of cards he draws will clarify your status. If he draws three, you will feel confident, but should keep the kicker. If he draws one, you should draw three and fold unless you improve.[8]

Drawing Strategy

The probabilities shown above in Table 12.1 also suggest how many cards it is sensible to draw to various hands. With one important exception, you should usually draw to maximize your chances of improving to the winning hand. The exception concerns drawing to trips, where a one-card draw is usually best. The small increase in the probability against

8. It would be foolish to keep an Ace kicker to your pair of Kings when the opener draws one. If he had two pair, one of which was Aces, your chance of catching the last Ace is tiny. With any other two pair, Kings-up will be good enough. And if the opener has trips, you need to give yourself the best chance to catch a third King.

improving (from 9 to 1, to 11 to 1) is more than compensated by the reduction of your opponents' ability to read your hand. If an opponent thinks you were drawing to two pair, or to a straight or flush, he may well call a post-draw bet with a hand that you can beat. Of course, if you discover a pat hand against you, you should draw two cards to trips.

Other two-card draws are seldom sensible, although mixing your strategy to keep your opponents confused is always worth doing some of the time. If I've opened with a pair of Jacks or Queens and been called, I sometimes draw two to discourage an opponent from calling after the draw with a pair of Aces or two small pair (though standing pat may be just as effective). If the opener draws three, I would keep a high kicker to a pair of Aces or Kings some of the time to confuse him, but also as a potential tie breaker in case the opener has the same pair. But despite the exceptions, two-card draws are so revealing that they should almost always be avoided.

Answering the Exercise

Table 12.3 summarizes my answers to the exercise that was given on pages 205–6. Most follow directly from the discussion of the previous section.

A few additional comments may be helpful.

(i) Queens are barely better than Jacks. The Ace kicker helps only in decreasing the chance that someone else holds Aces.

(ii) The Aces are worth opening with in any position and calling with unless the opener is raised. An immediate raise by you behind the opener will discourage one-card draws and put you in the driver's seat if the opener draws three.

(iii) This is the hardest hand. Two pair are probably best before the draw, but they can easily be beaten if sev-

Table 12.3 Suggested Actions in Draw Poker Situations

SITUATIONS

Key cards in hands	A under the gun	B 2nd position; 1st opens	C 6th position; 1st–5th check	D 6th position; 4th opens	E 7th position; 3rd opens; is raised
(i) Q♥, Q♠, A♦	check	fold	open, draw 3	fold	fold
(ii) A♠, A♦	open, draw 3	raise	open, draw 3	call, draw 3	fold
(iii) 10♥, 10♦, 7♠, 7♣	check	raise	open, draw 1	call, draw 1	fold
(iv) 8♠, 8♥, 8♣, K♦, 10♥	open in limit poker, check in pot-limit	call, draw 1	open, draw 1	raise, draw 1	reraise, draw 1
(v) 8♠, 9♥, 10♥, J♣	check	fold	check	fold	call, draw 1
(vi) 9♣, 8♠, 7♠	check	fold	check	fold	fold

eral people are drawing. You want to discourage others from doing so if you can.

(iv) Trip 8's will probably win, so you want to keep as many players in as possible but also build the pot. A sandbag check under the gun is risky, but is likely to pay big dividends in pot-limit poker, though not in a limit game. In most cases you should draw only one to this hand. Keeping the 10 kicker is marginally better than keeping the King, since the opener may have Kings.

(v) A four-card straight (or a four flush) requires good pot odds, and that means other callers. It is a better call in pot-limit than in limit poker.

(vi) The three-card straight flush may seem appealing, but the odds against being able to beat a pair of Jacks are 11 to 1.

The Number of Competitors: Why Jackpots Is a Dull Game

Because the principles of sound play are so clear, the opportunities for skillful play are relatively limited. Only with weak players at the table is there ample opportunity for much action.[9] In a competently played Thursday-night game the number of players who will choose to meet the normal-size opening bet is small, and for good reason. Of all five-card hands that are dealt, only 20 percent have a pair of Jacks or better, and at most another 8 percent have a straight or flush possibility worth considering. Hands that meet neither of these criteria are not worth keeping, and as we have seen, position and pot odds dictate that many

9. Mike Caro stresses picking your opponents as the major element of skill required to win money at draw poker. He says: "Look for [a table] . . . where no one's taking poker too seriously. . . . Try to spot players who sit upright and who seem attentive. Avoid them. Select a table where there are distractions— an attractive woman, a boisterous drunk. . . ." See Caro's essay in Doyle Brunson *et al., How I Made over $1,000,000 Playing Poker,* pp. 56–57.

hands that do meet these criteria are not worth calling with either. A realistic estimate is that only about one hand in five dealt is worth the cost of even an unraised opening bet. If this is the case, the number of players expected to stay to see the draw is shown in Table 12.4

Table 12.4   Expected Number of Players Who Pay to See the Draw in a Seven-Person Game of Jackpots

Number of Players	Percent of Deals	Result
None	21%	Redeal
1	37	Opener wins ante
2	28	Head to head
3 or more	14	Big pot possible
	100	

As the table shows, about 58 percent of draw hands will either be redealt or be opened but have no caller. If poker-playing time is a scarce resource for you, this is a disadvantage. Even where there are two or more players drawing cards, there is often little post-draw action since the hopes that motivated the calling of the opening bet will more often than not go unfulfilled. Since there are only two rounds of betting, big contested pots are infrequent.

To be sure, there are occasional major confrontations, usually between two players who both have hands that are well above average. These become episodes of cat-and-mouse in which you hope to be the cat and lure a player with a good but second-best hand into at least calling your post-draw bet. The strategy required to do this (and avoid the role of mouse!) involves a good deal of caution and slow-playing of hands such as high trips or better. Such confrontations may make it all worthwhile, but they are much more frequent in other forms of poker.

Play After the Draw

Because draw poker confrontations usually devolve into a two- (or at most three-) person game, your post-draw play depends entirely upon your reading of the other players' hands while keeping them uncertain about yours.

If, as the opener, you must act first, you will normally check unless you have a big hand. If you have not improved to at least two high pairs, a bet gains little and risks much. A beaten opponent will fold, and an opponent who has improved will either call or raise. With Aces-up or better, a bet is usually indicated except into pat hands or one-card draws that did not raise before the draw. (If a skilled player raised you and drew a card, his most probable holding is two pair, and you can beat that hand.) Of course, you must vary your behavior enough to make your checks and bets after the opening hard to decipher, as well as to invite an opponent to try to bluff you out when in fact you hold the best hand.

If you are acting second—that is, if someone else opened—you have additional information. In what position did your opponent open? How many did he draw? Did he make an unusual bet? You now have three options: fold, call, or raise. There is little general advice to give; every hand is situation-specific. But be sure to remember your own earlier behavior, since your opponent will. Bluffs in limit draw poker seldom work unless they have been set up *before the draw.*

Pot-limit draw differs from limit draw primarily in the post-draw round. The opportunity for (and risks of) big bets and raises is substantial. Here everything depends on knowing your opponent.

Variations on Jackpots

Several common variations on Jackpots are designed to increase the number of big and contested pots. One way to do so is to eliminate opening requirements, playing *Guts* instead of Jackpots. Among players used to Jackpots this variation seldom makes much difference since they will tend to stick to their Jackpots strategy. But you will find players opening with very little in the late positions just to steal the ante, and thus there will be less redealing.

Another way to increase the amount of competition is to raise the ante substantially relative to the size of the permitted bet, thus improving the pot odds for potential callers of an opening bet. (With a large enough ratio of ante to bet, everyone will call.) But few players like a high-ante, low-limit combination. Other variations that keep the main features of Jackpots but do increase confrontations and/or big pots, at least occasionally, are also available.

Raising the opening requirements—say, to requiring Kings or better—will result in about one deal in three requiring double antes and one deal in nine requiring triple antes. If the size of the permitted bet is not increased, this will often lead to more callers when the hand is finally opened. Now low pairs with an Ace or King kicker may become playable, and even inside straights may face pot odds that are attractive. If, however, the stakes are raised in proportion, this effect will not occur, and raising the opening requirements will do nothing more than increase haphazardly the stakes for some hands. A similar change, called *Jacks progressive,* raises opening requirements only after a hand is passed out. If it is, the next deal requires Queens to open, and if passed out again, Kings. (The progression usually stops with Aces, and then works down again.) Jacks progressive haphazardly creates a few large ante pools and can add some spice, and a good deal of randomness, to an evening of draw poker.

There are also some more radical variations of draw poker. Here are three.

Use of the Joker as bug.   The present low popularity of draw poker is suggested by the fact that at a major poker-playing casino (the Mirage, in Las Vegas) none of its thirty-one poker tables is regularly devoted to draw poker. Where draw survives, in many California poker parlors, it is played with a fifty-three-card deck that includes the Joker as *bug*—as an Ace or as a wild card in straights or flushes. This improves the competitiveness of draw poker by increasing the number of players who are willing to call an opening hand. It is not, however, a readily available alternative in the kind of dealer's choice that is played in most Thursday-night games, since adding or removing the Joker between hands is a nuisance.

Adding the Joker doesn't make major changes in the distribution of hands, as Table 12.5 shows:

Table 12.5   The Effect of Adding the Joker as Bug

Odds to 1 against holding indicated hand in five cards

HAND	52-card deck	53-card deck (with bug)
4 of a kind	4,165	3,466
Full house	694	657
Flush	509	368
Straight	255	140
3 of a kind	47	45
Any of the above	35	30
Two pair, but not more	21	21

The bug does two things. First, it greatly increases the value of an Ace relative to other cards, since it is much easier to get multiple Aces than other ranks.[10] If you hold Kings or Queens, they are greatly devalued. Second, it greatly increases the frequency of straights, and to a lesser degree flushes.[11] In both of these respects, the bug tends to keep more players in the game during the early rounds, and it often keeps the person who has the bug in for the draw since his options are substantial.

Nevertheless, the addition of the bug does not greatly change the character of draw poker. What it adds is perhaps more psychological than material, but even small increases in the possibilities of improving one's hand can increase participation, and increase opportunities for bluffing if one holds the bug.

Jacks-or-back, or Kings-or-back. These variations, which I prefer to the ones mentioned above, avoid most of the redealing caused by opening requirements. If the hand is not opened for high, it reverts to lowball draw, and only if no one wishes to open low is there a redeal and a reante.[12] Lowball provides a nice change of pace, and no one has sacrificed a first-rate high hand to play it. It increases somewhat the number of competitors, since the number of legitimate drawing hands is greater in lowball than in high draw poker.

---

10. Thus the apparent constancy of the odds of getting two pair or trips is somewhat misleading since a much larger number of them now contain Aces.

11. The change in relative frequency of straights and flushes occurs because there are many more ways to improve four cards to a straight than four cards to a flush when there is a bug present. Without the bug, if you hold four cards to a flush there are nine cards that can fill it; with the bug there are ten. With four cards to a straight, there are (at most) eight cards to improve it without the bug. But suppose you hold 5, 6, 7, Joker. Any 3, 4, 8, or 9—sixteen cards—will make a straight.

12. My preferred form is Kings-or-back, which will play high about two-thirds of the time and low one-third. Jacks-or-back is more common, and will play low about one-quarter of the time.

In general, it pays to draw for a low hand if you need only one card to achieve an 8-low or better.[13] This may be a bit loose, but it is roughly right. If all players follow this rule, the distribution of expected players in a game of Jacks-or-back is shown in Table 12.6.

Table 12.6   Expected Number of Players Who Pay to See the Draw in a Seven-Person Game of Jacks-or-Back

Number of Players	Percent of Deals	Result
None	2%	Redeal
1	41	Opener wins ante
2	34	Head to head
3 or more	23	Big pot possible
	100	

Comparing this distribution with that shown in Table 12.4 on p. 216 shows the expected increase in the amount of confrontation relative to Jackpots. Most hands get opened in one direction or the other. This reduction in the amount of redealing makes for a livelier session, as well as providing a change of pace.

If the hand is played for low, the major decisions are whether to open, and whether to stand pat on hands headed by a 9, 10, or Jack. Position is crucial to each of these decisions. Avoiding a likely second-best situation is particularly important, especially if the post-draw betting can be large, as it is in pot-limit poker.

Strategic play in lowball is a big subject in itself, but its flavor can be suggested by a couple of examples. Suppose you are dealt a K, 8, 7, 6, 4. While an 8-low usually wins,

13. This is based on the assumption that the best low is 6, 4, 3, 2, A (see Chapter 14).

this would be a dangerous hand to open in an early position, or to call with if even two others are competing. The reason is that even if you draw an Ace, deuce, or trey (12 chances in 47), anyone else with an 8-low or better will almost surely beat you, though you will probably feel obliged to call. But in a late position, or against only one competitor, this is not a bad drawing hand.

Next consider a hand of 10, 8, 6, 5, 2. This hand is worth playing in any position, even against three other players. Against one competitor who is drawing a card, you should stand pat: if he hits a 7-low or better he'll beat you even if you improve; if he gets an 8-low he may well beat you, and the rest of the time he will not be able to call your post-draw bet. But with two, three, or more drawing callers, you had better hope to make an 8-low, about a 1-in-3 chance.

High-Low draw poker. As a final variation, draw poker can be played high-low with no opening requirements. This is a very good game for limit poker, but it is much more complicated. The appropriate strategy is much closer to that of 7-card Hi-Lo (discussed in Chapter 14) than to 5-card draw. The essential element of strategy is to position yourself to be going in the opposite direction from your opponents if you have a mediocre hand, or in the same direction if you have a monster hand.

FOUR PROBLEMS

1. The game is 5-card stud, $20 limit, and after the last card is dealt you still have the high showing hand, holding:

Behind you sit

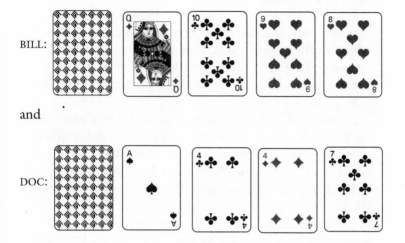

There have been no raises to your bets since you received the second 10. You now check. Bill bets $20, and Doc calls. There is now $110 in the pot. What should you do?

2. You open in Jackpots in second position with a pair of Kings. Duke, sitting in third position, raises and everyone else folds. You call, draw three, and Duke draws one. You find you have now caught a second pair, 7's. Should you check or bet?

3. It is pot-limit Jackpots. You are sitting in the sixth position and no one opens in front of you. You hold two pairs, Aces and fives. You open for the combined amount of the ante, expecting everyone to fold. To your surprise, Doc, sitting under the gun, raises, and Ty, behind Doc, calls him. You reraise, and both of the others call your raise. There is now $150 in the pot. Doc draws two and Ty draws one. What do they hold, and what should you do now?

4. You are playing Kings-or-back, and, sitting under the gun, find that you have been dealt A, A, 3, 4, 7. What should you do?

ANSWERS TO THE PROBLEMS
(AS I SEE THEM)

1. You should fold. While it is quite likely that Bill is bluffing with his scare cards, as he might well do if he holds a Queen in the hole, the fact of Doc's call must mean that you are beaten. Doc surely has either an Ace or a 4 in the hole.

2. You should bet the maximum allowed. Duke's raise on the previous round was intended to get people out. With trips, Aces-up, or a drawing hand he would have called, not raised, your opening bet. So you now have him beaten, but he'll call any bet that you make. Remember, he's the Iron Duke.

3. What your opponents hold is not hard to discern; what to do about it is. Ty almost surely is drawing to a flush or a straight. Doc, who didn't open originally and then raised and drew two has trips. In a way you are relieved that he drew two: you feared a pat hand when he called your reraise. You could draw one, but your chance of getting a full house is only about 1 in 12. You have two better choices: one is to draw three to your pair of Aces, giving yourself 1 chance in 8 of getting the highest trips while hoping that Ty fails to make his hand, which is, of course, likely. The other choice is to stand pat and come out after the draw with a big bluff bet. This won't work if Ty hits, but it makes your original bet and reraise look like a genuine pat hand. Which choice to pursue depends on your reading of how Doc reads you. If you don't bluff very often, this is a good spot.

The three-card draw, long shot though it is, is probably the soundest, and certainly minimizes your downside risk. If you don't get a third Ace you will have no trouble checking after the draw and folding if anyone bets.

4. You are in a perfect position to check, even though you have solid openers. Your drawing hand for low if no one

opens high is superb; your pair of Aces is worth calling with if someone opens for high. By checking now you can see how much strength is out there. If a high opener is raised, you can fold without having spent any money.

13

♠ ♣ ♥ ♦

7-CARD STUD

My group was asked how they felt about 7-card stud. Beauty is in the eye of the beholder; here are their replies:

TY TASS: *It's great. My bets on good hands get called because they are well concealed.*

HARDLUCK HARRY: *I hate it. My hands get beat too often by someone drawing out on me.*

BLUFFALO BILL: *It's tops for bluffing opportunities.*

DUKE STEELE: *I do not care for it. You've got to call too many hands to keep your opponents honest.*

DOC WRIGHT: *I relish the opportunity to apply ever-changing probabilities against players who play their hopes rather than the probabilities.*

LUCKY LOU: *So where else do you have the chance to fill a flush, a straight, and a boat at the same time?*

KNOTT WAH CHIN: *It's too much like work to have to keep track of all those cards. I prefer Holdem.*

HUGH: *I enjoy all poker games, but this one certainly rewards your skill in processing all that information.*

Seven-card stud (sometimes also known as Seven-Toed Pete, or Down the River) is the most widely played poker game of the last half-century, even if everyone doesn't like it. The explanation lies in its structure, which underlies each of the comments above. With its three down cards, it combines the multiple closed-card feature of draw poker, which means that surprising things can happen, with lots of information from the four open cards. Moreover, its five betting rounds create opportunities for lots of action and don't require high antes to produce a worthwhile pot. These features make it anything but a simple game to play well, and thus put a premium on the skills already discussed:

Estimating probabilities.[1]   Because the open cards come one betting round at a time, the ability to approximate quickly the changing pot odds facing you is much more important than tables that show how likely a given hand is to improve when you know nothing about the rest of the deck. In a seven-person game, if five players see the fourth card, each player will have seen 14 of the 52 cards.[2] Your chances of getting the card or cards you need out of the remaining 38 are dramatically affected by the ones you have seen. While a mathematician calculates that if you hold a pair of 8's, a King, and a 3, each of a different suit, and know nothing else about the other 48 cards, your chances of improving to trips or better in seven cards is about 14 percent, this number goes out the window once you've seen 14 cards. If none of them except yours is an 8, your chances *increase* to 18 percent; if one is an 8, they decrease to 10 percent; and if both the remaining 8's are showing, they fall to 2.6 percent.[3] Further, these numbers assume that neither your King nor 3 is matched by any of those showing.

As soon as the fifth card is dealt, you will have seen more cards and have more information and there will be fewer cards left, so you'll have to recalculate your chances. This means that you need to pay close attention to the cards dealt, and to remember those folded to give you an approximate notion of your chances of improving to a winning hand.

1. Discussed in Chapter 5.
2. You will see your own four, all six of your opponents' *door cards,* and the four second-round cards of your remaining competitors.
3. This last number is the maximum chance of getting either two Kings or two treys in the next three cards. There is also a very small probability that the final three cards will themselves be trips.

Reading cards.[4] Putting together what you know about a player and what you see in his open cards, combined with his earlier betting or raising, will give you many clues about what he's likely to have and what he's likely to be looking for. This is critically important in 7-card stud because almost everything is possible. Suppose after all of the cards have been dealt, a tight-playing opponent such as Ty Tass shows 8♥, K♦, 4♠, and 10♦, received in that order. With three cards in the hole, he could conceivably have anything from a total bust to a royal flush. Neither is likely. The first thing you know is that Ty stayed in with [X, Y], 8♥, and paid to see a fifth card after adding the apparently unconnected K♦. What kept him in? It is unlikely to have been the flush or straight possibilities that were there only after the diamond 10 appeared on the sixth card. A good guess is that he had either a pair in the hole, or an 8 with a high kicker. How he bet will provide some help. If he raised after getting the King, I would suspect that he now has at least Kings and 8's. If so, neither the 4 nor the 10 have improved his hand. If he merely called when he got that King but raised later, I would suspect he has at least three 8's, and possibly a full house. But this guess should be refined by remembering the other cards you have seen. Remember, too, that the better your showing cards, the better his hand is likely to be; after all, he stayed in despite your apparent strength.

Pot management.[5] Suppose you have a monster hand after four or five cards. Your challenge is to build the biggest possible pot. Will you do this by making a big bet now, or by a smaller bet that keeps opponents around so that they will improve their hands enough to call your later bets? Or if you have a good drawing hand, but one that is worthless

---

4. Discussed in Chapter 11.
5. Discussed in Chapter 9.

unless you get a good card on the next round or two, can you manage to keep your costs low while you get additional cards and information? How you should behave will depend both on which of your own cards are showing (since that is the context in which your opponents will evaluate your action) and who the opponents are.

Avoiding second-best.[6]   Hands are seldom made in 7-card stud until the sixth or seventh card, so most players in the early rounds are looking for the cards that will improve, rather than make, their hands. But improvement to what? Holding a pair of 8's, you may welcome a second pair—say, 10's—but with several other players staying in, this hand is unlikely to win unless it improves to a full house. When holding 8's against several opponents, anything less than Aces-up or trips may well get you into trouble; if so, you ought to figure your odds that way. Similarly, drawing to a straight when someone who is betting shows three diamonds invites being second-best to his flush even if you catch your straight. While he may not have two diamonds in the hole, he is likely to have at least one. To win you need both to make your straight and to have him miss his flush. The worst scenario—that is, the most expensive—is for you *both* to hit. You will feel obliged to call him, and will end up with what the pros call a *bad beat,* but one that you should have avoided.

WHAT WINS AT 7-CARD STUD?

What wins depends on both how many players are in the hand at the start and how many stay until the end. The old poker maxim that says you can't win if you don't stay in is of course true, even if it may be misconstrued as advice to

6. Discussed in Chapter 8.

stay in more often than you should. Mathematics can answer the question of what is likely to be the winning hand for any given number of players if *all* the players stay in to the showdown. Such showdown probabilities are listed in Table 13.1 and provide a good starting point for understanding 7-card stud.

Table 13.1 Winning Hands in 7-Card Stud Showdown (Seven Players)

Winning Hand	Percent of Deals	Percent This Good or Better
Full house or better	18%*	18%
Flush	16	34
Straight	20	54
Trips	15	69
2 pair	28	97
1 pair	3	100
No pair	—†	100
Total	100	—

*The "or better" accounts for 1.4 percent.
†Less than 1 percent.

As the first column of the table shows, two pair is the most frequent winning hand, but full houses, flushes, straights and trips are all frequent enough winners to occasion no surprise when they occur. A look at the second column of the table shows that in aggregate these hands far outnumber two pair. Indeed, under these circumstances the winning hand is expected to be trips *or better* more than two-thirds of the time. The median winning hand is a 7-high straight.

But Table 13.1 applies to showdown. In an actual deal, many hands are folded, and thus the quality of actual winning hands is poorer than that shown in the table. The reason is that many hands that would lead to *backdoor*—that is, unexpected—straights, flushes, and full houses are folded before they mature because they seemed too unpromising to justify paying to get the additional cards.

How good the actual winning hand is depends on how loosely or tightly the players play, which, in turn, depends upon the stakes and culture of the game, as discussed in Chapter 2. Poker writers usually pinpoint the median winning hand somewhere between Aces-up and three 10's, based on their own experiences in the games in which they play.[7] These estimates are good enough for practical purposes and should be borne in mind, although my experience in Thursday-night games would put the median at three Kings or Aces. But of course while playing a given hand, you have a lot of additional information in the showing cards of your opponents, not to mention their past betting behavior—if you've paid attention to it. In general, the more players who have stayed in a deal to the fourth or fifth card, the better the winning hand is likely to be. You may be happy with Aces-up after five cards, and it is usually a powerful holding against one or two other players. But the same hand will tend to be dangerously weak against three or more experienced opponents, especially if your Aces are there for all to see. One player might still be in with only a small two pair, hoping that you had nothing to back up your Aces, but if three people call, you can be virtually certain that one or more of them already has you beaten, and that you'll need a full house to win.

7. David Spanier, *Total Poker* (New York: Simon & Schuster, 1977), points to Aces-up as the expected average (p. 225); A. D. Livingston, *Advanced Poker*, (N. Hollywood: Wilshire Book Co., 1971), and Albert H. Morehead, *The Complete Guide to Winning Poker* (New York: Simon & Schuster, 1967), report that it is trip 8's, 9's, or 10's (p. 178 and p. 114, respectively).

STARTING STRATEGY

The keys to a sensible strategy about which hands to hold and which to fold lie in the discussion of what proves to be a winner.[8] You usually have to have Aces-up or better to have much chance of winning a contested pot, and you will be a good deal more comfortable with high trips or better. Straights, while good hands, are by no means hands you should be prepared to bet the ranch on, nor should you be afraid to fold them if the information you have suggests that a flush or full house is present.

As a general matter, promising hands after the first three or four cards have been dealt are those that have a reasonable chance to make high trips or better, and marginal hands are those that have a reasonable chance of making Aces-up or low trips. What constitutes a "reasonable chance"? In a seven-person game, a hand picked at random has 1 chance in 7 of winning, a probability of 14.3 percent; thus it takes a probability above that—say, 18 percent or higher—to be significantly better than average.

Whether the critical moment for decision is at the first betting round (after three cards have been dealt to each player) or at the second round (after a second up card has been dealt around) depends upon the structure of the game. For games that were characterized as aggressive in Chapter 2, you need to have a pretty good hand to call any bet on the deal or you risk getting sucked into expensively chasing someone who *has* such a hand. Making your stay/fold decision after three cards makes sense in such games. There you can expect many hands to be folded and, as a result, many uncontested pots, or deals that are quickly reduced to only a couple of players. Most of the experts who write about a strategy for 7-card stud seem to have

8. I neglect here the opportunities for bluffing and for stealing the ante against tight players, independent of the cards you hold.

such a game in mind, and propose strict rules for staying in even to receive the fourth card.

By contrast, most Thursday-night games are restrained ones, with nominal betting and raising patterns in the first round. When there are five betting rounds and restrained early betting it usually pays to see the fourth card since it will greatly clarify both your hand and those of your opponents.

Starting Three-Card Holdings for Aggressive Games

While I do not believe your three-card initial holding to be the critical decision point for most Thursday-night poker games, it is worth considering because it is relevant for some games.

The best possible three-card holding is three of a kind, the higher the better. If you have trips, you already have a hand that may win without any improvement, and you also have better than a 40-percent chance of improving to a full house or better after seven cards. Together you have a high probability of winning the pot. Unfortunately, getting trips on the deal is going to happen to you fewer than three times in every thousand hands you are dealt, and will happen to someone at the table only about once in every sixty deals, so it is not worth holding your breath for. If you do get trips in three cards, simply rejoice silently and direct your attention to how best to build the big pot you expect to win.[9]

Open-ended three-card straights (for example, 8, 9, 10) and three-card flushes are each promising starting cards, and if they are held to the end they will lead to straights or flushes almost 20 percent of the time. Since either holding can also improve in other ways, their overall chance of leading to a hand of trips or better is about 25 percent.

9. If the trips are low in rank, you may well want to get people out soon so they do not have a chance to outdraw you, but with high trips, say 9's or better, I would advise slow-playing them to keep people in. Even if you do not improve, high trips are likely to win about half the time.

Any pair in three cards has about an 18 percent chance of making trips or better if held to the end, and high pairs (say, 9's or better) are usually worth playing for a round or two unless the other players' showing cards and betting have convinced you that someone already has a higher pair.[10] (About a third of the time that you hold a pair in three cards, one of the other six players will also hold a pair, which is why high pairs are a lot safer than small ones.)

It is useful to distinguish between *pocket pairs,* where both of the paired cards are concealed in the hole, and *split pairs,* where one is showing. The probability of improving is, of course, the same in each case, but if you do hit trips, the pocket pairs will prove more profitable: opponents won't see a showing pair and be as likely to read your now-powerful hand. Pocket pairs, even deuces or treys, are usually worth playing for a round or two for this reason, as long as none of their kind is showing. Low split pairs are not worth much unless they become trips right away, or unless they are accompanied by an Ace or King. While any pair after three cards has a 43-percent chance of being improved to two pair by the seventh card, drawing to achieve anything less than Kings-up is not recommended; even if you hit, you are all too likely to end up with an expensive second-best hand.

To summarize, most authors who advise making the stay/fold decision before calling the first-round bets suggest folding unless you hold one of the following combinations in the first three cards:[11]

---

10. It is virtually never worth playing an underpair.

11. This is representative of the advice found in each of the books cited above in note 7, as well as many others. Herbert Yardley, in his famous book (*The Education of a Poker Player,* p. 82) suggests an even tighter standard; he would, for example, advise folding an opening pair of Queens unless it is accompanied by an Ace or King. If you follow his rules you'll play only one out of seven hands, and unless the other players are wholly unobservant, they will tend to drop out whenever you do play unless they have really powerful hands.

trips
high pairs
three-card flushes
three-card straights open at both ends
low pairs only if pocket pairs or if accompanied by an Ace
    or King.

You will have one of these three-card holdings only 20
percent of the time, so if you follow this advice you will be
doing a lot of anteing and then folding, a combination that
most Thursday-night players do not relish. Moreover, if everyone in the game follows this advice, two or more hands
that meet this test (and thus lead to a pot amounting to
more than the ante) will occur less than half the time.
There will be only three or more hands meeting these
starting conditions about one-sixth of the time. Played
this way, 7-card stud can become almost as boring as
5-card stud! Of course, if most players do play the opening
round this tightly, there is an opportunity for you to bet or
raise on the first round and steal the ante. This is attractive
only with sizable antes, of the kind not usually present
in Thursday-night poker. (If you try to steal the ante, be
wary of the player who stays in with you, and be prepared
to exit quietly if he shows any improvement in the next
round.)
    Unless, therefore, you are playing in an aggressive game
with lots of first-round raising, or in a game where you are
the one preying on the geese, it is sensible (and not dangerous) to be more flexible in how you play the opening
round.

Starting Four-Card Holdings for Restrained Games

My strategy in Thursday-night 7-card stud games, whether
limit or pot-limit, is to stay in for the fourth card unless
there is obvious behavior (such as a raise) to suggest that

someone has a power hand.[12] Many attractive four-card holdings are made so only by the fourth card. The profits on these more than repay a lot of what seem to be loose first-round calls. For example, an opening hand of 9, 10, Q, can become very promising if you catch a Jack, an 8, or a King, or if you pair one of your cards on the next round. This means that twenty-one cards can help you, and if none of them is showing, it is about an even-money chance that you will get one on the next card. If you do, you are in a good drawing position. Of course, when you play loosely on the first round you must have the discipline and courage to fold after seeing the fourth card.[13]

Here are the four-card combinations I consider playing in Thursday-night poker:

any trips
any two pairs
any four-card flush
a three-card flush with a pair, or with two high cards
a three-card flush with three straight cards (e.g., 6, 7, 9)
a four-card straight with no more than one gap (e.g., 6, 7, 8, 10)
a three-card straight with a pair (e.g., 8, 9, 10, 10)
any pair of Queens or better, if none show in other players' up cards
any other pair with an Ace kicker
any three cards each 10 or higher.

12. This overstates it a bit. If I am dealt a 9, 5, 2, of three different suits, or any other holding that has little chance of making one of the four-card holdings I list in the text below, I will fold rather than meet even a nominal bet. I will do so also if two or more showing cards match my own and I do not have realistic straight or flush possibilities.

13. If the pattern of your game is for virtually everyone to stay for the fourth card for, say, $2, it will save time to add $2 to the ante and then just deal four cards, two down and two up. While this eliminates ante-stealing raise opportunities for players in the first round, it speeds up the game considerably.

This list will seem pretty loose to a conservative player like Ty Tass, but I have found it to be acceptable—indeed, profitable. Even if you played *every* such holding for another round (which I do not suggest), you would play only about 50 percent of the possible four-card holdings. Still, I do not suggest *playing* all such hands, but merely *considering* them. Whether to bet, or call a bet, depends critically on the large number of open cards you have seen by now, on the betting on this specific hand, *and* on the betting patterns that your fellow players usually follow. It depends also on your position: with one of the weaker combinations, it is safer to call if there are no players behind you who might raise than if there are several.

Here are the results of an experiment I conducted in which I compared my proposed "loose" strategy with the tight three-card strategy suggested in the previous section. In each case I have compared the results to a game in which every hand was played out to the end. The first question focused on how frequently a potential winner would have been folded and thus never given a chance to develop; it asked: "Did the showdown winner 'pass the starting gate'?"[14] The answer was yes about 25 percent of the time for the three-card rules (listed on page 235) and 66 percent for my proposed four-card rules (on page 236). This represents a lot of folding errors for the conservative three-card rules. The second question asked: "How frequently did hands that were played under these rules turn out to be the best of the seven hands if all seven were played out to the end?" The answer to this question measures the *efficiency* of the rules. This efficiency (which should be compared to the average efficiency of 14.3 percent) was 22 percent for the three-card rules and 25 percent for the

---

14. A three-card starting holding also had to pass the four-card test to be retained to the end.

four-card rules.[15] What this experiment shows is that winning efficiency does not suffer by remaining flexible until the fourth card is dealt, and that a great many additional winning holdings are retained under the four-card rules. Of course, staying to get the fourth card is not free; the cost is the size of the first-round bet you must meet to do so. When this bet is small relative to the ultimate pot, as it is in restrained games, the extra expenditure will be justified by the increase in your number of winning hands.

PLAY ON THE SECOND ROUND
(FOURTH CARD, OR FOURTH STREET)

Generally you can afford to see an additional card on the second round more easily in a pot-limit game than in one with a small limit, and you need to be more conservative if there are raises than if there are none. These propositions both result from paying attention to the implied pot odds. If the cost of getting an additional card is small relative to the expected future bet sizes, it is easier to do than if the reverse is the case.

With three cards to come, any four-card holding might become the winning hand (four of a kind, for example), but only those listed on page 236 are sufficiently promising to consider. Before you call a second-round bet, it is advisable to count how many different cards you can get that will make you comfortable on the next round. The fewer there are, the more reluctant you should be to call.

---

15. The efficiency of the 50 percent of all hands that met neither test was about 10 percent. Notice that efficiency is interesting only in connection with how frequently the hand occurs. For an extreme but revealing example, one might specify a four-card strategy that dictated always folding without four of a kind. The "efficiency" of this rule would be very close to 100 percent, but you would go broke meeting the antes if you played such a strategy.

It is worth distinguishing four kinds of four-card hold-ings:[16]

1. Holdings that are already probable winners.
With a powerful hand, such as high trips or Aces-up, you probably do not need to improve to have a winner, and your attention should turn to pot management. Either make a normal bet or check with such a hand, but do not raise. You want to keep others in (even if it means letting them get a free card), and hope they improve enough to stay around as the bets get bigger.

2. Mediocre holdings that can become very good hands with one more card and may win even without it.
Such a hand is two middle or small pairs, or small trips. These hands are vulnerable, and you will usually wish to bet or raise the maximum now in order to induce some or all of the drawing hands to fold.[17]

3. Drawing hands that have no chance without im-proving but can become winners with one card.   Four-card straights and flushes are examples, and if there are only one or two competitors, a pair of Aces or Kings may also qualify. With one-card needs you should usually expect to stay around for two rounds of betting and two more cards. You will want to get them as cheaply as possible. Check if it is your bet and never raise.

4. Holdings that require two of the next three cards to become a probable winner but have multiple ways of hitting.   Such hands include three-card straights or flushes that also contain a high pair, or a hand that has both a three-

16. Holdings that fit none of these categories should be folded without regret.
17. A bet at this stage can also set up a bluff bet at a later point if you do not improve.

card straight and a three-card flush. When you need two cards to make your hand, your tactics should be aimed at getting the fifth card as cheaply as possible, and if you do not get one of your cards then, to fold. You must catch a promising additional card as the fifth card in order to continue because you never want to be in the position of needing to be helped on *both* the sixth and seventh cards, not merely because the odds will be against you, but also because you face the prospect of having to call two rounds of bets before you even know whether you have a hand that can win.

Enough of generalities. Here are six four-card holdings that you may face as the second-round bet comes to you. Treat them as an exercise and think about how to play them before reading my suggestions:

1. This holding is strong and you should bet if it is your turn, or call, but not raise another's bet. You want both to build the pot and to keep most players in. Don't advertise your strength this early. You have almost as good a chance of improving as people drawing to open-ended four-card straights or flushes, and you have the best hand if no one improves. Your time to get people out is not now but on the next round or two if you fail to improve.

2. This is a good drawing hand unless a number of Jacks or 6's are showing or have been folded. Since only 8 cards out of the roughly 35 to 40 that you haven't seen can help you, you probably have to expect to see more than one more card to make your straight. Plan to see two more cards, even if there is a raise or two at this point. But you want to get the next card as cheaply as possible. Your secondary possibilities here (the two-card flushes) don't add much value to your hand. Even a spade, a heart, or a pairing card on the fifth card isn't going to alter your chances very much.

3. Even though this can become a winner with only one more card, your chances of getting the full house are small: only four cards can help you. If you stay for three more cards you have less than 1 chance in 4 of getting one of them, even if none of them is already showing. This below-average two pair might survive to be the best hand at the end if you can greatly reduce the number of people drawing against you. Your best strategy is to bet or raise the maximum now. If one of your pairs is showing, this is likely to get people out, but even if not, you should try now to eliminate some of the competition. If, despite your best efforts, two or more others stay in, plan to get out in the next round unless you make your full house. Staying too long with two pair is a common but expensive mistake.

4. This hand has ten cards—any J, 7, or 10—that would put it in a strong position after five cards, and fourteen others—any Queen, 6, 9, or 8—that offer some chance of drawing for a winner. It is usually worth staying in for one more round.

5. This hand looks promising but it can easily lose if there are several players in at the end, even if it improves to two-pair. Your best chance is to reduce the number of competitors if you can. If both of your Aces are showing, this can usually be accomplished by making the maximum permitted bet. With only one of your Aces showing, a bet is not going to chase most players who have strong drawing prospects, so I would check but raise if someone else bets. And with both Aces in the hole, you are in a wonderful position to lie low and see what happens. A pair of Aces has so many ways to improve that you will almost always want to see a fifth card unless both of the other Aces have already shown up. The mistake players make with this holding is to fall in love with it and stay beyond the fifth card even if doesn't improve.

6. Fold this hand now if there is any bet. It would take two or three perfect cards to make it a winner, and you will probably have to call three bets before you find out.

PLAY ON THE THIRD ROUND (FIFTH CARD) AND BEYOND

The most critical moment in a 7-card stud game is after the fifth card has been dealt but before the third-round bets have been made. As a player, you have received five of the seven cards that are going to be available to you, and so you already have well over two-thirds of your hand. You also already see three of the four cards your opponents will expose. While most of the information you can glean from the cards is already there, you have only had to meet two rounds of betting; three more rounds lie ahead, and they will almost surely be larger than the two that have gone before. Thus, while your information is mostly complete, the investment you will have to make to see the hand to a showdown is not. It is time to fish or cut bait. You must now be ruthlessly realistic in balancing your chances of winning against the cost of staying in.

Your Chances of Winning

At this point there are no absolutes, only relatives: a pair of Kings may be a good hand or a sure loser, and the same is true of a straight. Everything depends upon the cards you have seen. Given those, you must form a judgment of what help, if any, you need to achieve a hand good enough to stay in with until the showdown. You will have seen so many cards by this point that you ought to be able to count quite precisely how many of the remaining cards will give you such a hand.

The hand you hold at this stage will usefully fit one of four categories:

1. *Probable winning hands.* I would include here any hand with Aces-up or better.

2. *Vulnerable leading hands.* This category includes hands such as other high two pairs or a pair of Aces. While such hands are likely to be the best at this stage, they are unlikely to remain best unless they improve, especially if several opponents stay in the pot.

3. *Drawing hands.* This category consists of small two pairs and four-card flushes and straights, holdings that have no chance of winning unless they improve, but which will become highly probable winners with the right additional card.

4. *Useless hands.* This category includes everything not included above, and particularly includes holdings such as three-card straights or flushes and single pairs (except

Aces, and possibly Kings) that will require two more cards to become probable winners.

Hands in the first category should surely be played; hands in the fourth category should be abandoned. Hands in the second and third categories must be evaluated according to their chances of becoming winners, measured against the pot odds facing you. Your sense of what it will take to win depends on your skill in card reading and on your knowledge of your opponents. Once you have identified the card you want, your chances of getting it are easily calculated if you have kept track of the cards that have been folded.

The relevant odds are given in Table 13.2, which has been calculated on the assumption that you have seen eighteen cards, your own five and thirteen others.[18] If you have correctly evaluated your chances, the table gets you halfway to a decision about how to play from here to the showdown. You must also estimate how much it will cost you, and the potential profits to be won.

From this point on it is necessary to distinguish between fixed-limit and pot-limit 7-card stud, because the two games diverge sharply in the subsequent betting scenarios. While your chances of getting the card you need are the same in either game, the implied pot odds facing you are not.

THIRD ROUND AND BEYOND: LIMIT POKER

The key to your strategy during the last rounds of limit 7-card stud is to have a good fix on what the other players are either holding or drawing for. You can seldom be cer-

---

18. The fewer the cards you have seen (that is, the more cards that are potentially available), the worse your chances are. The data in Table 13.2 are approximately correct for any number of remaining cards in the range of 30 to 36. For example, the number of cards you need to have for an even-money chance of getting one of them increases from 9 to 11 as the number of unseen cards increases from 30 to 36.

Table 13.2   Getting 1 Card out of 34 in Two Tries

Number of Cards That Will Make Your Hand	Probability	Odds
4 or fewer	.22 or less	3.5 to 1 or more *against you*
5	.28	2.6 to 1 *against you*
6	.33	2.1 to 1 *against you*
7	.37	1.7 to 1 *against you*
8	.42	1.4 to 1 *against you*
9	.47	1.2 to 1 *against you*
10	**.51**	**even money**
11	.55	1.2 to 1 *in your favor*
12	.59	1.4 to 1 *in your favor*
13	.63	1.7 to 1 *in your favor*
14 or more	.66 or more	2.0 to 1 or more *in your favor*

This table shows, for example, that if any of eight cards will help a drawing hand in 7-card stud after the fifth card, the odds *against* being helped are 1.4 to 1.

tain, but you must make a judgment, and it can often be better than a mere guess. You have seen a lot of cards, and so has each of your opponents. If he is not a mindless *calling station*, each player who is still around is there for a reason, and you will have several clues as to what it is. One is when and how he has bet or raised; another is how he has reacted to your up cards.

This last is often overlooked. Suppose you have been showing a pair of 10's since the fourth card and after betting you were raised by one player and then called by another. Your opponents are evidently not worried that you may have 10's-up, nor do they seem very concerned that you may have a third 10. This ought to tell you that 10's-up is not going to be good enough to win, and it may also tell you that one

or more of the 10's you'd like to catch is already in someone's hole cards. If one of your opponents is showing cards
for a high straight this latter is all but certain.[19]

A key factor to remember is that the third round of a limit
game is probably the last opportunity to influence your opponents to drop out by the size of your bet. After this point
there is usually enough money in the pot, relative to the
fixed limit, that the size of a bet is not going to have much
impact. While big enough bets can usually drop players, it is
not usually possible in limit poker for one player to make a
big enough bet at this stage unless a second player is raising.
If there is another bettor, you can raise him, but be cautious. You must weigh your chances specifically against the
guy who is betting or raising; you don't want to spend
money merely to eliminate the others and then come in second-best.

Playing a Probable Winning Hand

With a big hand in five cards—say, you've already made a
high straight, a flush, or a full house—it is sound strategy to
keep as many other players in as possible (although not by
giving them a free card) even though you may yet be beaten
by someone whom you might have induced to drop by
more aggressive play. You should tend to bet modestly if it
is yours to bet, or simply call another's bet. Reserve the raise
you are itching to make for the next betting round. Bets
that might drop opponents on the fifth card are likely to be
called on the next round; and in any case, bets will tend to
be bigger after the sixth card has been dealt.

Once the sixth card has been dealt, you are likely to be
facing two or three other players, and you can safely assume
that whether they stay in or drop out at this stage depends
not on what you do but on whether that sixth card helped

19. Every high straight must have a 10.

them. If you are still pretty sure you have the winning hand, you should bet the limit now and expect to be called. However, if you are raised, you will want to rethink your level of confidence—and this will depend in good part on which opponent raised you—before either calling or reraising.

The same strategy is appropriate on the final betting round. With a hand that you expect will win, you should bet the fixed limit at every opportunity. You will lose some of the time, but if you have learned to evaluate your hands correctly, the losses you suffer when another player hits his draw and beats you will be clearly overshadowed by the extra bets you have collected when your hands win. If you find yourself suffering a great many bad beats, ask yourself whether you are being realistic in classifying your cards as probable winners at the critical decision point after getting the fifth card.

Playing a Vulnerable Leading Hand

Most of the time with the leading hand you will not be so confident of winning that you want to keep a great many players in, any one of whom may outdraw you. The fact is that most hands that prove to be winners in 7-card stud showdowns are not fully formed until the sixth or seventh card. But with a vulnerable leading hand you have to gamble on the third round and attempt to increase your chances by reducing, if you can, the number of your competitors. This should be your objective also if you have only a fair hand, even though it is presently the best one around, or if you are trying to *quasi-bluff* when you have scare cards showing but in fact have only a mediocre hand.[20] In limit poker if you try these tactics at this stage to eliminate com-

20. A quasi-bluff is a bet made on a hand that, although much weaker than you are representing, nevertheless has some chance of being the winning hand. Two middle-size pairs is an example of such a hand; another is a four flush with a pair of Aces as an out.

petitors and they do not work, you should abandon them. Stubbornness in this respect is a major weakness of poor players who are likely to persist in a bluff or quasi-bluff once started, even against an opponent who seems undaunted.[21]

With several opponents still in the hand at the time of the sixth card, and a leading hand that is only fair—say, Jacks- or Queens-up—a check is in order. It is a good way to see who is proud of his hand, and while there is some danger of the round being checked around, this sign of weakness itself will be helpful to you in the last round. When your bet after the fifth card did not cause a competitor to drop out, another bet on the sixth card is unlikely to drop him, so such a bet should be made only if you have improved to a winning hand. Your Jacks-up are likely to lose against two or more opponents, and you would like to see the next card cheaply in order to see if you can catch the full house that will win. A check is the way to do that.

On the final round you should almost always check unless you have improved to a hand that you believe will beat even the hands that the others were drawing to achieve. There is no point in betting otherwise: an opponent who has busted won't call any bet you make, so there is nothing to gain, and one who has hit a straight or better will call and beat you. Indeed, he is likely to raise, and you will feel obliged to call the raise in most cases. If you check and one opponent bets, you should almost always call if you are the only remaining player, not only because the pot odds are likely to be in your favor but to make it clear that you won't be lightly bluffed out on the seventh card when you had the best hand at the end of the previous round. But if one opponent bets after your check and another calls or raises, you should fold; your lead has surely evaporated.

21. This phenomenon is not unlike that of poor bridge players who feel insulted when an optimistic bid is doubled by an opponent, and feel they must redouble to vindicate their honor.

Playing a Drawing Hand

If you are in at the fifth card and need to improve to have any chance, you will want to get the next card as cheaply as possible. Usually this involves checking if it is your bet, or merely calling another's bet. Occasionally a less than limit-size bet by you can forestall a bigger bet, particularly if it is misread by an opponent to be a come-on.

The biggest mistake you can make with a drawing hand is to misread your chances so that you are either *drawing dead*—that is, drawing in a situation where no card can give you the winner, even though it may improve your hand—or drawing to a hand when others are drawing to superior holdings. Watch a mediocre player and see how often he draws for two pair when someone else already has trips; or he'll draw for a straight when another player is going for a flush or a higher straight. Such draws don't always lose, but they are a sure way to come out a loser in the long run. You lose not only when you bust but even more expensively when you get your desired card and end up second-best.

How do you figure the implied pot odds facing you with a drawing hand and two cards to come? Suppose that after the fifth card has been dealt in a $10/$20 limit game, you have determined that only four cards can help you, and thus, using Table 13.2, that the odds against your hitting a winning hand are 3.5 to 1. There is $40 in the pot after your only opponent bets $10. Since you can get the sixth card for only $10, this may look like a better-than-pot-odds proposition. But what if you do not make your hand with the sixth card and then your opponent bets $20? Those odds of 3.5 to 1 assumed that you would have chances to hit on both the sixth and seventh cards. To assess your necessary investment correctly, you need to compare your expected loss if you fail to hit the card you seek, with your expected winnings if you get the winning hand. How much will it cost you if you fail to get your required card on either the sixth or seventh card? In addition to the $10 bet to get the sixth card, you can anticipate having to spend an additional $20 for the seventh card if there is a bet but no raise. This expected expenditure of $30—$10 plus $20—with odds of 3.5 to 1 against you would require winnings of $105 (3.5 × $30) or more if you hit your card to give you a positive expected value. Against only one player this is not likely to be the case given your maximum allowed bet of $20 after the seventh card. But if there are two or more potential callers, your expected winnings may well be good enough to call on a drawing hand, provided that you are confident that you will win if you get the hand you are drawing for. This proviso is important: to repeat, you don't want to draw into second-best. If you don't get the card you need on the sixth card, you will want to keep the betting as modest as you can, and after the seventh card you either will have caught your hand and will play it as a winning hand or you will be busted and have to fold.

The reason to think two betting rounds ahead is that, in a typical limit poker game, if you call the bet on the fifth card, you most likely will try for the seventh card if the sixth card does not help you.[22] You won't feel sucked in if you have properly anticipated it.

THIRD ROUND AND BEYOND: POT-LIMIT POKER

In contrast to the limit game, where players who stay for the sixth card usually stay for the showdown, in pot-limit the anticipated big bets on the last two betting rounds lead to frequent folds of both credible drawing hands and vulnera-

---

22. Your own bet on the previous round is now part of the pot, and improves your pot odds at this stage. This, as we have seen, is the meaning of being sucked in on a later call by your own earlier bets.

ble leading ones. While the objective probabilities of getting the right cards are the same as in limit poker and are as easily calculated, the expected costs of staying to the showdown are larger in pot-limit poker relative to the pot. In pot-limit your staying mistakes are likely to be much more expensive.

Another important difference is that it is much harder to interpret big bets in pot-limit at the fifth card because the game invites bluffing bets at this point by any player who has scare cards showing. A large bet by someone showing three cards to a flush or to a high straight (or even by someone with a showing pair) may win the pot from a higher showing pair or a four flush, not so much because of the bet now but because of the fear that it will be followed by even bigger bets on both the sixth and seventh cards. Even someone holding a high two pair, who would be unlikely to fold in limit poker, may well get out, especially if any of the other cards that might have improved his hand have shown in others' hands.

If the hand has not already been decided by the sixth card of a pot-limit 7-card stud game, there are usually only two players still prepared to continue. The great majority of hands do not go to a showdown, and the ones that do tend to be *mano a mano*. When contested one-against-one, the last two rounds of pot-limit 7-card stud depend heavily on nerve, intimidation, and card-reading ability. They test skill and reward it. This can be a difficult game against strong opponents, and you are advised to play it cautiously, if at all, until you develop confidence in your ability to read cards correctly. At least at first you should err in the direction of folding errors rather than calling ones—for your own self-esteem as much as for your bankroll.

Playing a Probable Winning Hand

Pot management is, as always, the key to playing very strong hands. You want to keep opponents in so that they will call big bets at the end. So much depends upon the style and habits of your opponents that there is little general advice to be given. It is usually sensible to bet modestly but not raise on the third round, and to make a big but not necessarily maximum bet on the next one. Such a bet at the sixth card is likely to be called by players with drawing hands. The reason not to wait until the final round for a near-maximum pot-limit bet is that at the final round you will be called only by those players who have hit their hands, and you will have missed receiving the contributions of those who drew but did not hit. They were drawing dead, and you don't want to let them do it for free.

Playing a Vulnerable Leading Hand

The key here is to reduce your vulnerability by reducing the number of competitors—indeed, if possible, by eliminating them all. In pot-limit poker, making a big enough bet to drop opponents at the fifth card is quite easy, not merely because you may be able to make a bigger bet than in limit poker at this stage but because your big bet now will create the fear that you will make an even bigger one in the next round. This will worsen the pot odds facing opponents who are thinking of drawing against you.

If only one player calls, you may want to repeat the big bet on the next round, but only if you are playing against someone you are convinced is conservative enough to give up now. Against such a player, a bet the size of the pot will more often than not win there and then against a drawing hand. He would need to have at least 1 chance in 3 that the last card will help him to have the pot odds in his favor.

If your objective is to protect a mediocre hand or to bluff, be careful if there are several opponents still in the hand; a call by one of them is likely to make the pot odds worthwhile for others to stay in. If there is $50 in the pot and you bet $50, the pot odds facing your first opponent are 2 to 1 if no one else calls. Once a first opponent calls, the next player is getting 3-to-1 pot odds, and if he too calls, a fourth player will face 4-to-1 pot odds. With several players behind him, the first player may anticipate that others will call, and this will increase his likelihood of doing so. The point is that tactics that work wonders against a single op- ponent may be self-defeating against several.

As the leading hand, if you make a maximum-size bet on the sixth card and are called, the correct play on the last round is to check, no matter what else happens. Here too the reason not to bet is that if your opponent has failed to hit a hand that can beat what he thinks you had, he won't call; if he has, he will raise. Even if you have improved and now know you have him beaten, whether or not he hit his draw, your check won't discourage him from betting, and you can then raise.

Playing a Drawing Hand

The critical differences between limit and pot-limit poker become clearest when looked at from the point of view of a player who *must* improve to have any chance to win. If you hold a drawing hand against pot-limit bets on the fifth and/or sixth cards, you have a difficult decision, one of the hardest in poker. A player with a leading hand at the sixth card will usually make a near maximum-size bet. If he does not, he is either missing a clear chance or is a player trying to induce you to call his almost unbeatable hand. (As Hugh tells us, beware of bargains.) It is seldom sensible to call against only one opponent who bets heavily since he is likely to continue doing so, even if you think he may be doing his best to get you to fold. Against several opponents a call at this stage, although expensive, may be justified, but only if you are sure that you will win if you hit, *and* only if you are also confident that if you do, at least one of your opponents will call a bet on the next round. But if there is a significant chance that you will lose even if you hit, or that a bet after you hit may not be called, you will need pretty good pot odds now to make a call worthwhile. It is often prudent to drop rather than chase the leading hand.

FOUR PROBLEMS

1. Here is a 7-card stud deal after the fourth card has been dealt:

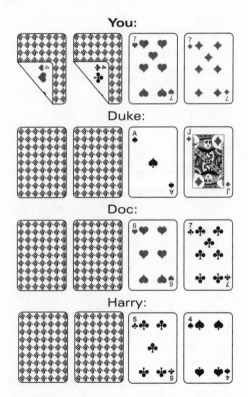

You:

Duke:

Doc:

Harry:

On the first round Duke had bet his showing Ace, Doc raised and Harry called. You called too on your pocket pair. With the fourth card you improved to two pair, and with your showing pair it is your bet. What should you do?

2. After the final card has been dealt, Knott is your only remaining opponent. Here is what you see:

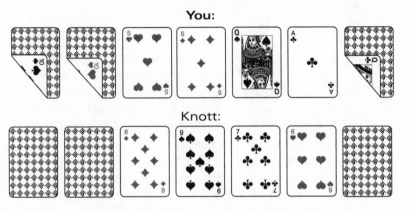

You:

Knott:

The folded cards that have relevance are a 9, 7, 10, and 5. There is about $80 in the pot, and you check. Knott now bets the maximum. What should you do?

3. You have made a 9-high straight in six cards. Ty, to your left, is apparently drawing to an Ace-high four-flush, while the only other player, Hugh, is showing a pair of 4's with an Ace. You made a maximum bet on the fifth card and both of the others merely called. It is still your bet, and there is $75 in the pot. What should you do now?

4. You are in a tough pot-limit game, and have been losing more than your share, but you are still in the game with money on the table. You are dealt a pocket pair of 9's with an 8 up. On the fourth card you get a third 9 and simply call a bet by Doc, who is showing A, K. The only other caller, Bill, shows two hearts to the King. On the fifth card you

catch a Jack and Bill gets a third heart. Doc catches trash and checks. You bet modestly, and Bill raises. Doc folds and you call. The sixth card pairs your showing 8, giving you 9's-full. Bill gets a fourth heart. It's your bet. How do you play from here?

ANSWERS TO THE PROBLEMS
(AS I SEE THEM)

1. You should check, expecting to fold if anyone bets. Even though you caught a second pair, your hand got worse, because one of your 4's and one of your 7's fell elsewhere. Sevens-up is not going to win, and only two cards can give you a full house. Even though you probably have the best hand now, it is unlikely to stand up, and you are not going to get the others out with a bet or raise at this moment.

2. You should call, whether this is limit or pot-limit. Knott has been drawing to either a straight or to two pair, possibly 8's and 9's. While he may have you beaten, lots of his cards are dead—he needs a 10 or 5 for his straight, and a 9 or an 8 for a boat. He may have them, but given his scare cards, he would bet this way in any case. Even an $80 bet is giving you 2-to-1 pot odds, and your Queens-up are worth calling with.

3. Here the answer depends entirely upon whether this is limit or pot-limit. In limit poker with a maximum bet of, say, $10 or $20, both of the drawing hands will draw, and there is a good chance that one of them will beat you, if indeed you are not already beaten. Hugh probably has trips or Aces-up at this stage, so you should check. If Ty bets, you may want to fold. If Ty checks and Hugh then bets, you can raise, and probably will get Ty to fold.

In pot-limit, this is the time to bet: you surely won't want to after the seventh card. A $75 bet now is likely to fold one or both of your opponents, but even if it doesn't, the pot odds probably favor you. Of course if Ty already has his flush, he's likely to raise you now, and if he does so you will find out more cheaply than you might have later on. If he does raise, a fold is probably wise. If either player calls your $75 bet you will surely want to check on the next round and reconsider your chances if one of them bets.

4. This is your big chance for a killing, if you want to take it. You should check. You can be sure that Bill will bet heavily whether he has his flush or not. When he does, simply call. On the last round, check again. Since you have given no hint of strength Bill will now bet the maximum if he has failed to hit, and may do so as well if he has his flush. At this point, you can raise with the rest of your chips. He'll call if he has hit. On this hand the question isn't whether you will win, but how to make the most of your monster hand.

14

♠ ♣ ♥ ♦

7-CARD HI-LO[1]

You are one of two remaining players in a hand of 7-card Hi-Lo and the final card has been dealt.

You

Your Opponent

You are disappointed that your promising start toward a 7-low did not work out. Your opponent has the bet. It is pot-limit, and with $80 in the pot he bets $60. What should you do?

Seven-card Hi-Lo is structurally identical to 7-card stud and thus much of what was discussed in Chapter 13 is the case here as well. This applies to the differences between an ag-

---

1. Chapter 13 should be read before reading this one.

gressive game and a restrained one, and to the consequent shift of the focus from a three-card starting strategy to one based on the first four cards. It applies also to the middle rounds, where your betting strategies will vary if you hold a probable winning hand, a vulnerable leading hand, or a drawing hand. And of course the importance of accurately reading your opponents' cards still applies—indeed, to a heightened degree. However, there are critical differences to this game that affect strategy.

HOW WINNERS ARE DETERMINED

The most important differences between Hi-Lo and high-only poker arise from the additional dimension created by the division of the pot between a high winner and a low winner. In fact, this creates at least three very different games, depending upon the rules of play. This can be seen by examining the hand in the example above. Your hand is mediocre; the best you can do is a 10 for low and a pair of Aces for high. But even though your opponent has three hidden cards, yours is surely the best hand in at least one direction. It is the best low hand if your opponent does not have three low cards in the hole that can combine with his 7 and 2 to beat your 10, 7, 5, 4, A. But if he has such cards, your pair of Aces is the best high hand. Indeed, it is possible that yours is both the best high and the best low hand—for example, if your opponent's hole cards are 10, 8, and 4.

Whether you will win all, half, or none of the pot depends, however, upon more than your cards; it depends also on the method for determining how hands are to be evaluated. The primary distinction is between whether the cards alone determine the winner or whether players must declare how they want to have their hands considered—high or low. If declaration is required, it may be either simultaneous or sequential. Strategy necessarily varies with the three cases, and it will be necessary to treat them separately in this chapter.

Cards Speak

The phrase *cards speak* is shorthand for: let the cards speak for themselves. In cards speak, after the last round of betting all remaining players expose their hole cards. The best high hand and best low hand are determined by the showdown and split the pot.[2] If the hand illustrated at the beginning of the chapter is played under cards-speak rules, you cannot lose and should fearlessly raise your opponent's bet by the maximum amount allowed. *You are sure of getting half the pot, and may win it all.* Indeed, unless your opponent is confident of winning one way he may not even call your raise, and thus let you win the whole pot by default.

Declaration

In either of the two declaration methods, the players, at the conclusion of the fifth betting round, must choose and announce whether they are going high, low, or both, and their hands are valid only in the direction claimed. A player declaring both high and low must win both ways. If he "declares Hi-Lo" and has the best high hand but is beaten or tied for low by a player declaring low, he is out of the pot and the best remaining high hand takes the high half of the pot.[3] If there is no other high hand, the player winning low takes the whole pot.

---

2. It is possible for one player's hand to be the best in both directions and take the whole pot, or to be the best in one direction and tied for best in the other direction and thus take three-quarters of the pot.

3. Some games allow a player declaring Hi-Lo to be tied in one direction, and claim three-quarters of the pot, but the win-both requirement is far more

Simultaneous declaration.   Here each player declares high, low, or both by using chips to reveal his decision. The usual method is for each player to place one fist on the table and, at a signal, to declare by revealing chips: none for low, one for high, or two for both ways. *If the hand illustrated above is played under simultaneous declaration, you will be forced to guess to have even a chance of winning half of the pot.* Your opponent's bet suggests that he has a strong hand in one direction or the other, but you don't know which. If you guess randomly you'll win half of the pot half of the time, and none of the pot the rest of the time. When—as in the example above—his final bet was anything more than half as large as the size of the pot at the time he bet, your expected value is negative and you should fold rather than call the final-round bet.[4]

Sequential declaration.   In this method, after the fifth betting round, the last hand to bet or raise must declare first, and other players declare in sequence, moving clockwise around the table. If no one bets, the high hand showing must declare first. If the hand illustrated at the chapter opening is played under sequential declaration, you should call the final bet, but not raise. *Since your opponent must declare first, you can be sure of half the pot by declaring in the opposite direction from the one he chooses.* Thus it is a riskless

---

common. In another variation, a player must actually have the best hand (or be tied for it) to claim any part of the pot. Thus, in the example here described, the second-best high hand would not collect the half of the pot that the Hi-Lo declarer has forfeited by being beaten for low, and it too would go to the low hand.

4. If you call his $60 bet there will be a $200 pot to divide. Half of the time you'll collect $100, and the other half of the time nothing. Your expected value is: $(.5 \times \$100) - \$60 = -\$10$. Only if your opponent had bet $40 or less would the expected value of a pure guess have been positive.

call.[5] You do not raise because that would shift the first declaration to you and force you to guess. Since your opponent
may be strong in either direction, you will lose the whole
pot if you guess the wrong way. A raise gains you nothing
but risks losing half the pot.

Defining the Best Low Hand

Another way in which Hi-Lo games can differ from one another is in how the low hand is defined, though this factor
is not nearly as crucial as the method of declaration. The key
distinction concerns whether straights and flushes are
counted against a low hand or whether they are disregarded
in determining it. If they are counted, the best low hand is
6, 4, 3, 2, A, as long as the five cards are not all of the same
suit.[6] This method of evaluation, in which straights and
flushes are considered as high hands only, and which I will
call the 6-4 method, is the usual rule in Britain and in most
Thursday-night games in the United States, but *not* in
American casinos.

When straights and flushes are disregarded in determining
lows, the best low hand is 5, 4, 3, 2, A—called a *wheel*, or a
bicycle. This definition of how to evaluate low hands, which
I will call the 5-4 method, is sometimes called the California
method, for it originated in casinos there. A detailed comparison of the two methods is shown in Table 14.1.

---

5. What if, in a show of bravado, he declares Hi-Lo even though he cannot be
best in both directions? He is offering you an even-money bet that you will
guess wrong. You can either take his bet if you think you can predict which way
he is going, or hedge by yourself declaring Hi-Lo. If there are only two players and each declares Hi-Lo and each wins one way, the rules revert to those of
cards speak and they will split the pot. When there are three players in a pot,
and two of them each declare Hi-Lo and win one way, the lucky third player
takes the whole pot.
6. This assumes that the Ace is allowed to be *either* a high or low card, which
is virtually always the case in Hi-Lo games. If the Ace is considered high only,
the best low hand is 7, 5, 4, 3, 2.

Table 14.1   Distribution of Low Hands in 7-Card Hi-Lo

HAND	Individual Hands (Percent of Hands)		Best of Seven Hands (Percent of Deals)	
	5-4 rules	6-4 rules	5-4 rules	6-4 rules
5-low	*	0%	4%	0%
6 or better	3	2	19	13
7 or better	8	7	46	42
8 or better	18	17	76	73
9 or better	33	32	94	93
10 or better	50	50	99	99
Worse than 10	50	50	1	1
Total	100	100	100	100

*Less than one percent.

Surprisingly, the two methods of defining low hands do not make a great deal of difference in the distribution of hands. A wheel is found in a seven-card hand only about 1 time in 170, so that with seven players each dealt seven cards, a wheel occurs in only about 1 deal in 25. Thus, holding a 5-low is a rare occurrence in 7-card stud, and any 6-low is a superb hand that usually wins under either definition. Of all the low hands that have a high card of 8 or smaller—and this includes most good low hands—less than 7 percent turn out to be either straights or flushes and thus are treated differently in the two methods.[7] The importance of the difference in the definitions of what is the best low hand concerns not how frequently it occurs, but rather the possibility that a low straight gives its holder in the 5-4 method of winning the whole pot. This is particularly important when playing under cards-speak rules.

7. The overwhelming majority of these—more than 90 percent of the total—are straights.

POT-LIMIT VERSUS FIXED-LIMIT HI-LO

The difference between pot-limit and fixed-limit poker is so much greater in Hi-Lo than in high-only poker that it becomes a difference *in kind*. The reason is that in pot-limit an opponent with a lock one way can make it so expensive for you that even if you hold the leading hand the other way, you will be forced to concede the whole pot. Faced with the prospect of a succession of pot-limit bets, the pot odds facing you may simply be too unfavorable to buck. By contrast, in a fixed-limit game, you may well be in a position to stay till the end and reap a small profit without taking too big a risk.

An example will make this clear. Suppose you are playing pot-limit and there is $50 in the pot after the fifth card. You hold [A, 2,] 6, 5, 6, a very promising low hand, but your chances of winning the high half of the pot are slim since your only opponent shows 7, 7, 7. He now bets $50. You are clearly ahead of him for low, but if you call you can expect him to bet $150 on the next card and at least $300 at the end. To call all three bets will cost you $500. That is a big investment to make for a chance to win $25—half of the pot before his bet—which is what you will win if you do indeed prevail for low and he wins high. You would be giving 20 to 1 that your opponent will not end up with a hand that will beat you both for high and for low and thus win the whole pot. Meanwhile, his chances of doing so are better than 1 in 20. If this were poker with a $10 limit you could see the hand to the end for $30 and would be on sound ground to do so, since risking $30 to win $25 is surely justified by the cards you see.

Pot-limit Hi-Lo is a very difficult game to play and involves a great deal of intimidation. I do not recommend it to any but the most experienced amateurs. It is not an appropriate game for Thursday-night poker, in my view, and I will not discuss it further in this chapter. *Either* Hi-Lo *or* pot-limit make for an interesting, challenging Thursday-night game, but together they are likely to prove destructive.[8]

CONSIDERATIONS APPLYING TO ALL FORMS OF HI-LO

Before treating the varieties of 7-card Hi-Lo separately, there are some general considerations that apply to all, but that are different from those that apply to a high-only game.

First and foremost, in Hi-Lo poker **low cards are much more valuable than high ones,** especially in the early and middle rounds. (Any card from a 9 to a King should be considered a high card.) Low starts such as A, 7, 5, or 8, 6, 5, are valuable not only because they may turn into low winners but because they may turn into high winners as well.[9] Moreover, a promising low holding that doesn't work out—that busts as a low hand when its low cards become paired—may become a high winner and thus let its holder escape with half the pot. This fallback can prove to be an important one. By contrast, high starts that would be highly valued in 7-card stud, such as K, Q, J, or Q, Q, 5, have virtually no chance of becoming winning lows and thus are fighting for half of the pot at best. When these promising high starts bust they have no recourse—*outs* they are called. Some Hi-Lo players will simply never play high starts; while this is extreme, it is suggestive.

---

8. The main reason is that it will tend to break up a poker group as less experienced or less skilled players suffer big losses by chasing hands that are promising one way but either bust or are beaten by a two-way hand.

9. The low hand with the Ace may well end up with another Ace, or Aces-up, and have a chance as both a high and a low hand. The straight possibilities of an 8, 6, 5, are obvious, and if two are of the same suit, there are also flush possibilities.

A second general consideration is that when playing Hi-Lo it is important to recognize that winning both high and low halves of the pot—*scooping* or *sweeping* the pot, it is called—is where the big swings occur. To see why, suppose there is $400 in a pot with only two players in at the end, each of whom has contributed $150 to the pot. If they split the pot each collects $200 and earns $50, a return of only one-third on the money he risked. If one of them wins the whole pot, he collects $400 and his profit is $250, five times as great. With more than two players the numbers change, but there will still be a big difference in the reward-to-investment ratio. For example, had there been three final players, each of whom had contributed $120 to a $400 pot, the profit for winning half the pot would be $80 and the profit for scooping, $280.

A key element of Hi-Lo strategy is to play for situations where you may be in a position to scoop. As important as seeking to scoop the pot, and more frequently encountered, is the necessity to avoid situations where you are struggling merely to escape with half the pot. How best to do this varies in the different games, as will be seen, but identifying your objectives is a big part of playing any of the games well. **An ideal situation is when you are sure of winning half the pot and have a chance to win it all.** Evaluating hands to see if they have this potential is an important skill.

A next general principle is that determining the direction in which your opponents are going is vital in Hi-Lo poker and requires close attention to showing cards and betting behavior. These will affect your decision to stay or fold, as well as your betting tactics. Even mediocre cards can become valuable once you are confident that your opponents are locked into going the other way; conversely, what are usually good cards may be hazardous if you are already second-best. For example, if you hold a 7, 6, 3, 8, after four cards—normally a wonderful start—against two opponents who are betting, one of whom shows a pair of Aces and the other a 2 and a 5, your prospects are unattractive. You are fighting for the low half of the pot against an opponent who may well be ahead of you for low, and you can be reasonably sure that the high hand is going to make it expensive to find out whether you have a winner. With a small number of players in the hand you must win the great majority of the split pots you go after in order to break even because the payoff is not high and you are sure to lose some in any case. Put differently, the proper pot-odds calculation must compare the risk of losing *all* of your bets with the chances of winning *half* of a split pot. These chances depend critically on what your opponents' cards tell you.

Another important common feature of limit Hi-Lo games is that multiple raises (and maximum bets) are likely to occur as soon as any players become confident about their chances in even one direction. Thus, calling can become expensive in the later rounds for a player who is chasing only half the pot. It is necessary to correctly anticipate the future bets you expect to be required to call before you know whether you have made your hand. Inexperienced Hi-Lo players systematically underestimate how much it will cost to try to escape with half the pot and get sucked into early calls as long as they feel that they still have a chance to win one way. Such calls can lead to expensive failures.

Finally, just as you must evaluate your opponents' hands, you must be aware of how they will read your showing cards and your patterns of betting. Put yourself in their seats and interpret your own up cards. Do they correctly reveal your direction? If they do, you have to decide whether to bet heavily in order to eliminate competitors, or more modestly to keep them in and build the pot. If your cards are scare cards but misrepresent the real strength of your hand, you may have many promising options. Suppose you show an A, 7, 3, after the fifth card. This will strongly suggest a powerful low hand, but it ought to be played differently when you hold a pair of Aces in the hole than when you hold a 4 and 2. Just *how* you should play each of those holdings depends on the method of declaration.

CARDS SPEAK[10]

Cards speak with fixed limits and a limited number of raises is the easiest variety of 7-card Hi-Lo. It is easier than games where declaration is required because playing well depends much less on the ability to read the cards and figure out which way your opponents are going. In cards speak you don't have to worry about misdeclaring a hand that would have won in the other direction, and you don't have to weigh the risks of losing everything in order to have a chance to scoop the pot when you feel sure of winning in one direction but are merely a possible winner in the other. As a result, the game can be played more mechanically, with more of your attention devoted to your own cards and the probability of their proving a winner. Further, efforts to deceive your opponents about the direction of your hand are less important. There is thus less scope for skill and experience to give a big advantage to some players. Cards speak is well suited for a Thursday-night poker game that does not wish to put its less experienced members at a big disadvantage. It is, however, less demanding and, to ex-

---

10. As 7-card Hi-Lo is typically played in American casinos, cards speak disregards straights and flushes and thus considers 5-4 the best low hand. This creates the possibility of scooping the pot with a low straight, and makes holdings such as 7, 8, 9 more attractive than they would otherwise be. I shall discuss cards-speak Hi-Lo in this form, although it is sometimes played in Thursday-night games under the 6-4 rules. The essentials of strategy are not much changed if it is.

perienced players, less challenging than Hi-Lo played with
a declaration.[11]

What Wins in Cards Speak?

Because low hands dominate the strategy of Hi-Lo poker, it
is well to begin there. Table 14.2 repeats the relevant part of
Table 14.1 and shows both the frequency of holding particular low hands and the quality of the winning low if seven
different hands are considered.

**Table 14.2   Distribution of Low Hands
in 7-Card Hi-Lo Under 5-4 Rules**

HAND	Individual Hands (Percent of Hands)	Best of Seven Hands (Percent of Deals)
5 low	*	4%
6 or better	3%	19
7 or better	8	46
8 or better	18	76
9 or better	33	94
10 or better	50	99
Worse than 10	50	1
Total	100	100

*Less than one percent.

11. The use of cards-speak rules in casino Hi-Lo poker, or in games among
strangers, is explained not by its ease but by its manageability. With a declaration there can be frequent arguments about who declared what, and when, and
this means an increased burden on the dealer or whoever is supervising the
game. With cards speak, there is an unambiguous division of every pot once
the cards are all exposed at the showdown. Though the division may be complex—for example, if there are side pots—it is orderly. A further reason for preferring cards-speak rules is that the opportunities for collusion between two
players, although never completely absent, are reduced.

A look at the right-hand column makes it clear why hands worse than an 8-low are underdogs in a contested pot of Hi-Lo poker; three-quarters of all deals of seven hands produce an 8-low or better. In fact, there are frequently two or more such hands with seven players, and thus attention must be paid to the second-highest card. Of all the 8-lows, more than half are 8-7's, and the median winning hand in seven-player showdown is an 8-6-low. Your chances of holding an 8-6-low or better are 1 in 8.

A 7-low or better occurs in 46 percent of all deals, and to *you* about 1 time in 12. When it does occur it is the only such hand two-thirds of the time.[12]

Actual winning low hands are somewhat worse than the figures in Table 14.2, because some low hands are folded before they materialize. However, because Hi-Lo strategy is heavily weighted in favor of going for low, the actual distribution of winning low hands is rather close to what is shown in the table. How close depends upon how tightly the game is played, and how vigorous the betting is in the early rounds. The more aggressive the game, the worse you can expect the average winning low hand to be, since fewer players will stay in. In a typical game this means that any 8-low has a good chance of winning, and any 7-low or better should be treated as a probable winner—unless, of course, the up cards and betting patterns suggest otherwise. And in hands that quickly reduce to two or three players, a 9-low winner is not unusual.

How good the winning *high* hands are in 7-card Hi-Lo is a different story, as Table 14.3 shows.

The first column of Table 14.3 shows, as was seen in Chapter 13, that more often than not better than three-of-

12. Even if you hold the worst possible 7-low, a 7, 6, 5, 4, 3, you'll hold the best hand about 30 percent of the time, and if you hold a 7-5-low or better the odds in your favor are at least 6 to 1.

Table 14.3   Winning High Hands in Seven Cards with Seven Players

	Playing Showdown (Percent of Deals)	Playing Hi-Lo (Percent of Deals)[†]
Full house or better	18%	8%
Flush	16	13
Straight	20	10
Trips	15	11
2 pair	28	20
1 pair	3	33
No pair	*	5
Total	100	100

*Less than one percent.
[†]Experimental results.

a-kind is required to win high in a 7-card showdown. But many of those hands started out with just the kind of high cards that it is not sensible to play with in Hi-Lo because they have no chance of leading to a scooping hand and have no low outs if they do not improve. More than half of the hands that would win in 7-card high are discarded before they mature when playing Hi-Lo. The second column of Table 14.3 gives a more realistic distribution of likely winning high hands in Hi-Lo.[13] Two pairs, and even one pair, are frequent winners in cards speak, and a high winner without even one pair is not unknown.[14] This does not mean you should keep mediocre high hands, only that the high hands that emerge as players strive for low often become

13. It is based on experimental data for a restrained cards-speak game with the players following the strategy appropriate to it.
14. Indeed, Table 14.3 underrepresents the decrease in the value of winning high hands at Hi-Lo, since within categories, the winning hands are poorer. For example, in the two-pairs category, many Kings- or Queens-up are folded, and hands with 8's- or 7's-up emerge as winners.

backdoor winners for high and, indeed, lead to many hands that scoop Hi-Lo pots with mediocre highs.

Starting Strategy in Cards Speak

The dominant principle of starting strategy in all Hi-Lo games is to aim for low, with the special incentive to look for potential two-way hands. This general advice is essential in cards speak, since low starting hands frequently turn into backdoor high winners.

More specifically, this leads to a first operating rule that comes hard to 7-card stud players: any hand with two or more high cards in the first four cards should be folded virtually without fail and without regret.[15] This is true of high pairs and even of high trips, since you will surely be fighting to win only half the pot, and are in significant jeopardy of losing it all unless you end up with a full house.[16]

Estimating the number of competitors is critical in Hi-Lo poker, and is directly related to the distinction between aggressive and restrained games. The fewer the competitors, the smaller the potential winnings but the greater the chance that the low hand will end up scooping the pot. The more aggressive the game—the heavier the first-round betting and raising—the fewer the number of players who will stay in, and thus the greater the advantage of the player with a low-card holding on the deal. In games of this kind, a conservative three-card strategy is appropriate. Following the rules suggested by professional poker writers (who are thinking of amateurs playing against professionals in such a game), no more than one hand in five is worth playing; if

15. This does not include Aces, which are considered low cards even though they may also be used for high.
16. An exception to the always-fold-high-trips advice is when there are five or more players still in the hand and likely to stay for a while. Then the pot odds are usually favorable enough to make half the pot worth going after.

played this way by everyone, about 60 percent of all deals will be uncontested after the first round, and most of the rest reduced to a two-person contest.

By contrast, in restrained games of the kind frequently found in Thursday-night poker, a looser four-card starting strategy is sensible and leads to most players seeing a fourth card, with about 40 percent able to continue beyond that. In this kind of game, about 90 percent of deals will have at least two players seeing a fifth card and usually there will be three or four. (This greater participation, for reasons that will become clear, is even more likely where declaration rather than cards speak is the rule.)

Three-card starting strategy for an aggressive game. This is the sort of game contemplated by most poker writers, and their advice is appropriate for casino play. It suggests a strategy that is too conservative for most Thursday-night players in most circumstances, but it provides a useful benchmark, and is appropriate in cards speak in any deal on which there is heavy betting and raising on the first round.

The very best starting hand would be one with three unpaired cards, each 5 or less (*babies*), all of the same suit. But *any* holding of three unpaired cards of which the highest is a 7 is excellent. You'll have such a hand about one time in ten deals. Three unpaired cards headed by an 8 occurs about one time in six hands dealt, and is a good start, especially if one of the three is an Ace, or if the three have either straight or flush possibilities. A pair of Aces, 7's, or 8's if accompanied by a low card is usually worth playing because of its two-way possibilities. Other pairs, or these pairs with a high card, are unpromising because they almost surely have no two-way prospects. Any hand with a picture card (*paint*), whether suited or not, whether paired or not, should usually be discarded. What of trips, the ideal starting hand for 7-card high? I would play trip Aces, 8's, 7's, and

5's, but throw away all others. Each of these has clear high prospects *and* some possibility of becoming a good low.[17]

Marginal starting hands that can safely be played if there is modest betting or raising on the opening round are hands such as 9, 8, 7, or 9, baby, baby, all of the same suit. But these hands require immediate reinforcement in the next round or they too should be dropped. Remember, it is the road to ruin in cards speak to chase with holdings that, even if they hit, will win only half of the pot.

Betting tactics depend on what you hold. With a 6, 5, 4, your chances of having a scooping hand are good enough that you want lots of competitors and don't want to drive too many away by raising. But if you have a hand that has only slim chances of becoming an excellent two-way hand, you'll usually want to reduce the size of the field in order to increase your chances of winning both ways. For example, with an A, A, 5, you have a good chance of having either Aces-up with a fair low, or a good low and a pair of Aces. Head-to-head, either hand could scoop the pot, but against multiple opponents you would be likely to lose at least one way, and possibly both. With this holding your opening strategy should be to bet or raise as much as possible to re-duce the field. There are some hands that you should play only if you can anticipate a head-to-head showdown. Some-thing like an 8, 8, 3, has some two-way prospects head-to-head, but few in a multi-way pot.

In an aggressive game a reasonable rule of thumb would be to play between 20 and 25 percent of the hands you are dealt. There is, however, so much information revealed by the fourth and fifth cards, and by the way your opponents react to them, that on those deals where it is cheap, you may want to stick around and reevaluate your chances. Thus it is

17. Trips lower than 5's are vulnerable to the higher trips that come in by the back door. I include 5's but not 6's because the greatest threat to trips is a straight, and a 5 (or a 10) is essential to any straight. Holding trip 5's greatly reduces the chance that someone going low will catch a straight and beat you.

easier to stay in late betting positions than in early ones. In general, in an aggressive game you will do well either to be the aggressor or to wait for a better hand. Playing more than a quarter of your opening cards is probably risky. The best rule of thumb is: *if in doubt, don't.*

If you stay for the fourth card in an aggressive game, the usual advice is to continue beyond this point only if your fourth card improves your hand. David Sklansky suggests a "paint rule": If you catch a picture card on the fourth card, you should usually get out of the pot.[18] While normally this is good advice, it is too rigid. You are likely to be playing against only one or two competitors, and what matters is not the absolute quality of your hand, but how it stacks up relative to the others. What you do not want to do is to be chasing half the pot when that is the best you can do and an opponent has got you clearly beaten one way.

Four-card starting strategy for a restrained game. In a Thursday-night Hi-Lo game there is usually only modest betting on the first round. When this is the case, I recommend seeing the fourth card almost all of the time unless you are dealt two high cards. At the fourth card in cards speak I would normally play any one of the following:[19]

> any three unpaired cards 8 or lower
> a pair of Aces with one card 7 or lower
> two low pair
> a low pair with an Ace if three cards are of the same suit
> a four-card flush with two low cards
> four-card straights that have two low cards and flush possibilities.

18. David Sklansky, "High-Low Split, Vegas Style," in Doyle Brunson, *et al., How I Made over $1,000,000 Playing Poker,* p. 256.
19. Of course either the up cards in opponents' hands or heavy raising ought to be considered and may lead to tighter modifications of these suggested guidelines.

This strategy, scandalously loose by professional standards, will keep you in the hand about 40 percent of the time. But it is appropriate to play this loosely only if you have the courage and discipline to fold your hand after the fifth card is dealt.

Here, too, attention to the number of your competitors is important. The larger the number, the more willing you ought to be to pursue hands that have little two-way promise but that are strong probable winners in one direction or the other. With four or more players it is not likely that anyone will scoop the pot, and you should calculate your pot odds on the assumption that you are playing for half the pot. With only one or two opponents, your strategy should still be oriented toward scooping the pot—and to avoid being scooped.

Fifth-Card (Third-Round) Strategy

This is the critical stage of a limit cards-speak hand. If a player stays for the sixth card, he is probably in for the duration. After getting your fifth card you should either be confident you have a winner one way or feel you still have a credible chance to win both ways.[20] If you don't, drop. Your chances of getting one card in two tries are approximately those given in Table 13.2 (see page 245).

The reason for taking the third round of betting very seriously is that if you stay then, the pot odds are likely to be such

---

20. How confident you have to be depends upon the betting scenario you anticipate. If you only have one-way prospects, Sklansky ("High-Low Split, Vegas Style," p. 262) suggests you need at least a probability of .75 of prevailing that way to stay in. These numbers are based on a specific anticipated betting scenario, head-to-head. The specific numbers are not important (and they will be lower if there is more than one opponent), but what they emphasize is that the fifth card is the time when you ought to get out if you are not reasonably confident of winning half of the pot.

that you will choose to stay for the next two cards and hope you at least get your money back. This is the familiar problem of being sucked in. The looser you have played the opening cards, the more critically you should view your chances at the fifth card. In cards speak, as distinct from declaration Hi-Lo, chasing for (at best) half the pot when you have no chance for the other half is almost always bad strategy.

If, however, you sense weakness on the part of your opponents at this stage, and if you have scare cards showing that suggest you can go either way, you have the opportunity to bet heavily and possibly take the whole pot then and there. A different situation exists if you have a lock one way but, despite your scare cards, have no chance for the other half of the pot. Here you must try to figure out whether you are better off keeping opponents in and taking half of a bigger ultimate pot or being aggressive and possibly taking the whole pot now. Against good players a maximum bet will often cause them to fold at this stage. Against poor players the choice may not be yours, for they are likely to stick around in any case.

Fourth- and Last-Round Play

There is little more that needs to be said. By the time you have six cards, you want either to be virtually certain of winning one way or to still have a credible chance of winning both ways. In the first case you'll want to bet the maximum possible and hope that perhaps your opponents will give up. In the second case you probably want to keep the betting low and get your final card as cheaply as possible. If you are merely trying to escape, you are having to live with a bad decision made earlier, but the pot odds probably make it sensible for you now to grit your teeth and hope.

After the last card has been dealt, you certainly should have a good sense of where you are, and can bet accordingly. Some of the time you will be distressed to find that your inferences were wrong and that you have been beaten both for high and for low, either by someone else's good play, or (as seems to happen all too often) by someone else's hanging in there when he had no business doing so and catching his long-shot card. Instead of brooding over your bad beat, think about how much this is going to cost the other guy next time.

Cards Speak, 8-or-Better for Low

Because the cards-speak game is so dominated by low cards and strategy that focuses on trying to scoop the pot, it makes high cards bad cards and discourages many players from staying in hands. One method to counteract this is to require declaration, and this tack will be discussed below. An alternative is to add to the usual rules of cards speak the requirement that the low must be no worse than an 8-low. In about one-quarter of all deals of seven cards, the best low hand is worse than this. In such cases, the high hand automatically scoops the pot.

This variation, called Hi-Lo, 8-or-better, is a distinctly different game, with a different strategy, and I shall not discuss it at length.[21] But some things are immediately apparent. First, good high hands such as high trips, or even high pairs, are suddenly given starting value. Second, players in a head-to-head situation who were previously confident about having the *better* low must now worry about meeting the minimum requirements. For example, the illustrative hand that appears at the head of this chapter is wholly worthless under these rules. Third, a made high hand before the last card is now in a position to bet

---

21. It is discussed at great length by Ray Zee in *High-Low Split Poker, Eight-or-Better for Advanced Players* (Las Vegas: Two Plus Two Publishers, 1992), pp. 1–170.

or raise the maximum because it stands to scoop the pot if there is no low, and it may discourage potential low hands from trying to make hands that meet the minimum requirement.

SIMULTANEOUS DECLARATION

The differences between Hi-Lo and high-only still apply when considering simultaneous or sequential declaration. But the differences between cards speak and simultaneous declaration are also enormous. This is true even if the game is played under 5-4 rules, and it is even greater under the usual, and recommended, 6-4 rules.

Major Differences from Cards Speak

Scooping the pot remains an important objective, but it occurs in a different manner. Having the best hand in both directions is less likely under simultaneous-declaration rules both because typically there will be more players in the hand and thus fewer scoopers on mediocre highs, and also because the 6-4 rules eliminate the power of low straights to be two-way hands. More importantly, having the best hand both ways is neither sufficient nor necessary to scoop the pot.

It is not sufficient because to win both ways against opponents in each direction you must declare both high and low. This risks losing everything if you are beaten or tied either way, and the risk is often not worth taking. Suppose you have an unbeatable low and three 6's for high against two opponents, each of whom is clearly going high. If you declare Hi-Lo you are betting the half of the pot that you are sure to win, at even money, that you can beat both of the others for high. While this may be sensible, it may not. And if you hold two pair or a pair of Aces (hands that might win high) instead of trips, it almost surely would not be a good percentage declaration.[22]

Having the best hand in both directions is not necessary to win the whole pot since you may be able to get your opponents to call in the same direction as you are going when you have them beaten in that direction. This is frequently the case against one or even two opponents if your showing cards and betting have suggested a strong hand in one direction while your real power is going the other way. For example, showing an A, 2, 2, 6, with two Aces and a 7 in the hole, you have a lock for high but a terrible low. But if you bet vigorously you will surely be read as having a powerful low hand, and will win the whole pot when, to your opponents' surprise, you declare high.

This example reveals a second major difference from cards speak: scare cards can be decisive. This is so, whether they mislead your opponents, as in the example immediately above, or whether they suggest more strength than you actually have in the direction you are in fact going. With a K, J, 10 of hearts showing, for example, and vigorous betting on your part, you are likely to win high even if your hand is a total bust, since mediocre high hands will almost surely have folded, and even a hand that catches a low straight or trips is not likely to want to challenge you for high if it can escape with the low half of the pot. This fact makes it possible to stay in and play many hands that were automatic folds in cards speak.

A related difference is that declaration puts a large premium on the ability to read your opponents' cards and intentions, and thus provides major advantages to skilled players. Looked at from the negative side, it is dangerous to be in a position where you have to guess which way your

22. A risk-neutral player who is certain in one direction should declare both ways if he thinks the odds are even money or better that he will win in the other direction. A risk-averse player may properly want a bigger edge before doing so.

opponents are going in order to have a chance to escape with half the pot. If your opponent has a strong hand one way and he knows that you don't know whether it is for high or for low, he will do his best to reduce the competition to head-to-head against you. He is sure of half the pot, and may well win the other half if you guess wrong.[23]

Starting Hands in Declaration Hi-Lo

It is more difficult to generalize about what quality hands actually win the high and low halves of pots where declaration is required because so many hands are uncontested in one direction or both. A greater number of players stay in at the start, and this tends to lead to better final hands. However, the greater leverage that scare cards provide often causes hands that would have won at cards speak to be folded. More important than the absolute quality of your hand is positioning yourself to be the only one declaring in a particular direction.

Low cards are still strongly preferred to high ones because they have the possibility of ending up as two-way winners since they have the out of becoming a high hand, and because of the possibility of looking low while being high. But low starts are not nearly as dominating here as in cards speak. High cards showing will indicate that their holder is playing for high, and if he plays aggressively he will usually discourage high declarations by those who started with low cards but end up with mediocre high hands such as a pair of Aces or two pair. Indeed, the promising low start that evolves into a possible high winner is likely to be folded in the face of active betting by a hand showing high cards from the start.

---

23. This is the reason why pot-limit Hi-Lo under declaration rules is such a tough game, and usually ends up without a showdown.

Because high showing cards are more valuable than is the case in cards speak, it pays to stay for significantly more hands in the first two betting rounds.[24] Assuming a restrained game, here are the four-card holdings that I consider potentially playable for one more round in simultaneous declaration:

> any three unpaired cards 8 or less
> a pair of Aces with any two other cards
> two pair with a high card showing
> any high pair with another high card
> any pocket pair
> a small pair with an A, K, or Q kicker
> any four-card flush or straight
> three-card straights that have either low or flush possibilities.

Hands in one of these categories will occur about 60 percent of the time. Whether to actually call the bet on the second round will depend upon what else is showing and how the betting has proceeded. Hi-Lo played under declaration rules tends—and properly so—to be a good deal looser game at the start than is cards speak, and it is not unusual to have four, or even five, out of seven hands still in play after the second betting round.

How to play any of these hands depends on how you read your opponents' as well as your own cards. You will want to bet relatively aggressively under two alternative circumstances. First, if your showing cards are misleading about your hand's real direction; second, if you have the only high showing cards and want to establish a high-end position that will discourage the low starting hands from eventually

---

24. Part of this increase is offset because some hands that were playable in cards speak, such as 7, 8, 8, 9, become less valuable with declaration. This hand can too easily end up second-best in both directions and force its holder to guess in order to escape with half the pot.

declaring high. With low scare cards that are in fact strong low hands, slow-playing is a good idea. If you hit a lock for low, you want to have as many people in as possible, since you are unlikely to end up with more than half the pot.

When you face aggressive betting on the part of an opponent at this early stage, it is necessary to try to determine what he is doing. This will depend as much on the pattern of his play as on the cards showing in his hand. Here is where a superior player's skill makes the difference. Indeed, a sufficiently skilled player will often stay in on worse hands than those listed above because of his ability to figure out how he can position himself to win half of the pot.

Play in the Third and Later Rounds

The fifth card is again crucial, but in a somewhat different way than in cards speak. Play on the fifth and subsequent cards is dominated by how you can position yourself for the declaration, and how you can represent—or misrepresent—your hand. Here the number of players is important. While many players properly pay to get the fifth card, not more than three should go further. If you are one of these two or three you must be sure of winning one way either by the quality of your hand or by your ability to persuade the other player(s) to go the other way. If there are four or more players, it is unlikely that the other three will all declare the same way, so you had better have a hand that has at least a 50-percent chance in one direction. (With four players, if you win in one direction half the time you will come out slightly ahead. With only three players and the same success rate you will usually lose money.)[25]

25. Suppose there is $30 in the pot and you expect four players (including yourself) to each put in another $40 before the declaration. Suppose, too, that you will win high half of the time in such a situation. At the end, there will be $190 in the pot. The half of the time when you win you will collect $95 and

The greatest danger in High-Lo declare is to drift along on vague hopes that either you will catch a winning hand or that your opponents are all going the same way. This behavior too often leaves you in the middle between a better high and a better low. Yet by the last round the pot odds make it worthwhile to call even multiple bets and raises, and you end up with a big loss on the hand.

A variation on the rules that is sometimes used in declaration Hi-Lo is to permit a sixth round of betting after the declaration. These rules make it even more important to be confident of winning at least one way. In a three-man game this variation puts the player who is uncontested in a dominant position, and squeezes the second-best hand in the other direction. I do not recommend this variation because it tends to punish poorer and less experienced players without adding anything significant to the excitement of the game.

SEQUENTIAL DECLARATION

Play in sequential declaration is similar but not identical to that in simultaneous declaration until the endgame, when maneuvering for position becomes a dominant objective.[26] This maneuvering requires some attention, but it is a good

---

win $55; the other half of the time, when you lose, you will have spent $40. Your net expected profit of $15 is half of the pot as it existed before the fifth-card betting. By contrast, if there had been only three players, the final pot would have been $150, and winning half the pot would let you collect $75 for a profit of $35. But the other half of the time you would lose $40. Your net expected loss is thus $5.

26. It is not identical, since the player with the best high hand on the board must declare first unless there has been a bet or raise by someone behind him. Having the high hand showing after the sixth card has been dealt is thus a disadvantage, and may indeed cause such a hand to fold. This possibility, in turn, makes high showing cards, such as a pair of Kings or Queens, something of a disadvantage even earlier and makes it less attractive to play them than would be true in simultaneous declaration.

deal less demanding than the card-reading skill required in simultaneous declaration. The position you want to occupy on the last round depends critically upon the number of opponents you face.

Play Against One Opponent

In head-to-head situations, being in position to declare second is of overwhelming value. If you have a sure winner in one direction, you can hope your opponent declares that way so that you can scoop the pot. If you are weak but can declare second, you only need fear an opponent who will call Hi-Lo, since you can declare the opposite way from any other call he may make. This gives the player with the lower showing hand a major advantage, and he should take full advantage of this by betting as heavily as possible on the sixth card, both to eliminate any potential third caller and to build the pot in case he can scoop. He should, of course, call but not raise any bet on the seventh card so as not to lose his preferred position.[27]

If you have the high hand showing here and thus must declare first, you should check and hope your opponent is foolish enough to bet and take over the position of first declarer. When he does not, you must use your knowledge of his prior play to make your best guess. Players sometimes rely on all sorts of conversational gambits, body language, or pauses at this stage, but rarely to any avail. If being in first position is too painful, you should have folded on the previous round; after all, your position was determined then.

---

27. A conceivable reason to want to declare first in a head-to-head hand is to discourage an opponent who is thinking of declaring both ways from doing so by your apparent willingness to have him declare in the direction you choose. With low scare cards showing, this may work, especially against a less than first-rate opponent. A really good player will be deterred, if at all, by your cards and previous betting behavior, but not by your last-round bravado.

Play Against Two Opponents

This is the most common final-round situation and is more interesting than the one above. Here, too, it is usually best to be the last to declare. If you know you have the best hand in one direction, you can scoop the pot if the other two players both declare in that direction before you. If you are quite weak, you can hope that the other two will declare in the same direction and you can take half the pot by calling the other way.

But declaring last is not always best in a three-handed finish. A player with a weak hand in the middle position will usually declare the opposite way from whoever declares first. Thus, if the player to your left has shown weakness, you may wish to declare first, declaring, say, high when you expect the third player to declare low, in this way inducing your neighbor to go low. There are even times when you might prefer to be in the middle and declare second. One example is if a strong player has been driving the pot and must declare first, but you are not sure which way he will declare. You can make life tougher for the person in the third position by declaring the opposite way from the first player no matter what you hold. Some of the time this will leave you the uncontested winner of half the pot; even if not, some of the time you may beat the third hand.

While position is important, you may not be able to control it. Hi-Lo generally has a fixed maximum number of raises, and if you do not like your position as it is, you may raise the bet to change it. But this then gives players behind you the chance to raise or not as best suits their own positional interests. A player who is trying to escape with a weak hand may make a nominal raise to preempt a larger one. And a player with a strong hand who believes he has a lock one way but no chance to scoop the pot is likely to raise at every opportunity without regard to how it affects his—or your—position. Usually you must choose between pot building and playing for position, but occasionally you can do both at the same time.

Play Against Three or More Opponents

The likelihood of scooping a pot with four or more players is so small that it should not figure heavily in your strategy on the last round unless you hold a genuinely powerful two-way hand. You should stay in a multiplayer confrontation only if you believe you have at least an even chance of winning one way or the other. And if that is the case, position will not matter very much. If you are not that sure of your chances at the sixth card, you should either drop out then or try your best by raising to reduce the field to a size in which maneuvering for position gives you a reasonable chance for half the pot.

FIVE PROBLEMS

1. After the fifth card in cards speak you hold [8♥, 7♣] 2♠, 6♠, 2♦, and are now the high hand showing. You bet, Lou to your left raises, and three others call both bet and raise. Should you call, fold, or reraise?

2. After six cards in simultaneous declaration, there are three of you left in the pot with the hands shown in Figure 14.2. You are discouraged by your second 10 because the other two 10's have been folded. Doc, who is sitting to your left, has the bet and he bets the limit. Bill is next in line and he raises. You think for a minute—none of you has a credible flush possibility—and then call. Doc reraises, and so does Bill. What do you do now?

FIGURE 14.2

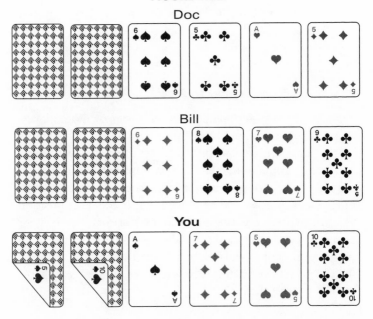

3. It is simultaneous declaration and after six cards you hold [4♥, 6♠,] 4♣, A♠, 5♥, 6♦. Harry, to your left, bets and Ty calls. Each of them shows middling lows with either three-card straight or flush possibilities. Everyone else folds, and it's up to you. What should you do?

4. It is sequential declaration and after six cards the remaining players are you, Knott, and Duke. (See Figure 14.3.) Knott has been betting, but now Duke has the high hand showing and bets. You call, thinking it is probably a mistake, but you've been on a winning streak and feel lucky. You expect Knott to raise on what looks like a good low hand, but to your surprise he just calls. What does this tell you, and what should you do next round?

5. It is sequential declaration, just you and Duke, head-to-head, after all seven cards have been dealt. (See Figure 14.4.) Duke checks to you. What should you do?

FIGURE 14.3

You

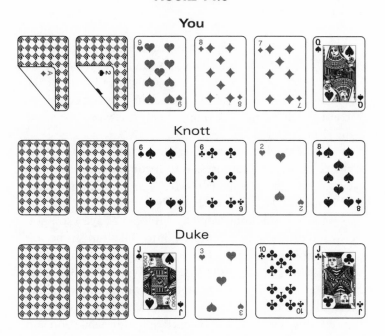

Knott

Duke

FIGURE 14.4

Duke

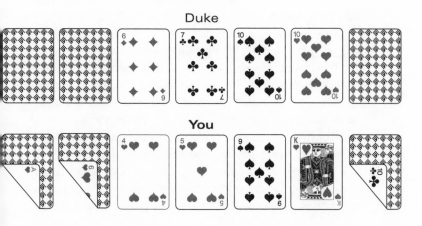

You

ANSWERS TO THE PROBLEMS
(AS I SEE THEM)

1. Fold. With four opponents you are clearly behind for low and have virtually no chance to win high. This is going to be an expensive hand, and you would need both of the next two cards to be on target even to have a chance for half the pot. Against one or two opponents this would be a fine hand, but now it is a probable loser.

2. You should call even though you expect Doc to reraise if the rules permit four raises. Your mediocre hand has been elevated to a likely winner by what you have learned from the betting! Doc is almost surely going low. Since he doesn't share your knowledge that Bill can't have a straight, he would not have bet and raised into Bill's cards if he was going high. Moreover, his low is apparently very good since your possible 7-low doesn't faze him. What does Bill have? Either he is foolishly betting an 8-7-low into Doc's low, or, more likely, he is reading you for low and is positioning himself to win half the pot by declaring high while you and Doc declare low. He'll keep it up next round. Either way, you should win half of a nice pot. If he calls high, your 10's-up should beat him.

3. You should raise, and if reraised, keep on raising. You might catch the nuts either for high or for low, but even if you bust—say, by catching a King on the last card—you stand to win half the pot by calling low. Harry's bet into your low scare cards was to set up a high declaration, and Ty, with a pretty good but hidden high hand, has correctly read Harry's bet. Harry may fold when you raise, but even if he doesn't, you should win at least half the pot.

4. Knott's play can be explained in two different ways. Either he has a lock for low and is trying to keep you in so you'll call the final-round bets, or he has trip 6's and really was disappointed to get that 8 on the sixth card. Against Knott you should probably believe the latter, in which case

you can stay in until the end, declare low, and win half the pot as both of your opponents declare high. If possible, you should be sure to get into position to declare before Knott. Against a more sophisticated player, such as Hugh, you would have to suspect that he was trying to keep you in. He would have realized that even if he had no low, a raise on the sixth card followed by a reraise by Duke would have led you to fold. In this situation he would be in position to declare behind Duke and win half the pot.

5. You should bet the maximum and then declare Hi-Lo. While you could check and settle for half the pot, your flush is almost surely the high hand, and your 9-low can be beaten only if Duke has three low cards in the hole. That is possible, of course, but it is much less than the even-money proposition that ought to deter you.

15

HOLDEM

EXERCISE: Here are ten different holdings you might be dealt. Arrange them in rank order from best to worst.

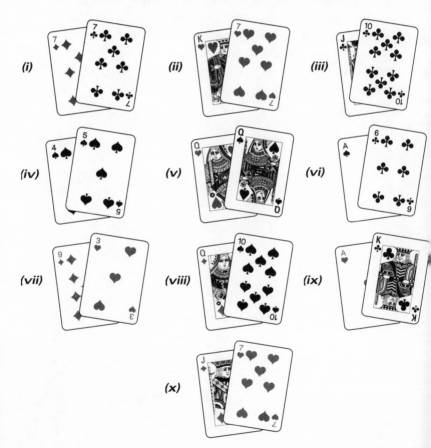

It is possible, though subject to argument, to rank the ten holdings illustrated above, and indeed, doing so is a key step in developing a strategy of play for Holdem. To take the second step—to proceed from a ranking of holdings to deciding whether or not to see the flop with them—depends upon information not given here. Only for examples *vii* and *x* is the answer almost surely no, and for *v* and *ix* almost surely yes.

Holdem's takeover as the leading professional poker game has resulted in a deluge of written analysis on the game and how to play it. Much of this material is by leading professionals and stresses the opportunities for making money by employing skills of pot management and card reading. Most of these treatments assume a ten-person game, as played in leading casinos.[1]

My purpose in this chapter is more limited: to introduce the basic elements of sensible Holdem play in Thursday-night games with seven, or at most eight, players. It concentrates on how to evaluate holdings before the flop, and how to reevaluate chances after the flop. But even this limited objective requires a long chapter, and many subtle aspects of Holdem will have to be left to playing experience—especially how to maximize your profits with a given hand, and how to read whether your opponents have what you fear they may have.

Holdem is deceptively simple. Each player receives two cards down (his *holding*), which he will combine with five common cards (the *widow*) to form the best possible five-

1. Some of these books are very good indeed and suggest the subtleties of the game. One of the very best is also the earliest: David Sklansky, *Hold'em Poker,* first published in 1976 by Gambler's Book Club (Las Vegas) and slightly revised and reissued since. Its sixty-three single-spaced pages bear reading and studying by anyone who chooses to compete in big-time Holdem, though they will probably discourage you from trying, which is just as well. A somewhat less compact and more anecdotal treatment, but also insightful, is found in Doyle Brunson *et al., How I Made over $1,000,000 Playing Poker;* the 190 pages devoted to Holdem are coauthored with Bobby Baldwin, another top professional. A briefer treatment, though somewhat more elementary, is found in Edwin Silberstang, *Winning Poker for the Serious Player* (New York: Cardoza Publishing, 1992).

card hand. After the deal there is a round of betting followed by the three-card *flop*. Another round of betting is followed by the showing of the fourth common card (the *turn*); and a third round of betting is followed by the final common card (the *river*). All hands are now complete and a final betting round is followed by the showdown.

The deceptive simplicity begins before the flop, because, while the distribution of the 1,326 different possible two-card holdings fall into 169 distinct combinations[2] that are easily defined, and somewhat less easily ranked, the strategy aspect of deciding which ones are playable depends heavily on the type of game and the player's position at the table.

Figure 15.1 shows the different holdings in the form of a pyramid. Each square represents a two-card *couple*, the higher card identified by the column, the lower card by the row. The numbers in the cells represent the number of different hands fitting the description. For example, the identified cell *J, 10, not suited*, shows the number 12 because, out of the sixteen different couples of Jacks and 10's, four are of the same suit and twelve are of two different suits. Each pair—say, a 10, 10—occurs six times, each non-pair sixteen times.

RANKING STARTING HANDS

A two-card holding may be ranked according to the probability that it will prove to be the best hand after the full widow is exposed. If the game is showdown, this probability can be calculated with precision.[3] A pair of Aces (the best

2. There are 1,326 different two-card holdings in a fifty-two-card deck. I will call each such holding a *couple*. For poker purposes, many of them are equivalent. For example, the couple 7♥, 9♠, is equivalent to the couple 7♦, 9♠ (each being a 7, 9, *unsuited*). There are 169 relevant couples, treating as distinct suited combinations (e.g., 9, 7, of spades) and unsuited ones (e.g., 9, 7, of two different suits).
3. Which is not to say that it is an easy calculation. We know the distribution of all two-card holdings and we know the distribution of all five-card wid-

possible couple) would win *x* percent of the time, and a 7, 2, unsuited (the worst possible couple since it has low cards with no pair and with no straight possibility), would win *y* percent of the time. *x* is more than 30 percent, and is much larger than *y*, which is under 3 percent.

But *x* is nowhere near 100 percent, and *y* is not zero. **Any two-card holding, by the time the whole widow is exposed, can be a sure winner.** Consider the worst holding, a 7, 2, unsuited. The widow might contain three 7's, or three 2's, either of which would certainly give the holder of 7, 2, the lock hand. Or it might contain two 7's and a 2, making 7, 2, a highly probable winner. In actual play, the holding 7, 2, unsuited, will prove to be a winner a much smaller percentage of the time than *y* because it will have been folded before the widow could have proved it to be a winner. Indeed, it is almost invariably folded before the flop.[4] Conversely, the holding A, A, will win more than *x* percent of the time because many unpromising holdings that individually had a low probability of beating it will have been folded without giving the probabilities (individually small, but collectively not so small) a chance to occur.

Which holdings win and which are folded depends on the interrelationship between the one and the other. What wins depends on the probabilities of winning if everyone stays *and* on the holdings that are folded; which holdings are folded depends on the probabilities of winning *and* on the cost of staying in; what it costs to stay in depends upon the

---

ows. If there are seven players, we can calculate what percentage of the time a given holding (e.g., A, A, or 7, 2) will end up with a better hand than six other holdings chosen randomly from the distribution of all possible holdings. These answers can be more easily obtained experimentally or by computer simulation.

4. An exception is where it is the hand that was obliged to make a blind bet that is not subsequently raised; another is where there is no betting before the flop.

FIGURE 15.1 DISTRIBUTION OF TWO-CARD HOLDINGS

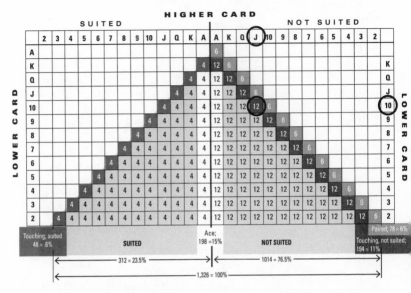

Every cell in this figure shows the number of different couples of a given character. For example, the cell *J, 10, not suited,* circled in the pyramid indicates that there are twelve different two-card holdings that meet this description. The number of couples of a particular description divided by 1,326 (the total number of different couples) gives the probability of getting that particular holding on a given deal. For example, since there are 312 suited couples, the probability is 23.5 percent ($^{312}/_{1,326}$) that the two cards of a holding will be of the same suit.

size of the bets, which, however, depend upon players' views of the probability of winning.

To penetrate this interdependence, it is well to start with the widow, which accounts for five of every player's seven cards.

What to Expect in the Widow

The composition of the widow is determined by the probability distribution of five cards taken from the fifty-two-card deck. After the full widow has been exposed you can depend on the following:

50 percent of the time it will contain at least one pair[5]

80 percent of the time it will contain three or more cards to a straight

40 percent of the time it will contain three or more cards to a flush

(Only 2 percent of the time will it contain none of the above)

34 percent of the time it will contain at least one Ace.[6]

The significance of these probabilities—for that is what they are—should be apparent:

1. A **pair** in the widow makes trips in the final hand a distinct possibility, since one of the remaining two cards that match the pair is about an even-money bet to have been dealt to one of seven players. The higher the widow's pair, the higher the chance that a card that matches it is in play: a player is much more likely to have folded a 3, 4, or 5 than an Ace, King, or Queen.

Even if there is no matching card to the widow's pair, the chance is excellent that one or more of the cards in the players' holdings will match one of the *other* three widow cards, thus producing two pairs. If the widow shows **5, 5, A, 10,**

---

5. In 42 percent of all widows it will be only one pair, 5 percent will have two pair, 3 percent will have trips, and a tiny percent will show four of a kind or a full house.

6. The same percentage is true of Kings, or 7's, or any other rank of card. But Aces are of particular interest because they are the highest rank.

9, there are nine outstanding cards (A's, 10's, or 9's) to create a second pair, as well as the possibility that one player's holding is itself a pair.

2. **Three-card straights** mean that the right two-card holding will complete the straight. While any particular two-card holding is not likely to do the job, it is certainly possible.[7] If the widow shows **K, 9, 7, 5, 3,** it is possible that someone holds a 6, 4, or an 8, 6. Of course, such a holding is likely to have been folded. But if the widow's cards include **K, Q, J,** the possibility of someone holding *and retaining* an A, 10, or a 10, 9, is reasonably good. A **four-card straight** in the widow requires only one card in a player's holding to complete it, and with three or more players it is more likely than not to be present.

3. **Three-card flushes** in the widow make a flush a possibility, and a **four-card flush** makes it likely.

4. An **Ace** in the widow is likely to be matched by an Ace in someone's holding.

In all of these cases, the number of players who see the widow greatly affects the likely winning hand. The greater the number of players, the more individual cards or couples are available to be fitted into a given widow, and thus the better the probable nature of the winning hand. Suppose the widow shows a pair of 9's on the flop. How likely is it that someone has a third 9? There are 49 non-widow cards at the time of the flop, and two of them are 9's. With seven players, 14 of the outstanding cards will have been dealt, and the probability that one of those cards is a 9 is 49 per-

---

7. To foreshadow, here lies the biggest difference between Holdem and Omaha. With seven players in Holdem, there are only seven two-card holdings to complete a straight or flush. But in a seven-person Omaha game, where each player has four cards, each one has six couples. With forty-two different couples among the holdings, completing straights and flushes is much more likely than with just seven. Straights and flushes, which occur only occasionally in Holdem, are commonplace in Omaha.

cent. In an eight-person game the chance rises to 55 percent, and in a ten-person game to 65 percent. Of course the matching card must not have been folded, which is why a high pair is more likely to be matched than a low one. The relevant number of hands is based on those that stay to see the widow.

Ingredients of Good Starting Holdings

The first element in defining good starting holdings is identifying which ones will mesh with likely widows. The more different widows a starting holding will complement to make a probable winning hand, the better it is. A second element, also important, is how soon the fit (or lack of it) will be apparent. If a call/fold decision will be clear as soon as you see the flop, it may not be very expensive to find out. If the decision is unlikely to be clarified until the turn, it will be more expensive, since you'll have to meet two rounds of betting rather than one; and if nothing is clear until the entire widow is fully revealed, it will be more expensive yet. The key estimate required is how expensive it will be to determine whether your holding promises to be the winner.

Pairs.   Pairs are attractive because their merit is likely to be quickly established. Any pair in the player's hand is a sure winner if it matches a widow pair.[8] It will be a very good hand if it matches *any* widow card, since trips formed in this way usually prove to be winners in Holdem. Further, the pair in the hole will produce two pair in the 50 percent of the time when the widow contains a pair.

But caution is required when holding a concealed low pair. Suppose the widow shows **5, 5, 8, 10, A,** and you hold a pair of 4's. Your two pair makes a poor hand because it will be beaten by anyone who holds a 5, an 8, a 10, or an

---

8. This ignores the minuscule probability of a straight flush.

Ace, or who holds a pair higher than 4's. If anyone else is in the hand, you can be sure that one of those things is the case. **After the flop, underpairs are virtually worthless.**

This means that a starting holding of a low pair such as 4's will prove to be valuable only if it makes trips on the flop, and this small probability (about 12 percent) is sometimes worth pursuing. If the flop does not make trips out of a hole pair, only high pairs are worth keeping. The higher the hole pair, the less its vulnerability. In general, a pair is valuable as long as there is no higher card showing in the widow.

While all pairs have some merit as starting hands, high pairs, especially Aces, Kings, and Queens, are powerful before the flop because they often will prove to be the high pair, or the high two pair, once the full widow is exposed. And if there is no higher card showing after the flop, they are likely to be the leading hand at the table. However, if you hold a pair of Queens—a premium starting holding— but the flop contains an Ace or a King but no Queen, you may already be second-best.

Touching cards. Because potential straights are so common in the widow, having both cards available to fill a widow's three-card-straight possibility is an important asset. A holding of 10, 5, has no such possibility, and this is true of more than 40 percent of all possible couples. The closer together the two cards are, the larger the number of possible straights they can make. A holding of J, 10, will complete any of four different three-card potential straights:[9]

A, K, Q; K, Q, 9; Q, 9, 8; and 9, 8, 7.

---

9. The focus is on three-card straight possibilities in the widow because any single card—a 2 as well as a King—can complete a four-card widow straight, and thus no initial holding is superior to any other in this possibility.

A holding of J, 9, will complete three different straights, a holding of J, 8, two different straights, and a holding of J, 7, only one, as can readily be verified.

Hence the value of touching or near-touching cards. But caution is required on two counts. First, because it is not enough to achieve a straight, but to achieve the highest straight that is held. This is a problem, because all players share the same widow and its possibilities. A holding of J, 10, is a much stronger holding than a 6, 5, because while each can make the same number of straights, the former holding is less likely to be beaten. Suppose a flop of **9, 8, 7,** of three different suits. Both hands are made straights, but the 6, 5, is already a loser. Beyond this, the 6, 5, is much more vulnerable. If either the turn or the river card is a **Jack, 10, or 6,** a straight higher than yours is readily made by a single card. Thus eleven cards (in addition to the J, 10, holding) promise trouble. Holding the J, 10, only another Jack or 10—one of six cards—will threaten to beat the Jack-high straight already held, and each of these would require a specific two-card holding to do so.

The second reason for caution with touching cards is that while a straight may be made on the flop, it is more usual that it will take four or even five widow cards to clarify your chances. With a 10, 9, holding, a flop of **K, 8, 7,** while encouraging, is worth nothing unless one of the next two cards is a 6 or a Jack. It is more expensive and thus less attractive to need to see two or three rounds of betting rather than only one before knowing whether to fold. *How* unattractive will depend on the probable bets, and will certainly be greater for low touching cards than for high ones. **You should not see the flop with touching cards unless you are prepared to see at least two rounds of betting, or unless your holding has other attractive possibilities.**

Touching cards, especially high touching cards, are valuable, at least until you see the flop. Near-touching cards, such as J, 9, or 10, 8, are weaker, but not so much weaker that their value is negligible, especially if they have something else, such as a flush possibility, to recommend them.

Both cards 10 or higher.   The high-card holdings A, Q; A, J; A, 10; K, J; K, 10; and Q, 10, though neither paired nor touching, are potentially powerful holdings for several reasons. First, if they make a straight it is likely to be the highest straight. Thus while a Q, 10, will make fewer straights than a 7, 6, it is a better hand because many of the straights that a 7, 6, will complete can be beaten. Second, two high cards have great potential to lead to the high two pair if the widow shows a pair, and to a high pair if it does not. For example, holding a K, 10, a flop of **K, 7, 5,** not only gives the holder the high pair, but not many cards threaten it.[10] Suppose the turn card is a Jack. Even if the river card pairs the board—for example, a 7—the King is still a winner unless someone has trips. Further, if there is no pair in the widow, only an Ace provides a new threat.[11]

A third advantage to holding two high cards is that the second one may prove decisive if two or more players hold the same pair or two pair, or even trips. If the widow shows **4, 4, 5, 8, 10,** and the betting does not suggest that there is a 4 in the wings (or a 7, 6), the holder of a 10, 9, may feel comfortable with his two pair, but your K, 10, will beat him by virtue of the King kicker. Finally, the merits of holding two high cards are quite likely to be clarified by the flop, without waiting for the turn.

An Ace and any other card (A, X).   The advantage of a holding of high cards is especially great if one of them is an Ace, even without a second high card. An A, 9, or A, 8,

10. Someone may already hold a pair of aces, a King with a higher kicker, or two pair, but that's one of the risks you have to take.
11. There are always other holdings that can threaten the high pair or high two pair, of course, but often the person holding them will have been induced to fold by a bet or raise earlier.

can be a useful holding even though it can fill no three-card straights. If the "X" card is paired, or becomes trips, or part of two pair, the Ace may well prove to be the decisive kicker. Indeed, this fact leads to an instructive anomaly: the holder of an Ace may be better off with a lower-ranked hand than with a higher one. Suppose you hold an A, 9, and could choose between these two potential widows:

(i) **9, 9, 7, 4, 2**
(ii) **A, A, 7, 4, 2**

You are better off with the trip nines with an Ace kicker than with the higher-ranked trip Aces. While a full house can beat you in either case, another hand holding an Ace with a higher kicker can beat you in the second situation but not the first.

Another advantage to holding an Ace is that if a flush is possible in its same suit, either you will have the nut flush or you will know (as no one else can) that it is not possible.

The A, X, holding, when X is a small card, is vulnerable to someone else also holding an Ace but with a higher kicker. This is a big threat in games with nine or more players, but a sufficiently smaller one with seven players, so that any holding with an Ace has merit.

Suited cards. Holding any two cards of the same suit—say, two spades—will prove very valuable if the widow ends up with three spades, because a flush is sufficiently rare that it usually wins. If two spades show up in the flop (about an 11-percent chance), there is a 35-percent chance that a third one will be added in the next two cards. This probability is usually worth pursuing for at least one more card.

The benefit of holding suited cards before the flop is, however, usually overestimated. To see why, suppose you hold two spades. While 40 percent of all widows contain three or more cards of the same suit, only one quarter of those will be spades. Next, recognize that only when the widow contains *exactly* three spades will your two-spade holding be a likely winner. If the widow contains four (or five) spades, your two-card spade holding—say, 8, 5—will be beaten if anyone has even a single spade higher than your 8. Finally, note that if you start with two spades in the hole, the chance of the widow ending up with three more spades is reduced. Indeed, the chance of getting exactly 3 spades out of the 11 that remain in the 50 cards you don't see is under 6 percent, and will happen only once in every 17 deals. This is too small a chance to rely on if there is any significant betting.

The exception to the generalization that suited cards are usually overvalued is where one of the two cards is an Ace. Such holdings are valuable because they provide the nut flush not only when there is a three-card flush in the widow but also when there is a four- or five-card flush there. Besides, any hand with an Ace has multiple chances.

The value of suited cards is, however, an important plus factor when other possibilities are present. The couple 10, 9, of spades has all the possibilities of a 10, 9, unsuited, *plus* the chance (modest though it may be) of ending up with a flush. As a rough rule, the extra possibilities of a flush make a 10, 8, suited, about equal to a 10, 9, unsuited.

To return to the exercise that opened this chapter, it is possible to rank the 169 combinations shown graphically above in Figure 15.1 from best to worst. Sklansky[12] ranks the top half of them, with A, A, ranked number one and 5, 4, unsuited, ranked number eighty-five. His rankings of the holdings given at the head of this chapter are shown in Table 15.1.

One can quarrel with these rankings for a seven-person game. For example, I would rate the A, 6, holding as more promising than the 5, 4, suited. But a complete ordinal

12. David Sklansky, *Hold'em Poker*, p. 14.

Table 15.1   Example Hands as Ranked by Sklansky

	Holding	Ranking
(ix)	A, K	4
(v)	Q, Q	5
(iii)	J♣, 10♣	16
(v)	Q, 10	42
(i)	7, 7	43
(iv)	5♠, 4♠	57
(ii)	K♥, 7♥	62
(vi)	A, 6	(not ranked)
(x)	J, 7	(not ranked)
(vii)	9, 3	(not ranked)

ranking is not necessary. All that is required are groupings that can be used to guide appropriate starting behavior.[13]

The pyramid in Figure 15.1 (on p. 296) is a convenient way to define different qualities of hands and to get a quick sense of how frequently they occur. The more promising combinations are its slopes (pairs and suited touching cards), its central core (couples containing an Ace), and the top section (two high cards). As a general rule, the closer to the apex or to the sloping sides or to the center line, the more promising is the holding. Other things being equal, the left-hand side of the pyramid (suited holdings) is prefer- able to the corresponding cell on the right-hand side. (The pyramid is not symmetrical because the pairs are all on the right-hand side—the unsuited side.) Figure 15.2 shows the same pyramid, but highlights in its two parts the best 20 percent and the best 50 percent of starting holdings.[14] The

13. Is a K, Q, suited, a better holding than a pair of Queens? It doesn't mat- ter, since you would surely play either of them. Is an 8, 2, a worse hand than a 7, 2, suited? It doesn't matter, because you will almost surely fold either one.
14. Any ranking of holdings will be controversial to a degree, and this is mine. But having compared the rankings of several different Holdem experts who have written on the subject, I find the differences to be relatively small.

FIGURE 15.2 BEST 20 PERCENT AND BEST 50 PERCENT OF HOLDINGS

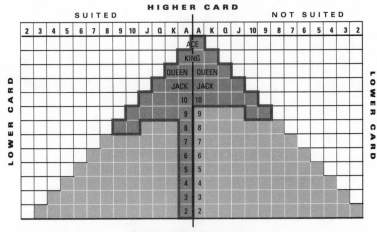

Best 20 percent

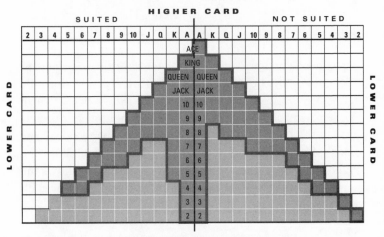

Best 50 percent

focus is on these because in a restrained game you may be willing to play as many as 50 percent of your holdings but in an aggressive one you are likely to play in the neighborhood of 20 percent.

CLASSIFYING STARTING HOLDINGS

For practical purposes, a five-way classification of holdings seems to me to be sufficient, and much easier to keep in mind than a complete ranking.

There are two relevant things to know about a holding: its frequency (how often does it occur?) and its efficiency (what fraction of the time that it occurs does it prove a winner?). The first can be calculated precisely; the second cannot, since it depends on the behavior of other players—for example, who drops out and who stays in. In the following classification, and in Table 15.2, which defines and summarizes its properties, I have followed two different assumptions: the first is the "showdown" assumption, in which everyone stays to the end on every hand; in the second, the holders of what are classified as "poor" hands always fold, but everyone else stays until the end. Even the second assumption underestimates the amount of folding of mediocre hands and thus understates the probable winning efficiency of better holdings. It is, however, useful, for it supplies a realistic lower boundary to the efficiency of different holdings.

Group I: Premium Holdings (occur 5 percent of the time)

These holdings have both cards Queen or higher. The strongest of these hands is the pair of Aces, the weakest the A, Q, unsuited. One doesn't get these hands often, but they are all excellent holdings, and prove to be winners close to 50 percent of the time they occur in a seven-man game.

Group II: Good Holdings (occur 9 percent of the time)

This group adds all holdings in which a 10 or a Jack is the lower-ranked card. The strongest holdings in this group are a pair of Jacks and a Q, J, suited, and the weakest is K, 10, unsuited. Holdings in this group prove to be winners almost as frequently, relative to their occurrence, as the premium hands, but they have the drawback that many times their status is not clearly defined by the flop.

Group III: Fair Holdings (occur 18 percent of the time)

This group contains all holdings in which a 9 is the lower card, all remaining holdings that are headed by an Ace, and a good number of pairs, touching cards, and near-touching cards in the middle ranks. Although holdings in this group, such as a pair of 8's, a J, 9, suited, and an A, 6, look attractive, they do not win often enough relative to their occurrence to be cherished. (I have included holdings headed by an Ace with a low second card only because their status is likely to be clarified very quickly, but these holdings are always vulnerable to an Ace with a higher kicker.) The efficiency of hands in this group is only about 20 to 30 percent, but this may be good enough for a call if the betting is light.

Holdings in one of these first three groups—Premium, Good, and Fair—occur nearly a third of the time, and prove to be the winners in most deals. They occur frequently enough that it is not a great hardship to limit your participation to them, and most conservative players do so. Indeed, many would regard the Fair category as questionable.

Group IV: Marginal Holdings (occur 13 percent of the time)

This group adds all pairs below sevens, all hands where the lower card is an 8, several holdings with a King and a mid-level companion, and some mid-level touching and near-

Table 15.2 Classification of Holdings (Percentages)

Holding	Frequency of Occurrence	Average Winning Efficiency*	
		W1	W2
I. PREMIUM			
• both cards Queen or higher	5%	30%	45%
II. GOOD			
• lower card 10 or Jack	9	25	40
III. FAIR			
• lower card 9			
• A,X			
• 9,8; 8,8; 7,7			
• suited: 10,8; 8,7	18	20	30
IV. MARGINAL			
• lower card 8			
• low pairs			
• K,7; K,6; K,5; 8,7			
• suited: 9,7; 8,6; 7,6; 6,5; 5,4	13	14	20
V. POOR			
• all other holdings	55	10	n.a.[†]
All Holdings	100	14	14

*"Winning efficiency" gives the percentage (to the nearest percent) of occurrences in that category that end up as the winning hand. (In a seven-person game the average efficiency is $\frac{1}{7}$, or 14 percent.) The percentages are derived experimentally. W1 assumes that all holdings see the showdown. W2 assumes that all holdings except ones classified as poor do so. With more than seven players the percentages in the efficiency columns would change. In particular, the efficiencies would decrease to a lower average.

[†]n.a. = not applicable

touching cards if they are suited. Holdings in this group win too small a fraction of the time to be worth pursuing unless the first-round betting is light and without raises.

Group V: Poor Holdings (occur 55 percent of the time)

This group includes all other holdings. There is great variety in this group (to which many experts would add the A, X, and K, X, holdings that I have included in higher groups). What they have in common is a low probability of winning if they are held to the end, and, equally important, little prospect of becoming likely winners at the time of the flop. Overall, their winning percentage, if all hands stay in to the showdown, is only 10 percent. Since the implied pot odds are unlikely to be as good as 9 to 1, these hands are usually folded if there is any betting before the flop.

This classification is summarized in the pyramid shown as Figure 15.3.

FIGURE 15.3   CLASSIFICATION OF HOLDINGS

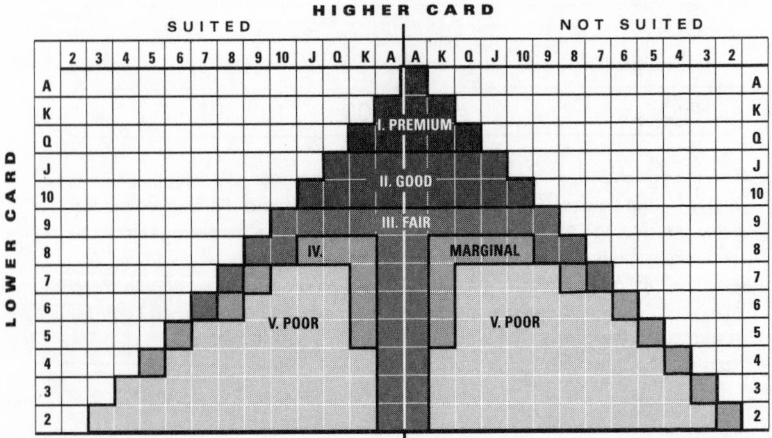

WHEN TO SEE THE FLOP

There are two key decision points in Holdem: first, whether to pay to see the flop, given your two-card holding; and second, whether to continue after seeing the fit between your hand and the flop.[15]

Table 15.2 (on page 309), by giving the frequency and winning efficiency of the different classifications, provides necessary information for a starting strategy in Holdem.

Notice first the drop-off—of about one-third—in the winning-efficiency percentages between the Fair and Marginal holdings. This explains why conservative players may well choose to stay in to see the flop on only Fair or better holdings—or about 32 percent of the hands they are dealt. Second, notice that the low winning efficiency of Poor holdings means that the pot odds are virtually never in their favor if there is significant betting before the flop. The dramatic rise in winning efficiency of the other holdings when Poor ones are folded (shown by the difference between W1 and W2 in Table 15.2) explains why players with better holdings will see to it that there is enough betting before the flop to encourage players with Poor holdings to fold.

The percentages in the last column of Table 15.2 suggest that the odds *against* a holding proving to be a winner are not worse than:

1.5 to 1 for Premium and Good holdings
2.3 to 1 for Fair holdings
4 to 1 for Marginal holdings.

---

15. At each of these points, the player has decisions beyond whether to fold or continue—whether to check or bet, call or raise. But the critical decisions are about whether to continue. (There are similar decisions required at the turn and on the river, but by then there is enough specific information available to the player that the decisions are, if not happier, at least simpler. They do not give the experienced player much difficulty.)

As usual, these odds need to be compared to the implied pot odds facing the player. The relevant odds will be the ratio of expected winnings if the holding becomes the best hand at the end, to the size of the player's contribution to the pot until he makes the decision whether to fold. Implied odds cannot be known with certainty, but the nature of the game—especially its usual betting patterns—makes it possible to estimate them. This is easier if you are sitting in late positions at the table rather than early ones, since you need to estimate how many players will be staying in and how big are the bets and raises that you'll have to call in order to see the flop.

Type of Game

In discussing Holdem it is useful to expand the two classifications of game types that I have been using (an aggressive game versus a restrained one) to three. First, an *aggressive limit game,* where players bet and raise freely before the flop but much more cautiously thereafter until the full widow is exposed. Second, a *restrained limit game,* where the betting is light before the flop, with raises a rarity—at least until the flop helps players to define the potential of their holding— and moderate thereafter. Third, a *restrained pot-limit game,* where the betting is light before the flop, but gets much heavier as the betting rounds proceed.[16] The betting scenarios are different in these three types and are the keys to when it is sensible to pay to see the flop.[17]

16. A fourth possible type, an *aggressive pot-limit game,* mentioned on page 22, doesn't occur often enough in Thursday-night poker to require attention. Indeed, even the aggressive limit game, while not unknown, is a relative rarity in seven-person games of the sort that are common where dealer's choice prevails. Where aggressive limit Holdem games are played, it is usual to have at least nine players, and to play the same game all evening.

17. I am focusing here on the ratio of the later-round bets to the earlier ones. There are, of course, other relevant aspects of different games, among them the number of players, how loosely they play, and how skillful you are relative

Aggressive limit game. Consider a $10/$20 limit game played by seven players where each antes $1 per hand. The pre- and post-flop bets are limited to the $10 level, and those after the turn and the river to $20. There is likely to be a bet and one or more raises before the flop, and another bet and up to two raises after the flop. If so, it will cost $20 or $30 to see the flop, and perhaps another $30 to see the final two widow cards. This requires $50 or $60, a steep investment compared to the minimal ante, and requires good probability odds to justify it. Thus, Marginal and Fair hands should usually be folded. After all the widow cards have been exposed, there is not likely to be much raising, and the $20 limit on final-round bets will not add enough to the pot to repay the heavy investment in low-probability starts. In this game, with seven competent players, you never expect more than three or four to see the flop, and no more than two or three to go beyond.[18]

The winning player in a hand of this game is likely to net about $150 on average, and thus any holding with less than a 1-in-5 chance of winning should be folded before the flop if the opening round costs as much as $30. Further, if it is likely to take two calls to clarify your chances (say, for a straight or a flush), you'll need at least 1 chance in 3 to justify a call.

Restrained limit game. With the same ante and betting limits as above, now suppose that the typical betting pattern is for a bet but no raises before the flop, and a bet and at most one raise after the flop. Here it will cost only

---

to them. As a general rule, the more players and the looser their play, the better the implied pot odds, and thus the weaker the holdings with which you can see the flop. Greater skill than your opponents works to the same end, but for a different reason: you are more likely to be able to decipher their hands and thus make intelligent decisions later in the play.

18. This high rate of attrition of competitors is what motivates Holdem players to seek games with nine or ten players rather than seven.

$10 to see the flop, and either another $10 or $20 to see the fourth widow card. Because the cost required to get the information the flop will provide is much less, the incentive is to see more flops, and more players will do so. Here perhaps four or five of the original seven players will stay for the flop, and perhaps three or four of those will stay for the turn. In this game the average pot will reward the winner with about a $100 profit, and hands with better than 1 chance in 10 of winning may be played if they will be decisively clarified by the flop.

Restrained pot-limit game.   Finally, consider a pot-limit game in which, to keep the game modest, there is but a small ante—say, $5 by the dealer. Before the flop there is likely to be no more than one $5 bet. If several players call, the bet after the flop can rise dramatically, but it is likely to be modest—say, $10 or $20. The expectation, however, is that big bets will be made on each of the last two betting rounds. Typically there will be lots of callers of the initial bet because the small cost of seeing the flop can be made up by a big bet later on.

In this game, among seven people there are likely to be as many as five or even six callers before the flop, and (if there are no raises) four after it. Because of the expectation of much bigger bets on the turn and river, and the consequent folding of holdings that haven't worked out, the number of competitors abruptly decreases after the turn. Indeed, many hands end without a showdown. But a typical contested pot will reward the winner with a profit of $200 or more. This may make it worthwhile to see the flop even on marginal hands.[19]

19. If it is an extremely loosely played game and you can see the flop for only $5, it may pay to see the flop on *any* hand at all if you have the discipline to fold if you don't get an exceptional flop. I hesitate to give this advice only because many amateurs will call with poor holdings, see them improve a bit on the flop, and then get sucked into calling after the flop with second-best hands.

Position Relative to the Dealer

Position at the table is important because of differences in the amount of information available to you depending upon where you sit. The person to the left of the dealer must bet first and is at a great initial disadvantage because he has to bet without knowing whether the bet he makes will be raised and without knowing how many other players will in fact meet the initial round of bets required to see the flop. Thus he will be unclear about both the cost of seeing the flop and the amount of money that will be in the pot at the end of the betting round—the key ingredients for figuring the implied pot odds. Under the gun it is usually wise to assume the worst and therefore, before you venture to put money in the pot, to have a holding robust enough to make you willing to call a raise if it should occur. (If you bet on marginal hands and are raised, you are likely to be reluctantly sucked into calling the raise.)

By contrast, the person playing last will have the information you lack, and be able to call with Fair or Marginal holdings when it is relatively cheap to do so, especially if several others have also stayed in and contributed to the pot. In a late position, you may well stay in on hands that you would readily fold in early or middle positions.

The way Holdem is played at casinos, this positional disadvantage of the early positions is present not only at the start but in every round. The person to the left of the dealer is obliged to act first every round, and this means he is always subject to being raised if he bets, or, if he shows weakness by checking, of having a late-round player bet as a bluff.

This subsequent-round disadvantage can be mitigated by having the responsibility for opening the betting rotate, round by round. For example, if a player in the second position has made the first-round bet, the next player who has stayed must open the bidding after the flop, the next remaining player must act first after the turn, and so on. The nuisance of this is that someone has to keep track of whose turn it is. But if the game is dealer's choice, something like this is necessary because the advantage of position is so great in Holdem. If no adjustment is made, players who choose not to deal Holdem will be at a persistent disadvantage.

Starting Strategy: Summary

The smaller the cost (relative to the expected winnings) of seeing the cards necessary to evaluate your holding, the weaker can be the hands on which you call. This cost varies with the nature of your holding, the betting habits of the particular game, and your position at the table.

Pot limit (paradoxically, it might seem) invites seeing the flop on marginal hands, even though the overall contribution of the winner to the final pot is typically a larger proportion than in limit games. The reason is that if you make a lock hand, the amount you can bet is much larger than in a limit game. **In pot-limit Holdem, more caution is needed when calling big bets in the later rounds than in paying to see the flop.**

A further consideration, however, is the danger of improving to a second-best hand that will prove expensive in the long run. This danger is greatest with hands whose promise lies in the possibility of middle-size straights or low two pairs, and it can be especially expensive in a pot-limit game. Experience is the great teacher here, and it suggests caution to the less-experienced player when it comes to investing in fair and marginal hands.

Taking all of these things into account leads to the starting strategies suggested in Table 15.3.

Table 15.3   First-Round Betting Strategies in Holdem in Games of Different Types

	Aggressive Limit: Heavy Betting Early, Light Betting Late	Restrained Limit: Light Betting Early, Moderate Betting Late	Restrained Pot-limit: Light Betting Early, Heavy Betting Late
A. For holdings that will usually be decisively clarified by the flop*			
Early Positions	Premium or Good holding required	Fair or better holding required	Fair or better holding required
Late Positions	Depends on raises: Fair or better required if none; Good if one or two; Premium if three	Depends on raises: Marginal sufficient if no more than one	Marginal (or even worse) sufficient if no raises
B. For holdings that will usually require two or three rounds of calling before they are clarified†			
Early Positions	Don't call	Good or better holding required	Fair or better required
Late Positions	Depends on raises: Fair or better sufficient if none; Good if one or two; Fold if three or more	Depends on raises: Marginal sufficient if none; Fair or better if one or more	Marginal (or even worse) sufficient if no raises

*This includes pairs and holdings headed by an Ace, King, or Queen.
† This includes touching cards and suited holdings without high cards.

PLAY AFTER SEEING THE FLOP

You never win in Holdem without the benefit of the widow; both directly, by the improvement of your hand, and indirectly, by the widow not giving someone else a better hand than yours. The decision point after the flop is critical because the flop—three-fifths of the widow, and five-sevenths of your final hand—redefines what are now playable holdings. A great many of the holdings that rightly led players to see the flop are rendered virtually worthless and thus can be folded without much thought. For the rest, you must quickly estimate whether the probability of ending up with the best hand outweighs the pot odds you are facing. You must also be aware of the risk of improving to only second-best. After all, a turn or river card that improves your hand will often improve other hands as well.

After the flop it is useful to think in terms of three kinds of hands:

1. Leading Hands: these are hands that are probably the best at this point. (These may be virtual locks to win the pot, but more usually in Holdem they are still vulnerable.)
2. Drawing Hands: these require only one more card in the widow to become the probable best hand.
3. Chasing Hands: these hands require *both* of the remaining cards in the widow to improve to the point where they become a probable winner.

Every starting holding (except perhaps a pair of Aces) can be any of the three kinds after the flop. **The first rule of sensible Holdem play after seeing the flop is to fold chasing hands in the face of any bet.** This advice is almost invariably correct, yet it is regularly violated. The cost of having to pay to see two more rounds of betting and having to hit both the turn and river cards to improve your hand is not an attractive combination.

Either leading or drawing hands may be worth pursuing. The key question to ask about a leading hand is: How many of the yet unseen cards are likely to turn mine into the second-best hand—or, in poker jargon, how many will *counterfeit* it? For a drawing hand the question is: How many of the outstanding cards will make me a probable winner?

To answer these questions you have to think through and count how many of the forty-seven cards you don't see will either spoil or make your hand if they occur on either of the

Table 15.4 Getting One Card out of 47 in Two Tries

A. Getting hurt with a leading hand

Number of Cards That Will Beat You	Probability	Odds
5 or fewer	.20 or less	4 to 1 or better *in your favor*
8 or 9	.33	2 to 1 *in your favor*
13 or 14	.50	1 to 1
20 or more	.67 or more	2 to 1 or worse *against you*

This table shows, for example, that if any of eight or nine cards will ruin a leading hand, the odds *against* being ruined are 2 to 1.

B. Getting helped with a drawing hand

Number of Cards That Will Make Your Hand	Probability	Odds
5 or fewer	.20 or less	4 to 1 or worse *against you*
6	.24	3.1 to 1 *against you*
7	.28	2.6 to 1 *against you*
8 or 9	.33	2 to 1 *against you*
10	.38	1.6 to 1 *against you*
13 or 14	.50	1 to 1
20 or more	.67 or more	2 to 1 or better *in your favor*

This table shows, for example, that if any of eight or nine cards will help a drawing hand, the odds *against* being helped are 2 to 1.

remaining widow cards. You want small numbers when answering the first question and large ones for the second. Table 15.4 translates these numbers into the odds that one of those cards will appear in the next two rounds. It is worth memorizing.

Once you've got the probability odds (shown in the table), you need to estimate the pot odds in your favor and then compare the two.

AN EXERCISE: PLAY ON THE FLOP

The number of cards that can help or hurt you depends upon both a given holding and a given flop. The range of possibilities is great, and no generalization is as useful as a situation-specific analysis. Consider the following exercise *before* you read my answers to it (given just below).

You have seen the flop with three other players. Their holdings are unknown. You hold (alternatively):

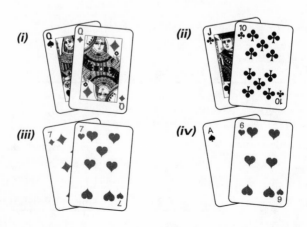

A. The flop is:

Should you call the bet and see the turn card if, as the last player, you estimate the immediate pot odds facing you to be about 3 to 1?

B. Repeat the exercise with the flop:

Questions to ask are: Does your holding give you the probable best hand at this point? If so, how many of the unseen forty-seven cards are likely to make you second-best if one of them shows up on the turn or the river? If you have a drawing hand, what card or cards do you need on the turn or river to make you a probable winner?

ANSWERS TO THE EXERCISE

A. Facing a Flop of A♣, K♥, 7♠

This flop will please those who stayed with Aces or Kings, and distress everyone else except the holder of a pair of 7's.

(*i*)   Although a premium hand before the flop, the pair of Q's has been greatly devalued. It is probable that one of the remaining players holds either an Ace or a King and thus makes the Queens already second-best. Only one of the two remaining Queens can improve this hand, and the odds against this are too large to buck. This hand should be folded if anyone bets. If you are in a late position and everyone has checked to you, a bet may be advisable. You could win the pot now, and if anyone calls, you'll at least clarify the situation, but you should plan to drop after the turn unless you get a Queen.

(*ii*)   Your J, 10, suited in clubs, has become a drawing hand, but only a Queen will make the hand with one card. There are two other long-shot chances: a 9 *and* 8 on the turn and river, or two more clubs. All of these chances add up to less than the 3-to-1 pot odds, but they are close enough that you might see one more card if there is only a modest bet and no raises. You can always hope for something like the 8♣ on the turn, but a fold is really indicated.

(*iii*)   Holding a pair of 7's, you now have trips on the flop, a leading hand. It can be hurt if either the Ace or King in the widow is subsequently paired, for it is likely that someone staying in already has an Ace or King in the hole. But no more than five cards can hurt you, and your hand is worth betting and raising on now. One reason is to build the pot, since the odds are in your favor in any case. Another reason is to decrease your risk. While someone who holds an Ace is likely to call in any event, you'll cut the threat against you in half if you cause someone with a King to fold.

(*iv*)   The A, 6, unsuited, was at best a fair hand originally, but it has been greatly improved by the Ace on the flop. The biggest danger is that someone else holds another

Ace with a higher kicker. In a seven-person game this is not probable unless someone raised before the flop. A bet or a call is certainly appropriate here, but anyone raising probably has you beaten.

B. Facing a Flop of 8♣, 8♦, 4♣

Only holders of an 8, a high pair, or two clubs will welcome this flop. The winning hand will almost surely be two pair or better, although the holder of an A, K, might eke out a win with the high kicker to the pair of 8's.

(*i*)   The pair of Queens is the leading hand here unless there is already an 8 in someone's hand (which is relatively unlikely since an 8 is not a prime card before the flop) or a pair of Kings or Aces, also improbable. But your Queens would be threatened by the addition to the widow of an Ace or a King or another club. That's seventeen cards, and it's better than even money that at least one of them will occur in the next two cards. With your pair of Queens you should try to reduce the risk by raising the maximum now in order to induce the holders of an Ace or King to fold. They are likely to do so unless suited in clubs. But even if this does not work, the pot odds are in your favor with this hand.

(*ii*)   The Jack and 10 of clubs will become a probable winner with any of the nine unseen clubs. The 2-to-1 odds against you are less than the pot odds you face. With this holding you should call as cheaply as possible, but not fold unless there are multiple raises. Four-card flushes with a Jack or better high card are usually worth drawing to twice.

(*iii*)   The pair of 7's, though giving two pair, which is quite possibly the leading hand after the flop, is extremely vulnerable because it is an underpair. Any 9 or above threatens a higher pair; any club threatens a flush. Only another 7, or both a 5 and a 6, would save this hand. It should be folded now.

(*iv*)   The A♠, 6♥, would be a possible winner only if another Ace appears, but even then it is vulnerable in many ways. This is an easy fold.

SOME GENERAL CONSIDERATIONS ON THE FLOP

Each of the examples was a special case, and each was vulnerable in ways other than those mentioned. But that is always the case, and that is what makes Holdem such a popular but difficult game. What is most important is to evaluate each holding at the time of the flop in the right frame of mind. Don't ask: Can I improve? Instead ask: What are my chances of being the clear winner at the end?

Playing Leading Hands

Some hands, such as a made full house or an Ace-high flush, are so strong that they are unlikely to be counterfeited, and playing them is merely a matter of pot management. You want to keep opponents in but not give them a free ride. Much will depend on who they are and on where you are sitting. A check in early positions is probably worth trying, for even if no one else has much, the player in last position is likely to try to steal the pot with a bluff. With a monster hand you should not raise. Holding trips on the flop is a very strong hand if two of them are in your hand, but is much more vulnerable if the pair is in the widow.

The main advice about playing hands that seemed good before the flop and are still leading after the flop is not to fall in love with them if the flop reveals several credible threats. A hand such as A♥, Q♦, still looks good when the flop is **Q♠, 8♦, 7♠**, but if several people call your bet, you can be reasonably sure not only that there is a potential spade flush against you but also that virtually every straight possibility is present. Only a 2, a 3, a Queen, or an Ace, none of them in spades, would leave you comfortable after the turn. This is only ten of the outstanding forty-seven cards. Betting heavily in this situation is sensible only if it will induce some of your opponents to fold.

There are a number of situations where you probably have the best hand on the flop but where the chances of ending up second-best are so great as to make the hand not worth calling. Suppose the flop is **7, 4, 4,** and you hold an 8, 7. Any card higher than an eight will likely pair someone, and anyone holding a 4 or a 7 will almost surely have you beaten. There are more than twenty-five cards that will probably beat you, and you might as well fold if there is any serious betting.

Suppose you hold a 4♦, 3♦, and the flop comes up with **5♥, 6♥, 7♥**. While you have a straight, not only is it potentially already beaten by either a higher straight or by a heart flush, but any other heart, or a 4, 8, or 9, on the next two cards will surely mean that you are second-best if anyone else is betting. Most of us grit our teeth and play out this hand, but better players give it up at the first hostile bet.

Another fatally vulnerable hand is a pair after the flop that is lower than the highest flop card. While possibly the leading hand and a possible eventual winner, this holding is so vulnerable to ending up second-best that it should be folded.

With vulnerable leading hands you can sometimes make them stand up by very aggressive betting on the flop—if your betting leads others to fold. Here, too, you must know how your opponents are likely to behave. If they are going to stay in any case, your efforts can become expensive.

Playing Drawing Hands

Since you must plan on seeing two rounds of betting to achieve the odds shown in Table 15.4 on page 319, the implied pot odds facing you after the flop will usually be less attractive than the immediate pot odds. The proper method is to add the expected size of the bet on the flop to one-half the size of the expected bet after the turn.[20]

Concerns about hitting but ending up second-best, when added to the prospect of having to see two rounds of betting before your draw succeeds or fails, should make for caution. Most Holdem players do not appreciate this sufficiently. **More money is lost on drawing hands that are overvalued than on any other aspect of Holdem.** The safest drawing hands are either two cards to a high flush when matched by two on the flop, or four cards to the best possible straight in the absence of two cards to a flush in the widow. In either of these cases, if you hit you can be pretty sure that you have the winner.

Here are some drawing situations where caution is in order, especially if there is more than routine betting or raising. Suppose you hold 10, 9, unsuited, when the flop shows **A, Q, J.** This looks promising: an 8 (but no King) will give you the nut straight, and a King will give you a high straight that will either win or tie for the best hand. With eight cards to help you, the odds are only about 2 to 1 against you, and the pot odds may make this seem an attractive proposition. But this is the high-card neighborhood, where holdings are likely to have been retained. It is always important to remember who bet or raised before the flop when evaluating your chances. Be suspicious if the bettors or raisers before the flop now bet and/or raise. One of them very likely has an A, K, and the other a K, Q, or a K, 10. If so, you will

20. See the discussion on pages 249–50, where a similar computation was appropriate.

need an 8 to do more than tie, even if no one holds a K, 10, and the chances of getting an 8 are not good enough.

Next consider the drawing hand 7, 7, when the flop shows **8, 6, 5.** Any 9 or 4 promises to make it a winner, and another 7 is also a good bet to do so, thus giving you ten chances for a win, and favorable odds. But with this same holding, suppose the flop is **8, 9, 10.** There may be no single card that will make the pair of 7's a winner, since a Q, J, is a likely holding. Even if this is not the case, you need a 6 *and* no Queen or Jack on the next two cards to be confident of winning.[21] With only four cards to help and eight to hurt, the odds against you are more than 5 to 1, and the hand should be folded.

Enough has been said to suggest the principles of sound play on the flop. The type of game and your position in the betting sequence will play a role in your decision to fold after seeing the flop or pay to keep going. It is more attractive to stay in pot-limit games than in limit ones because the biggest bets are yet to come. But the cost of being second-best can be much higher in pot-limit games. In them it is worth drawing to achieve a lock but never merely to get a credible hand.

PLAY ON THE TURN AND THE RIVER

Once the fourth widow card has been exposed, the same kinds of considerations apply as after the flop, but now the calculations are much easier. There is only one card to come out of the forty-six you don't see, and only one round of betting is required to see it, so figuring the pot odds is easy. The hard part is to be honest with yourself about the cards

---

21. There is also the long-shot chance of catching two cards (e.g., 7 and 8, or two 9's) that will give you a full house, but such a full house is itself vulnerable.

you either need or fear. Here much will depend on the number of opponents you face, as well as their behavior in the previous rounds.

There are almost always cards that can counterfeit your leading hand (and they will seem to do so with distressing frequency). But, of course, they do so in predictable ways, and if you take the trouble to calculate your chances you can make sensible decisions about whether to call, raise, or fold.

Once the last card has been exposed, everyone's hand is fully determined. If you have the best hand, your challenge now is to keep the others in and maximize your winnings; if you do not have the probable winner but feel you have a credible chance, you must decide whether this chance justifies the bets you have to make or call. The analyses discussed in earlier chapters about avoiding second-best, about card reading, about bluffing, and about deciding when to call the final bet in uncertain situations all apply. Knowing your opponents and remembering their behavior is, as always, likely to be a big help. What is essential to remember about widow games is that the common cards that have improved your hand may have improved others even more.

FOUR PROBLEMS

1. After the fourth card in a $10 limit game:

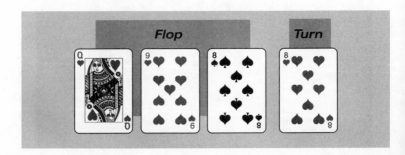

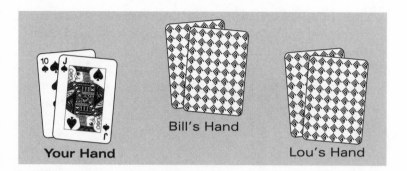

Bill's Hand

Your Hand

Lou's Hand

You had bet your straight on the flop and were called by both Bill and Lou. There is $40 in the pot, and you now bet another $10. Bill raises and Lou folds. What should you do now?

2. In the hand illustrated, the initial promise of your holding has not been fulfilled when the **A♣** falls on the river.

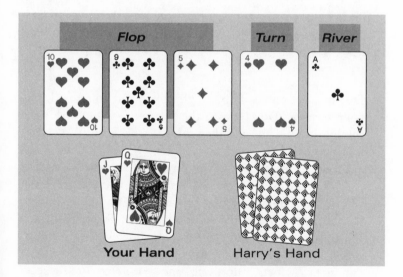

Flop   *Turn*   *River*

Your Hand   Harry's Hand

You had bet on the turn because of your many drawing opportunities, and only one opponent, Harry, called. It is your bet. What do you do?

3. In the illustrated pot-limit deal, your dubious decision to stay for the flop with the 3♠, 2♠, seems vindicated when the flop gives you a full house.

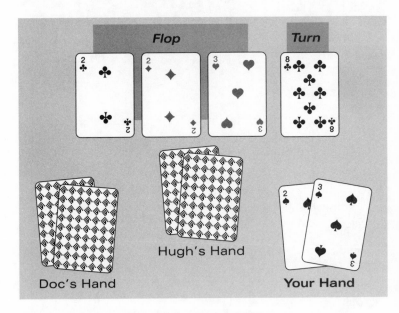

Doc had bet on the flop, Hugh called, and you raised. To your surprise, Doc reraised the maximum allowed. Hugh thought for a while and then folded. You called. When the turn produced the innocuous-looking 8, you bet and Doc again raised. What should you do now?

4. It is late evening in a pot-limit game, and you are dealt K♥, Q♥. When the betting is opened by the player under the gun, you raise in the second position, Ty reraises, and Knott calls. The opening bettor folds and you call. The flop is K♠, K♦, 5♦. You check, hoping not to discourage either opponent. Ty bets, Knott calls, and so do you. You suspect that Ty is holding either K, 5; A, K; A, A; or 5, 5—and all those couples but the pair of Aces have you beat. You guess that Knott has two diamonds. But the pot odds are attrac-

tive and you hope for a Queen. The turn card is the **K♣**! You hold the nuts and now want to maximize the pot, which presently is about $100. You check, Ty bets $25, Knott folds, and it's up to you. What do you do?

ANSWERS TO THE PROBLEMS
(AS I SEE THEM)

1. You certainly intend to call to the end with your made straight, even though the **8♥** makes either a flush or a full house possible. There is now $70 in the pot, and you can see what Bill has for only $20 more if you choose merely to call. Your alternative is to raise. Here your knowledge of your opponent is critical: Bill, who bluffs often, is likely to have done so as soon as the widow provided a threat to the straight, so a raise against him is a good idea. (Against someone like Hugh a call would have been safer.) While Bill may fold, that shouldn't bother you, for he might now have either two pair or a single heart and thus might outdraw you if he stays in. He is more likely to stay in, and if he does so you should check to him on the next round and call his bet. Notice that if the same cards had shown up in a pot-limit game, you would have been wise to fold when the raise occurred on the turn. Your hand cannot improve but your opponent's can, even if it is not already better than your straight. A pot-limit bet by an opponent on the river would be difficult to call.

2. You have no chance to win if you check, since Harry surely has at least one pair or a King to have stayed this long. Your only hope is to bet and hope that he folds. There is no chance that he holds the 3, 2, that would give him a lock, since this holding would not have survived the flop, even if Harry called the opening round with it. He might have a pair of Aces, and if he does he'll raise and you, of course, will fold. The alternative to the bluff bet is simply to give

up, and you probably should do this against someone who is hard to bluff out, such as Duke.

3. You should fold your full house! Since at this point Doc must surely suspect that you hold a deuce, what can he have? The only credible answer is a pair of threes! He would not have stayed for the flop with a 2, 8. He might have stayed with a pair of eights, but he would not have raised on the flop with that holding, since the chance of someone else having or catching a higher pair is too great. He would not have raised a second time with only two pair, even Aces. You have already contributed enough and should fold your full house: the only card that can help you is the fourth 2, and that is not likely, especially since Hugh may well have had it to justify his staying for so long.

4. You should call but not raise. Ty's modest-size bet is probing to see if you have the fourth King, and he surely has a full house. If you raise now, he will probably fold. You want him in the pot for the next round since the river card cannot possibly counterfeit you. Next round Ty will surely not fold if you bet then. Thus, reserve your bet for the last round and hope Ty raises. You might check on the last round hoping that Ty will bet into you, which he might do holding a pair of Aces. But if he does he would not call a raise on your part, and there is a good chance that if you check he will be cautious and do likewise.

16

♠ ♣ ♥ ♦

OMAHA

"Hey, Tex, do you still want to play in our game? Ralph's moving to Boston and we have an opening."

"I sure do! What games do you play?"

"Some Holdem, some 7-card, but mostly Omaha, high only."

"Omaha. Isn't that kid-stuff Holdem, with four cards to hold instead of two?"

"Not exactly. You're dealt four cards, but—"

"And does the widow still get built by a three-card flop and then one and one?"

"Yeah, and there's betting before the flop and then each time new cards are exposed. But—"

"No problem. Count me in. I've been playing Holdem for twenty years, so your game will be a piece of cake."

Omaha is a relatively recent offspring of Holdem-type games; it rapidly spread nationwide after reaching Las Vegas early in the 1980s.[1]

1. The literature on high-only Omaha has been relatively slim, although Michael Cappelletti writes a biweekly column on it in *Card Player* magazine. A useful introduction, first written in 1984, but revised several times since, is Bob Ciaffone's *Omaha Holdem Poker* (Las Vegas: Harris Printers, Inc., 1992). Where the game arose and where it picked up its name are unclear. Ciaffone's explanation of the name is that in Omaha, Nebraska, it was common to require a Holdem player to use both of his hole cards in forming his final hand and that this feature was retained as extra cards were added to players' holdings. A Hi-Lo version (requiring 8 or better for low) is becoming increasingly popular in casinos, and it is such an enjoyable game that it will probably grow in popularity in Thursday-night games.

Omaha is particularly well suited to Thursday-night poker. It has more action and requires less conservative starting play than does Holdem in either the limit or pot-limit varieties found in Thursday-night games. Many people, myself included, believe it to be a far better game for those who play poker for recreation rather than to make money by taking advantage of less skillful players. But it is hardly "kid-stuff Holdem." While chance plays a significant role in ruining or making hands on the turn and river, the game both requires and rewards card-reading skills.

OMAHA VERSUS HOLDEM

Omaha is deceptively similar to Holdem. The widow and the way it is generated are exactly the same in the two games, and the betting rounds and rules are identical. Once the widow is defined the same final hands are possible in the two, but there the similarity ends. People who come to Omaha by way of Holdem, such as Tex (quoted above), tend to underestimate the critical differences that make the carryover of strategy from Holdem to Omaha quite small.

The first, and most critical, source of the differences derives from the fact that in Omaha each player is initially dealt four cards for his holding rather than two. (The second is the requirement that exactly two cards from the holding must be used in the final hand—discussed below.) Dealing four cards creates six couples (or, six two-card combinations) for each player, as compared to one in Holdem, and totally changes the nature of what hands may be expected to prevail. Very good hands in Holdem, such as high trips or Aces-up, are seldom good enough to win in Omaha, where the winning hand is usually a straight, flush, or full house, and where it is not uncommon for three or more players to be holding hands of this quality after the full widow has been dealt. Further, a nondescript couple, such as 7, 5, unsuited, which is seldom retained in Holdem, is frequently retained in Omaha as part of a four-card holding, and may end up making a lock straight when the widow produces a K♠, J♥, 8♥, 6♦, 4♣. Such low straights are equally possible in Holdem, but they are not probable there. **In Omaha a straight or better is the expected result in the great majority of deals.**

A useful working assumption in Omaha (a variant of Murphy's Law) holds that if a better hand than yours is possible, given the widow, it probably *is* held by one of your opponents. While this may sound pessimistic, it is more often than not the case in Omaha.

An important consequence of the greater number of cards available to each player, which, in turn, lead to a greater variety of winning hands, is that the difference between better and worse starting holdings (as judged before the flop) is much less pronounced in Omaha than in Holdem. The winning efficiency of Premium and Good holdings is much lower, and thus on this ground alone it proves sensible for players to see more flops on average-quality holdings. When it is sound Holdem strategy to see, say, 30 percent of all flops (given the number of players, the stakes, and the culture of the game), the corresponding number for Omaha turns out to be 50 to 60 percent.

Moreover, the nature of the decision about when to call is different. In Holdem it depends heavily on the quality of a given two-card holding: a pair of Queens, for example, or an A, K, suited, is each worth at least a call in Holdem under almost any circumstances, whereas a J, 8, unsuited, would hardly ever survive. In Omaha the strength of your holding typically depends on the availability of multiple possibilities, which are called *multiway holdings.* If four, five, or six of the six possible couples in a four-card holding each would work with a different widow, the holding is more powerful than even the best couple taken alone. Thus, holding a pair of Queens with nothing more is a poor holding in Omaha, and an A, K, suited, accompanied by a 7 and a 4 is only a marginal holding.

Compare the value of the holding J♠, 10♥, 9♠, 8♥, with that of the holding A♠, A♥, 6♦, 3♦. The pair of Aces is better than any two of the cards in the other hand, but overall the first holding is much more attractive. It can fill any of twenty (!) possible three-card straights that the widow may produce, as well as a flush in either hearts or spades.[2] The holding with the Aces fits some possible low straights and a very low flush, but unless the widow ends up with *both* a pair *and* an Ace, this holding will not have much chance of being the winner.

Because it is sensible to see the flop much more often in Omaha than in Holdem, raises before the flop for the purpose of reducing the field to one or a few players are less likely to succeed, and thus such raises are seen less frequently. This, in turn, means more callers and better pot odds, which reinforces the incentive to call on more holdings.

All of this tends not only to increase the amount of action and the size of the pot in each deal but also to shift the game's most critical point from the initial round of betting and the decision whether to see the flop to the evaluation of your hand *after* the flop. Starting strategy is not of negligible importance, of course, but neither is it so critical to success as in Holdem. In either a pot-limit game or a restrained limit game, it pays to see the flop often. This assumes that you have the discipline to fold quickly if, as is often the case, the flop does not mesh with your holding. If you do not, you had better be conservative in your starting strategy or you will be sucked into many expensive misadventures.

2. As we saw in Chapter 15, touching cards (e.g., 10, 9) can fill any of four straights; near-touching couples that have a gap of one (e.g., 10, 8) can fill three straights, and couples with a gap of two (e.g., J, 8) can fill two straights. In the example J, 10, 9, 8, there are three touching couples, two near-touching couples, and one two-gap couple.

While an Omaha holding has six times as many couples as a Holdem holding, the requirement in Omaha (but not in Holdem) that a player's final hand must consist of exactly *two* of the cards from his holding and *three* from the widow modifies this numerical advantage. This requirement plays an important role, and it often confuses seasoned Holdem players and leads them to overvalue their Omaha holdings. Here are four hands that cost Tex a bundle when he started playing Omaha:

Tex's Holding	Widow (in the order revealed)
(i) A♠, A♦, Q♦, 8♥	A♥, J♠, 7♠, 6♠, 4♠

Tex thought he had a lock flush with his spade Ace, but of course he had no flush at all, since he had to use two cards from his hand. His trip Aces were his best hand, but were outranked both by someone holding an 8, 5, for a straight, and by someone else holding the K♠, 3♠, for a flush. He needed a pair in the widow after the third spade made a flush likely; with it he would have had the highest full house.

| (ii) A♠, K♦, Q♥, J♣ | A♣, K♦, 10♠, 10♥, 10♣ |

Tex thought he couldn't lose after the flop gave him the nut straight and the high two pair, but his hand was counterfeited when the second 10 appeared on the turn. Then the third 10 came and he worried about someone holding the fourth 10; but when everyone checked to him, he felt he was home free and bet. At the showdown he found he had lost to a player holding a pair of 7's! Because he had to use two cards from his holding, the best Tex could do was to use his Q, J, to make a straight, while his opponent put together a full house.

(*iii*) A♣, K♠, K♣, 10♣   Q♦, J♣, 7♣, 6♥, 8♠

Tex's powerful holding, which looked so promising both before *and after* the flop, was destroyed
by the last two widow cards: the best hand he
could make was a pair of Kings. This sort of thing
happens often in Omaha, but the disaster for Tex
was that he still thought he had a lock hand at the
end, and kept raising and reraising in a pot-limit
game. But both his imaginary flush and straight
required three cards from his holding.

(*iv*) J♦, 9♦, 9♠, 4♠   8♣, 7♠, 6♥, 5♥, 4♦

Tex stayed for the turn and river cards, hoping for
a 10 to give him a lock straight. When it didn't
come, but a straight showed on the board, he figured his holding was as good as anyone else's, so
he called the final bet. But all he had was a pair of
9's, and he lost to a player who held an 8, 6, and
thus had a straight.

While there is much experience that a Holdem player can
bring to the game of Omaha, he must start by completely
rethinking the power of his holdings.

STRATEGY BEFORE THE FLOP

What to Expect in the Widow

The composition of the widow, as discussed in Chapter 15,
is determined by the probability distribution of five cards
taken from a fifty-two-card deck. As mentioned above, after
the full widow has been exposed,

50 percent of the time it will contain at least one pair

80 percent of the time it will contain three or more cards to a straight

40 percent of the time it will contain three or more cards to a flush.

The significance of these probabilities is wholly different than in Holdem. This is shown in Table 16.1, which compares the best possible hand, given the widow, with the hand that will prove to be a winner in a seven-man game if everyone stays to the showdown. It addresses the question of how the *actual* winning hand relates to the best possible hand. Though a bit difficult to understand at first glance, the table is explained in the three paragraphs that follow.

Look first at the bottom ("Total") row of this table; it shows the probability distribution of the widow. When the entire widow has been exposed, 50 percent of the time it will contain at least one pair, and thus a full house is possible. Twenty percent of the time there is no pair, but there are at least three suited cards, indicating that a flush is the best possible hand. Twenty-eight percent of the time there is neither a pair nor three cards to a flush, but a straight is possible. And in the remaining 2 percent of all widows, there are none of the previous possibilities, and the best possible hand is trips.

The right-hand ("Total") column shows not what is possible but what actually occurs.[3] Thirty-four percent of all seven-person deals produce at least one full house. In a quarter of all hands the best hand is actually a flush, and for another quarter it is a straight. In the remaining 16 percent of hands the best hand is trips or less. This column explains why the Holdem player's experience can be so misleading,

---

3. To see why it differs from the bottom row, notice that while a pair in the widow makes a full house possible, that result requires the right matching cards in one of the players' holdings.

Table 16.1   Theoretical Best and Actual Winning Hands in a Seven-Person Omaha Showdown

(Numbers are percentage of all hands)

| | BEST POSSIBLE HAND | | | | |
	Full House or better*	Flush*	Straight	Trips	Total
Full House or better*	**34**				34
Flush*					
• two highest flushes	3	**10**			13
• other flushes	4	8			12
Straight					
• highest straight	2	1	**12**		15
• lower straights	1	1	8		10
Trips	4		5	1	10
Less than trips	2		3	1	6
Total	50	20	28	2	100

(left margin: BEST OF SEVEN HANDS)

*Four of a kind and straight flushes are so infrequent that I disregard them in this chapter.

since in Holdem, hands of trips or less are the usual winners, not the 1-in-6 long shot that they become in Omaha.

The interior portion of Table 16.1 adds some highly relevant detail. Look down the first column: when a pair is present in the widow, and thus a full house is possible, two thirds of the time (34 out of 50) a full house *will be* present. The significance of this for play is clear: if a pair shows in the widow, even the nut straight or flush is an underdog. When three or more cards to a flush are present, the odds of someone holding two cards in the same suit are very high—18 out of 20, or 90 percent. And in about half of these cases the winning flush is either the highest possible or second-highest one. This warns against relying on suited cards in your holding if they are not headed by an Ace, King, or Queen. Where a straight is possible, a straight is usually present—20 out of 28, or 71 percent—although not as regularly as a flush. In more than half of the cases where a straight is the winner, it is the highest straight, often among several that are possible. Look, finally, at the three boldface numbers arrayed diagonally in the table: more than half (56 percent) of the time, where a full house, flush, or straight is the best possible hand, it actually occurs in someone's hand. Anything less is thus an underdog to win.

Table 16.1 emphasizes the key feature of Omaha strategy. **It is essential to strive for the best hand made possible by the widow cards, because the chances are good that if you don't make it, someone else will.**

Since not all holdings in Omaha will survive to the showdown, the percentages in this table are merely important clues to sensible behavior, but the clues are significant. Here are three of them:

1. Whenever there is a pair in the widow, one or more full houses is very likely to be present, particularly if the pair shows on the flop.   Indeed, the possibility of two or more full houses is great enough that lower full houses are in danger of being second-best.

2. A three-card flush in the widow makes a flush likely.   Here it is well to distinguish between "front-door" situations, in which the flop contains two or three cards of the same suit, and that in which the flush comes via the back door—that is, when, with only one card in the suit on the flop, the fourth and fifth widow cards each match it. In the front-door case, it is likely that a player will have retained a holding with two cards in the suit if headed by an Ace, King, or Queen, and will either have the high flush or be drawing for it. In the backdoor case, it is unlikely to have been attractive to keep a holding on the chance of getting a flush unless the holding had other possibilities as well. Even two low cards in the suit may prove to be the backdoor winner if the river produces the third card to the flush.

3. A three-card straight means that the right two-card holding will complete the straight. In seven-man Omaha, forty-two different couples are created by the deal. With forty-two different two-card combinations among the holdings, completing any straight that the widow makes possible is likely, particularly if it looked promising on the flop.

The number of players who see the flop greatly affects the likely winning hand. The greater the number of players, the more couples are available to fit into a given widow, and thus the more often the winning hand will be the best possible hand. The fact that many players typically do see the flop in Omaha means that the best, or near-best, possible hands are likely to be realized.

Elements of Strong Holdings

Strong holdings are those that have multiple chances to lead to a winning full house, flush, or straight. The larger the number and strength of the couples that are present in a holding, and the more they complement one another, the better the holding before the flop. Even relatively unpromising couples can provide important alternative winning combinations (outs) if the primary apparent strength of a holding does not lead to a winner. For example, holding a suited J, 4, along with a pair of Aces, gives long-shot possibilities of a high straight, a low straight, and a Jack-high flush that provide outs in case the pair of Aces does not become part of a winning combination.

The elements of a holding that lead to particular types of winning hands are easily defined. A holding that can potentially become a winner of several different kinds is especially valuable.

Holdings for a potential full house.   Suppose the widow shows **A, 10, 10, 6, 4.** Any of six couples in someone's holding will make a full house: A, A; A, 10; 10, 6; 10, 4; 6, 6; and 4, 4. (They are listed in order of merit.) The first is the nut full house, but the second is pretty safe, and the third, while marginal, may well prove the winner. The last three (the lowest 10-high full house and the two full houses formed by the underpairs) are dangerous holdings, likely to be second-best if anyone else is showing strength. This example suggests why high pairs are valuable if they match a high card in the widow: they can lead to a high full house (Aces-full in the example) if the widow shows a small pair. If you match a board pair (say, with a 10, as in the example), you must worry about a player holding the other 10. You will be more comfortable if your other card is high (an Ace here) than if it is low (either a 6 or a 4 here). This shows why high cards are valuable if one of the player's lower cards matches a board pair. (About half of the full houses that win are made by holding a pair, and the other half by matching a widow pair and another widow card.) **Low pairs are not valueless, but they are vulnerable.**

Holding trips is not good news. A third King in your holding, say, adds no strength to the other two (since you cannot use three cards from your holding), but it cuts in half the chance that the widow will have a King. And being dealt quads is even more of a disaster, since then your Kings have no chance of being matched in the widow.[4]

---

4. Quad deuces is considered the worst possible holding, but quad Aces is not much better. For it to make anything better than two pair (usually not good enough to win in Omaha) requires trips in the widow, and then it is vulnerable to someone holding the fourth card to the widow's trips.

Holdings for a winning flush.   Having a suited A, X, before the flop is always promising, because if a flush becomes possible in your suit, you will be drawing for a lock unless the widow has a pair. The holding of K, X, suited, is almost as good, but a King-high flush can, and sometimes does, get beaten by an Ace-high in someone else's hand. A holding of Q, X, suited, is a frequent winner but also a frequent loser, because it is vulnerable unless the flop shows both an Ace and a King in the suit. Third-best flushes are bested so often in Omaha that before playing one you must be attentive to the betting and be prepared to give up if another player is betting strongly.

Suited cards can also have their value reduced by redundancy. Holding the A, 9, of hearts, your hand is poorer if either or both of your other two cards is a heart, since the redundant ones in your hand decrease the chance that the widow will end up with three or more hearts.

Low suited couples are of some value because they may come in by the back door, but they are virtually worthless if the flop shows two or three in the suit. When this happens, players holding a potential high flush will stay in and the holder of a potential low flush is likely to be drawing dead. Double-suited low holdings, however, such as 8♠, 6♦, 5♠, 4♦, provide a nice plus factor to straight or full-house possibilities and win a number of hands with backdoor flushes.

Holdings for a potential straight.   Here the multiway holding is the key. A sequence of four touching cards makes each of six couples a potential fit to a board straight, and four cards with a gap, such as Q, 10, 9, 8, are almost as good. Three touching cards with a stranger, for example A, 9, 8, 7, have only three couples to fit into a straight—half as many. Even one couple of touching or near-touching cards has some value if the holding has other promising possibilities. That value is much greater for the higher couples, such as Q, J, or Q, 10, than for low ones such as 7, 6, or 7, 5, because high straights are more likely to be winners and avoid second-best.

Starting Holdings

Experience is the best teacher of how to pull these elements together to form a sensible strategy for when to see the flop in Omaha.[5] In time you'll get a feeling for which holdings will prove to be winners significantly more often than 14.3 percent of the time—the average winning percentage in a seven-handed game—and, at least as important, which holdings will prove to be winners substantially *less* than average. But no holdings are so good that they win more than 25 percent of the time in Omaha, and few are so poor that they win less than 8 percent of the time if held to the showdown. (This brings us back to an important difference between Omaha and Holdem: the advantage of holding even the best starting hand is substantially less in Omaha.)

It is not necessary to be able to rank all holdings in order, but only to be able to set threshold standards for Premium, Good, Fair, and Poor holdings. Figure 16.1 shows twelve holdings, arranged in decreasing order of merit, that may serve as benchmarks.

Starting strategy, of course, depends on more than your holding. As in Holdem, it needs to take into account such factors as position, the size of the bets and raises, and the betting patterns of the game, and it will be different in pot-limit and in limit poker. But it is not as sensitive to those factors as it is in Holdem.

When playing in restrained games, whether limit or pot-limit, where there is relatively light betting before the flop, you can afford to play both Good and Fair holdings; in-

5. I, as well as others, have experimented with a point count to rank starting Omaha holdings. My experience is that by the time it becomes sufficiently accurate it has become too complicated to be practical.

FIGURE 16.1

HOLDING	CLASSIFICATION	COMMENT
K♣ Q♦ J♦ 10♣	Premium	This hand not only has most of the high-straight possibilities but is double-suited and has powerful high cards. Each of its six couples works.
A♠ A♥ K♠ K♥	Premium	Another powerhouse with two top flush draws and two high pairs.
A♥ K♣ Q♦ 8♣	Good	The straight cards combine with the high clubs to make this a strong hand.
A♥ Q♦ Q♣ 8♦	Good	Three different working couples make this an above-average winner. But it is weaker than the previous holding because of its shortage of straight opportunities.
10♥ 9♠ 8♦ 7♣	Good	Even without any flush draw, its many possible straights make this a good holding.
Q♣ 9♥ 8♣ 6♠	Fair	Five of the six couples work together, but the gaps are there, and the Queen-high flush, if it occurs, may be vulnerable.

HOLDING	CLASSIFICATION	COMMENT
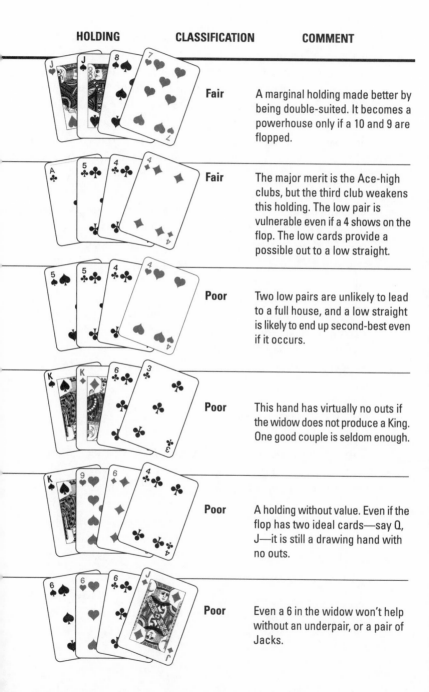 J♠ J♣ 8♠ 7♥	Fair	A marginal holding made better by being double-suited. It becomes a powerhouse only if a 10 and 9 are flopped.
A♣ 5♣ 4♣ 4♦	Fair	The major merit is the Ace-high clubs, but the third club weakens this holding. The low pair is vulnerable even if a 4 shows on the flop. The low cards provide a possible out to a low straight.
5♠ 5♣ 4♣ 4♥	Poor	Two low pairs are unlikely to lead to a full house, and a low straight is likely to end up second-best even if it occurs.
K♠ K♦ 6♣ 3♣	Poor	This hand has virtually no outs if the widow does not produce a King. One good couple is seldom enough.
K♠ 9♥ 6♦ 4♣	Poor	A holding without value. Even if the flop has two ideal cards—say Q, J—it is still a drawing hand with no outs.
6♠ 6♥ 6♣ J♦	Poor	Even a 6 in the widow won't help without an underpair, or a pair of Jacks.

deed, in late positions, when you are confident there will be no raise, playing some of the better Poor holdings may also be sensible. In early positions in all games it is well to be cautious with Fair holdings, since you do not want to have to call a raise, nor to have to fold after calling one bet.

In aggressive games, where raises are likely before the flop, or anytime there are raises in front of you, you should play only Good or Premium holdings if you are in any but the last betting position. But if you find yourself in the last position in a pot that has not been raised, you will sense weakness and may well call or bet on Fair holdings. Some players will routinely raise in this situation hoping to steal the pot there and then, or, failing that, to reduce the competition to a small enough number that their holding has more chance of winning. This is worth doing occasionally, but not as a regular strategy.

As a general rule, in virtually any game, in any position, holdings with only one or two working couples are not worth much even if the cost of seeing the flop is minimal.[6] **Good holdings offer outs, and the more the better.**

PLAY ON THE FLOP

Fitting the flop is the key to Omaha strategy. Starting strategy gets you to the flop, but not beyond. The only thing that matters then is how well your holding meshes with the widow. As soon as you see the flop you see five-sevenths of your final hand; this happens after only one round of betting, and often a light one at that. Further information and improvement is going to be much more expensive.

6. The major exception to this is a holding that has a suited A, X. It will become very promising if the flop shows two or three cards in the suit, and can be folded at once if it doesn't.

Generally, before you pay to see the flop you should try to define the cards you need, given your holding. If you are not going to be happy even if you get them, don't bother to stay in. If the best possible flop will excite you, and it occurs, wonderful. If it does not, you must ask whether you can still get the cards you need, *and* whether the flop is likely to give someone else an even better hand, even if you do eventually hit. **In Omaha the only sound flop strategy is to ask: What are my chances now of having or getting a lock?** Too often, "pretty good" is not good enough!

At the time of the flop, you must estimate what is likely to be the winning hand at the showdown, and how many chances you have to attain it. Table 16.2 gives the relevant probabilities for getting a particular hand with two widow cards to come in Omaha.

Relying on your post-flop evaluation is not difficult, but it requires discipline, for it is easy to fall in love with Premium or Good starting hands that may become mediocre or worse after the flop. The second of the sample holdings illustrated on page 346—a double-suited holding of pairs of Aces and Kings—was a powerhouse, but when the flop showed a **10, 9, 7,** of three different suits, rather than the high cards that the holding required, it became worthless. Meanwhile the holding J, J, 8, 7, retained in large part because it was double-suited, became a very promising hand with the same flop.

Looking for a Full House

If you are holding a pair, or high cards, the most secure flop is one that gives you the highest possible full house. For ex-

Table 16.2 Getting One Card out of 45 in Two Tries[7]

A. Getting Hurt with a Leading Hand

Number of Cards That Will Beat You	Probability	Odds
5 or fewer	.21 or less	3.7 to 1 or better *in your favor*
8	.33	2 to 1 *in your favor*
13	.50	1 to 1
19 or more	.67 or more	2 to 1 or worse *against you*

This table shows, for example, that if any of eight cards will ruin a leading hand at Omaha after the flop, the odds *against being ruined* are 2 to 1.

B. Getting Helped with a Drawing Hand

Number of Cards That Will Make Your Hand	Probability	Odds
5 or fewer	.21 or less	3.7 to 1 or worse *against you*
6	.25	3 to 1 *against you*
7	.29	2.5 to 1 *against you*
8	.33	2 to 1 *against you*
10	.40	1.5 to 1 *against you*
13	.50	1 to 1
19 or more	.67 or more	2 to 1 or better *in your favor*

This table shows, for example, that if any of eight cards will help a drawing hand in Omaha after the flop, the odds *against being helped* are 2 to 1.

7. This is very similar to Table 15.4 (p. 319). It differs slightly because in Omaha there are forty-five unseen cards after the flop, not forty-seven as in Holdem. This difference increases slightly the chance of getting any unseen card, but for practical purposes you can use either table in either game.

ample, suppose you hold K♥, K♠, 8♥, 7♣. While straights or a heart flush are possible outs with your holding, you should hope to see **K, 7, 7**, on the flop.[8]

What about the situations in which the flop merely gives you a credible draw for a full house? Many flops do this, but not all are worth drawing to. Here are three common situations where you may well be advised to fold, and the relevant odds.

1. You hold trips on the flop but have no outs. Suppose you hold K, K, 8, 7, and the flop shows **K, Q, J**. This flop gives you high trips, but it also makes a straight in someone else's hand likely. Your high trips will become a winner only if one of the next two widow cards pairs one of the existing flop cards (any of seven cards) or if the last two cards are a running pair. Together this is a 36-percent chance. Not bad, because if you hit you'll have a lock, but it is still an underdog. It's probably an easy call in limit poker but a tough one in a pot-limit game against one player who bets the pot.[9]

2. You hold K♠, 10♣, 9♣, 7♣, and the flop is K♦, 10♦, 9♥. Having the three high pairs looks promising, but both a straight and a draw for a flush are realistic hold-

---

8. This is better than the flop of two Kings because it is likely to be called by players holding either a 7 or a pair higher than 7's. Any pair on the flop along with a King will give you a full house. A pair of 5's, say, is not quite as safe as 8's or 7's, because there is some danger of quad 5's. And 7's are better than 8's here because someone else holding a pair of 8's may stay with you after the 7's appear, but the reverse would not be true. The pair you need to worry about is Aces, which would threaten your Kings-full with Aces-full.

9. It's tough because often you'll have to see two bets to get your full chance to hit, and the player with a straight is not likely to let you off cheaply. Against two or more callers, the pot odds may well make it worthwhile to try for the full house. Many risk-averse players, however, choose the more conservative strategy of giving the hand up rather than facing the prospect of two big bets against them. Big losses, even with slightly positive expected value, are what they seek to avoid.

ings for your opponents, so your only realistic hope is a full house. To turn your two pair (almost surely not good enough to win) into a full house requires you to hit one of only six cards that will pair the board, or to get a pair of 7's. There is less than a 25-percent probability of doing so in two draws, and the implied pot odds are often not that good, especially since you may need two draws to get there.

3. The flop is 10, 10, 9, and you hold A, 10, 4, 3. Duke bets and you suspect he holds either a 10, 9, or a pair of 9's. You will almost surely win if the widow adds the fourth 10 or an Ace, but those cards add up to only a 17-percent chance even if Duke doesn't have a 10. You have some chance if the widow shows another 4 or 3 or produces a running pair, but you may well end up second-best with those hands. Altogether your chances of getting any full house are less than even money.

In sum, while winning full houses are nice when they occur, the holdings that make a full house likely (high pairs and high cards) are underdogs to win the pot unless you make the full house on the flop, or unless your holding also has cards that could lead to winning straights or flushes.

A full house is almost never worth drawing to unless it promises to be the nut full house if you hit. This means that if the board flops a pair, it is never worth drawing to an underpair. If you hold an underpair and have already made a full house, it may be worth a probe bet to see if it can win, but many good Omaha players throw such hands away on the ground that they lose more money by ending up second-best than they win by being the only full house. If the flop was **10, 10, 9,** the only underpair worth anything is a pair of 9's, and that is vulnerable not only at once (if someone holds a 10, 9) but with each subsequent card. For example, if the next two widow cards are **6** and **Q,** you will be beaten by anyone holding 10, 6; Q, 10; or Q, Q.

If you have two callers, one of those three holdings is likely. Since the callers stayed in despite the pair in the widow on the flop, they have to be drawing for at least a 10-high full house.

In Omaha, more money is lost by pretty good players drawing for full houses *after* seeing the flop than in any other way. While a third of all Omaha hands are won by full houses, nearly half of those are made on the flop. It is the other half that are expensive when they fail and not enormously profitable when they hit. This is because as soon as the widow pairs, you are unlikely to get calls on your bets by those with, or seeking, straights and flushes. Thus the actual payoff to hitting a full house is often modest compared to the cost of drawing for it.

Looking for a Flush

Holding, say, the Ace and 5 of hearts you hope for two or three hearts—and no pair—on the flop. (You are more likely to win if three are flopped, but you will not get as many callers as you will if only two are.) If three hearts are flopped, the only people who will draw against you must be looking for a full house, and any pair on the board will counterfeit you. You may want to bet the maximum to discourage anyone drawing. The odds are about 2 to 1 against the widow producing the pair your opponents need, so if two or more opponents stay in despite your flush possibility, your expected winnings will be ample compensation for the times your flush doesn't stand up. Be wary, however, if you hold a flush that is not the highest possible flush. A conservative player like Ty, who merely calls your bets on the flop and the turn, may well have the nut flush and be waiting for the river card to make sure no full house is possible before he raises you.

If you've got an Ace-high four flush on the flop, you should usually stay in, even if your holding has no outs. In an unraised pot, the pot odds will typically favor you, though with heavy betting and raising, they may not. Your chances of hitting a third flush card in the widow and also not having the widow catch a pair are about 33 percent.[10]

Draws to anything less than the two best possible flushes are recommended only if you have significant outs. Suppose you hold Q♦, 7♦, 6♥, 9♣, and the flop shows 9♦, 5♦, 4♣. Either a 3 or an 8 can give you the nut straight, and the eight possible cards that do so provide important outs to go with your flush draw.[11]

With only one card in your suit showing on the flop, flush holdings are never worth pursuing if they are your only avenue for winning, but they may be useful backdoor cards if you also have a legitimate draw for a straight or full house. With a double-suited holding, each suit of which is matched by one of the cards in the flop, the backdoor chances of making a flush are about 1 in 9, a small but not negligible plus factor.

Looking for a Straight

When the flop shows neither a pair nor any two cards in the same suit, the hand is about even money to be won by a straight if all hands are held to the showdown. Since many holdings with pairs and suited couples will be folded when they receive no encouragement from the flop, the chance of a straight ending up as the winner increases to about two out of three. But not all straight draws are equally attractive. Suppose the flop is 10♠, 9♥, 5♣. Here are four alternative

---

10. If you hold three hearts instead of two, they fall to under 30 percent, and if you hold four, to less than 25 percent.

11. Indeed, you would prefer one of those cards, if it comes, *not* to be a diamond. If another diamond does show, and one of your opponents then becomes an aggressive bettor, he is a good bet to hold an Ace- or King-high flush.

holdings, each of which has an apparently promising draw for a straight:

(*i*) Q, J, 8, 7
(*ii*) K, Q, J, 5
(*iii*) Q, J, 4, 2
(*iv*) J, 8, 4, 4

Any one of these can make a straight for you; indeed, any one can end up as the nut straight. From your point of view with one of these holdings there are 45 cards you do not see. How many of them can make a straight for you? The answer is 20 for the first holding; 13 for the second; 11 for the third; and just 8 for the fourth.[12] With two chances to hit, the first holding (a "twenty-way" draw) is a 2-to-1 favorite to hit, while the fourth holding is a 2-to-1 underdog. Given the further chances that an opponent may get either a flush or a full house by the back door, it is not often that drawing to an eight-way (or less) straight is attractive. This emphasizes why, in valuing hands, having three or four cards in a string and working together is so much more valuable than having only two.

Of course, merely making a straight is not enough, since there is frequently more than one straight present. Indeed, even making the nut straight on the flop may not be good enough. Suppose the flop is 5♥, 4♥, 3♠, and you hold A♣, 7♣, 6♦, 3♦. You presently have the nut straight and may think you did well on the flop, but your hand is likely to be beaten if any heart, or any 3, 4, 5, 6, or 7, appears in either of the two remaining widow cards. Thus, twenty of the un-

---

12. For the first holding (*i*), any King, Queen, Jack, 8, 7, or 6 will produce a straight. For the fourth holding, only a Queen or a 7 will do so. The other two cases are intermediate. And of course there are even weaker holdings: the holding of A, K, J, 9, gives only a four-way draw for a straight (requiring a Queen).

seen cards can counterfeit your present nut straight, and the odds are 2-to-1 that this will occur.[13]

ON THE TURN

After the fourth widow card has been exposed, Omaha becomes a simple game analytically, but it does require discipline and a sense of reality. It is simple because you have seen 8 cards, and should be able to count how many of the unseen 44 will give you or keep you the winner. If the number is 22, you are even money to win. If it is 11, you are a 3-to-1 underdog. If it is 8 or less, you should probably fold at the first bet. But in making this calculation you will benefit greatly if you can put your opponents on their probable hands. While I have said that in Omaha it is wise to assume the worst about your opponents' hands, such caution may be unwarranted if their earlier betting has clearly indicated a different holding. And fortunately this is often the case.

Given your chances, it is necessary to compare them to the pot odds facing you. There are two rounds of betting to anticipate, the second of them after you know whether you have made your hand. In figuring the implied pot odds, remember to consider whether, if you get one of your good cards, your opponents will call your subsequent bets; and, further, if you get one of your bad cards, whether you will feel obliged to call if someone else bets. These implied pot odds should guide your decision.

The biggest difference between betting in pot-limit and in limit Omaha occurs on the turn. In limit Omaha a player

---

13. At this point you may wonder why you called the flop with your holding. The answer is that the Ace-high flush possibility in clubs was a big part of the incentive. When it was washed out, the hand had no outs, and should probably have been folded if anyone had shown strength. For some psychological reason, players find it very hard to fold hands that are currently the best, no matter how poor their long-run chances may be. So they call, lose, and grumble.

can rarely bet enough at this stage to cause someone with a pretty good drawing hand to drop, so maximum bets tend to be made by the hand that currently is leading only if the player feels that he is unlikely to be ruined on the river. Thus the turn bet is not likely to be raised. And when it isn't, you can usually afford to draw for a lock hand.

In pot-limit Omaha, by contrast, the biggest bets are likely to be made on the turn by the apparently leading hand, either as a bluff or to discourage drawing hands by worsening their pot odds.[14] It is thus likely to be expensive to pursue a draw for even the lock full house or flush, and many good players who have stayed after the flop on drawing prospects now give up their hands rather than meet a maximum bet on the turn. When facing such a bet, it is essential to try to decipher the motive behind it. Here experience and skill play a large role.

ON THE RIVER

There is little more that needs to be said: after all the cards have been dealt, the considerations in Omaha are the same as those at the same stage in Holdem. The decision is likely to be easier if you remember that in Omaha, as distinct from Holdem, after the full widow is shown you can not only define the lock hand but usually assume that someone has it. If that someone is not you, do not be lured into calling modest bets simply because they seem cheap relative to the size of the pot. (Hugh's frequent advice is "Be wary of bargains," and this is especially sound in Omaha after all the cards have been dealt.)

The size of the bets on the last round, and the decision to call them, has much more to do with psychology than with

14. In limit poker it takes at least two, a bettor and a raiser, to make drawing expensive. In pot-limit it takes only one.

probability. Is the big bet being made by someone who wants me to think he has a lock or by someone who has it and wants me to think that he is bluffing? The best clue to unraveling all of this is to try to remember what the bettor did much earlier in the hand. Did he raise or merely call before the flop? In what position? Was it the flop, the turn, or the river that seemed to turn him on? Was it credible for him to have called both before and after the flop with what he now seems to be implying he holds? What does he think about how I play in these situations?

Remember, too, in doing all of this that you want to balance your calling errors and your folding errors—not keeping their number equal, but keeping the dollar consequences equal. Keep in mind also that you know something about how a particular opponent plays. Use this knowledge. You cannot play mechanically at the showdown and come out a winner in the long run.

FIVE PROBLEMS

1. This is $10 limit Omaha. You've made a straight on the flop, as the illustration shows.

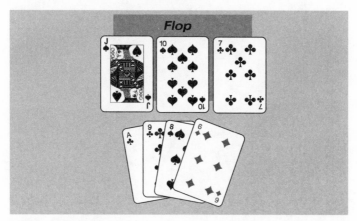

After two checks you bet, and are raised $10 by Harry. Two other players call, and it is up to you. What should you do?

2. Before the flop in this hand, you bet and were raised by Ty. When you reraised, it became a two-man game.

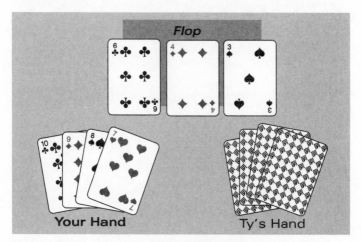

After the flop, it is your bet. What is your strategy now?

3. Your are sitting in next-to-last position with a very strong holding, but you didn't raise the opening bet before the flop in order not to reveal your strength. Four players saw the flop.

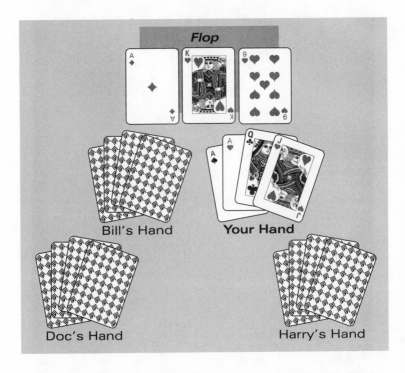

Doc bets, Bill raises, and it is up to you, with Harry behind you. What should you do now?

4. You are playing pot-limit Omaha, and by the turn, only you and Doc are left. Doc raised you on the flop.

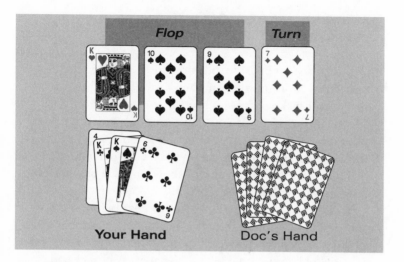

Your Hand Doc's Hand

You now check to Doc, who bets the pot. Should you call or fold?

5. It's pot-limit, and after the whole widow is exposed, there is only one other player, Hugh, whom you respect a lot.

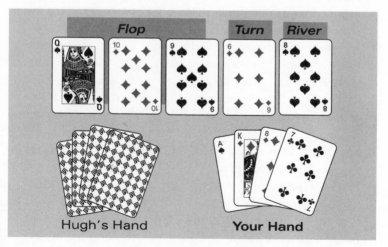

Hugh's Hand **Your Hand**

Hugh raised on the flop, bet heavily on the turn, but checks to you now. What do you do?

ANSWERS TO THE PROBLEMS
(AS I SEE THEM)

1. Your straight is an odds-on loser and you have no outs. You can't improve, but any card 7 or higher, or any spade, will make possible a hand that can beat you. That's 31 out of the 45 cards you don't know about! With three other players in the game, someone is looking for each of those cards, and there is better than a 90-percent chance that one or more of them will show up. You should fold now, no matter how cheap it seems.

2. Ty must have high cards for his raise before the flop, and probably also a flush draw. When neither of these possibilities were helped by the flop, he became a candidate for an early fold. You should bet or raise at every chance and expect him to fold. While the flop didn't help you either, Ty doesn't know this. Of course if he turns around and raises, you'll have to reconsider.

3. Continue to slow-play your hand and call but don't raise. You have a magnificent leading hand with your high trips and have draws for both the nut heart flush and the nut straight. Of the 45 unseen cards, 18 will give you a lock, and there are other ways to win as well. You want to keep as many of your opponents in the hand as possible. If you raise now, Harry will surely fold—what can he have that would lead him to call two raises?—and Doc may too. One or both of them may anyway, but Bill bluffs so often that at least one is likely to stay. After one more card, your opponents will probably stay in till the end. Thus you can bet or raise very aggressively at that point. Of course, your hand can be beaten if both of the next two cards are diamonds or if they make a low straight the best possible hand, but those are low-probability outcomes, and if you are afraid of them you ought not to be playing poker. Play this hand for the big win, and if you don't get it, at least you'll have a good story to tell.

4. You should take another look. Everything depends on the suit of that black 4. You can be sure Doc had a straight on the flop. If your 4 is a club, only 10 of the 44 cards you don't see will give you a winner; you need a pair on the board. This is not a good enough chance to call, since if you do get the pair on the board, your next-round bet will not be called. You should fold.

But if that 4 is a spade, your King-high flush draw is also alive, and you have 18 cards that can let you beat Doc's straight. The pot odds are in your favor unless you think Doc may hold an Ace-high spade draw. I'd call, hope for the Ace of spades on the river, but play as if I had the winner with any flush or full house.

5. Your key card is the Ace of spades. Hugh surely has a higher straight than yours. You know Hugh can't have the nut flush, and he is plainly worried by the fact that a third spade came on the last card. Take advantage of your knowledge and his fears. Bet the pot. He'll fold unless you are a notorious bluffer—or unless he has the straight flush. If he doesn't fold, tell yourself that the good news is that next time he'll call you when you do have a lock.

V

SOME CAUTIONARY NOTES

17

♠ ♣ ♥ ♦

CHEATING

An insight commonly attributed to Tex Sheahan is that
among poker players, professionals overemphasize skill and
amateurs overemphasize luck. Cardsharps add a third dimension. While you hope and expect that skill and luck are
the sole determinants of who wins and who loses in your
Thursday-night game, it is well to be aware that this is not
true of all poker games. As my father-in-law used to say (or
was it W. C. Fields?), trust all men, but cut the cards.

As the ad quoted above suggests, dishonesty is not merely
a phenomenon of the lurid past of poker but a clear and
present danger. Cheating can occur at several levels. There
is the dishonest game, whether arranged in a hotel room or
in a crooked casino. There is the crooked player, either professional or clumsy amateur, who enters an otherwise hon-

est game, sometimes with an accomplice, and can resort to either sophisticated or simple acts that give him an unfair edge over other players. Finally, there is a variety of relatively petty acts of dishonesty that tempt some otherwise honest people to take advantage of an opportunity that presents itself.

CROOKED GAMES

Listen to Vincent Teresa describe a mob-run poker game:

> We'd start a card game and ignore the sucker as though he wasn't there. Everyone in the game was a mob guy, a mechanic, a thief, a swindler . . . what have you. We'd all be betting and winning and losing money like there was no tomorrow. Pretty soon the sucker would want to get into the game. Before the night was out, he'd be cleaned out and never know he was in a rigged game. . . .
>
> When we had a sucker to clean in a game, Yonkers Joe would set up two duplicate sets of cards. One set was stacked and kept by Joe. We'd let the sucker shuffle the other deck. Then Joe would cut the shuffle. While the sucker was watching him, Joe would switch the decks, replacing the sucker-shuffled deck with the stacked deck.[1]

In earlier days, the expression "honest casino" was an oxymoron. Payoffs to the authorities and to the mob, as well as to the parties involved, were all financed in part by various forms of cheating. The skills of crooked dealers,

1. Vincent Teresa, with Thomas C. Renner, *My Life in the Mafia,* pp. 218, 223.

called *mechanics*, became highly valued, particularly in blackjack but also in poker. With the spread of legalized gambling and its profitable regulation, this seems to have changed. Today, in reputable casinos in places like Las Vegas, Atlantic City, and California, blatant dishonesty *on the part of the house,* such as using crooked dealers, marked cards, and stacked decks, is virtually unthinkable. The casino has many incentives to police its own operations. The same may not be true in small-town games, on riverboats, or on poker cruises. It matters a lot whether the casino is counting on a regular, returning clientele or on a transient population that it is efficient to fleece quickly and surely.

Your best defense against this is to avoid such games if in any doubt. Play with strangers always involves risk, and if the play is for high stakes, or even for moderate table stakes, be warned that there is a real chance that something is going to happen to leave you the loser. Be particularly wary if you are winning in such a game and someone suggests raising the stakes. All the videos in the world will not protect you from the professional crooks who choose card games as their medium. If you are going to play poker with strangers, do so in a casino that you are confident is run honestly and is content with the profits that can be made without resorting to dishonest devices and dealers. Or do so for stakes that are sufficiently modest that they are unlikely to provide much temptation to the professional cardsharp, and which, in any case, cannot hurt you much even if you are victimized.

CROOKED PLAYER(S) IN AN HONEST GAME

Most country-club games that I have played in have had at least an occasional episode of someone entering the game and eventually being caught systematically cheating in one of a variety of ways. There is less of a threat in a home game, since the number and turnover of players is usually much smaller and the participants are more likely to be connected by ties of employment or friendship. But if the stakes are large enough, the temptation is there, and it happens sometimes. If the cheater is relatively subtle, he will not cheat so often or so blatantly that it becomes obvious that his edge is an unfair one. I have little doubt that some players cheat for years without being suspected. It is not necessary for a player of average skills to improve the odds in his favor very much to become a consistent winner. Most crooked players get caught eventually, however, because they become impatient with only a small edge or they simply become greedy.[2]

Some awareness of the methods of cheating at cards can be of help.[3] Here are four types of deliberate and systematic dishonest behavior, which can be used singly or in combination: having illegal knowledge of the identity of supposedly hidden cards in a random deal; controlling and manipulating the cards that are dealt or played; engaging in collusion that can affect the betting in such a way as to give an advantage to the colluders; and playing with chips that were not purchased at face value.

1. Illegal Knowledge

There is a great variety of ways to mark some of the key cards in the deck and thus to have the critically important ability to know when to bet and when to fold. Marking is of

2. The same appears to be so with white-collar criminals generally. Their early success at minor embezzling gives them a level of confidence (or perhaps arrogance) that leads them to levels of criminal activity or lifestyle that become too large to ignore.

3. A good brief introduction may be found in A. D. Livingston, *Advanced Poker: Strategy and Smart Winning Play*, pp. 76–88. His sources include John Scarne, *Scarne on Cards* (New York: Crown Publishers, 1965); Frank Garcia, *Marked Cards and Loaded Dice* (New York: Bramhall House, 1962); Floyd Moss, *Card Cheats—How They Operate* (New York: William Frederick Press, 1950).

two general types. One is in the prepared deck in which the backs or sides of cards are doctored to reveal their face identities to anyone who knows the code. Cards can be marked with ink, with indentations, and by shaved edges, among other ways. They can even be bleached in the sun. Many so-called magic stores sell doctored decks, and provide them in sealed packages that appear to provide assurance that the deck is honest. Avoiding off-brand types of cards is a defense against this, as is the privilege of any player at a table to request a new deck at any time if he is prepared to pay for it. A second form of marking is the sort that is done at the table by a player who marks key cards during the course of play using his fingernails, or a pin concealed in a ring or bandage, or a hidden source of ink. Indeed, merely bowing certain cards may be sufficient to make them stand out from the rest.

The use of systematic knowledge of the identity of hidden cards can be decisive in games such as 5-card stud, where knowledge of the hole card tells the cheat everything. It is also an enormous advantage in widow games such as Holdem or Omaha when the nature of a yet-to-be-exposed card (on the turn or the river) can be known in advance.

Knowing the next card to be dealt before the current round of betting is finished would be highly advantageous. Since the easiest card to identify by the back is the one on top of the deck, it is a useful precaution to have the dealer always *bury* (or *burn*) the top card on the deck just before dealing each round of cards. This is routinely done in casinos, and it is good practice in all games. If it is done routinely it will occasion no alarm or implication of dishonesty, but it is an important tool against anyone seeking to use marked cards, and indeed may be a disincentive to try.

A second method of acquiring illegal knowledge is to use a *shiner*, some sort of mirrorlike device that enables a dealer to read the cards as they come off the deck. Such a device can be on the table, or on the dealer's person, perhaps on a ring or the underside of a long fingernail. Combined with a good memory, a shiner eliminates doubt about what is in opponents' hidden cards.

2. Controlling the Cards

Introducing a stacked deck (as described a few pages earlier by Vincent Teresa) is only the most blatant form of controlling hands. Perhaps the simplest is to arrange cards as they are picked up from the previous deal and put them on top of the deck. Then, using a fake shuffle and a false cut (or a *crimp cut,* which occurs at the point the cheater wishes), the cards are dealt in the intended order. This can most easily be prevented by having the cards gathered and shuffled by someone who is not the next dealer, and then cut by a third party.

A second method of controlling cards, reputedly commonplace, is used in conjunction with marked cards. It is called *dealing seconds* and involves saving the top card for an appropriate time or person. Here is a description:

> [A second-card dealer] holds the deck firmly in his left hand. In a normal deal, he pushes out the top card with his left thumb and takes it with his right hand for the serve. When he chooses to deal the second card, he still pushes out the top card with his left thumb; but his thumb then retracts the top card while his right hand takes the second card.[4]

This is not difficult to do well, and gives the dealer enormous power over the hands. It can be used only when the crook is himself the dealer. Direct detection of this kind of mechanic may be difficult, but one clue is to watch the thumb: if the person is dealing seconds, his thumb stays on

---

4. Livingston, *Advanced Poker,* p. 77.

the top card during the deal instead of coming off as each card is dealt. If you have good ears you may also hear the difference caused by the extra friction involved in pulling out the second card. But the main means of detection is indirect: you should always be suspicious if a player seems to win a highly disproportionate share of the hands on his own deal.[5]

Finally, there are methods for a cheating player to introduce an undealt card into his hands. These vary from the use of mechanical devices to deliver and withdraw a card up the sleeve, to the introduction of a fifty-third card from a deck of the same pattern as the one in use. Relying on standard brands of playing cards, such as Bicycle or Bee, while desirable for reasons of avoiding a premarked deck, may make it easy for a cheat to have extra cards on his person that match the deck in use.

Here is an example I witnessed that occurred in a game at the Mirage, in Las Vegas, which uses the same kind of card, in two different colors, at each of its tables. While decks are checked when they are introduced into play, they are not when they are removed. A player can extract a card on one deal (or at one table), hold it in reserve, and reintroduce it later to his advantage. In this particular Holdem deal, a player who held the Ace of spades would have a lock, an Ace-high flush. Two players in the final betting round kept raising each other the fixed limit until one was out of chips—after thirty-eight consecutive $20 raises! (Under the house rules there was no limit on the number of raises permitted once there were only two players contesting.) On the showdown, they each had an Ace of spades! Since the deck, which had been introduced about ten hands previously, was openly checked at that time to reveal only the standard fifty-two cards, what had happened? The logical

---

5. If the dealer has an accomplice, you'll need to notice if a particular player usually wins when this man deals.

conclusion was that in an earlier hand some player (almost surely not one of the two in the contested hand) had introduced an extra Ace of spades that he had acquired from another deck with the same backing. The additional card didn't show up until two players in a showdown each had a spade Ace. (Upon reflection, people seemed to remember an individual, whom no one could identify clearly, winning a big pot with an Ace-high spade flush and shortly thereafter leaving the game.)[6]

There is no foolproof defense against such an act, but since one can ask for a new deck at any time, it is a good thing to do so immediately after someone wins a big pot and then abruptly departs. This sort of a situation is much more likely to occur in a casino or club than in a game in someone's home, where a cheating player cannot readily leave the game without having everyone remember the fact.[7]

3. Collusion

A far simpler form of cheating is collusion. It requires no external devices, only an understanding between two (or more) players, and a means of communication. It is, I believe, much more frequent than other forms of cheating among amateurs, and may be present even in relatively low-stakes poker games. It does not require one or a few big killings to pay off, but can provide the colluders with a

6. The card-room manager's resolution of the problem was to try to unravel the present pot and redistribute funds to everyone who had been in it. Perhaps not surprisingly, the claims added up to more than the pot contained. Eventually the house made up the shortfall, but even this did not satisfy everyone. A woman who had recently lost to an Ace-high spade flush demanded to be reimbursed. She was not successful and left the casino in a huff.

7. For a cheater who is content with a small advantage, all he needs to do is to remove a key card—indeed, any card—from the deck in use. Having that card subsequently found on the floor does not even direct suspicion at him. But playing with a deck that has, for example, no 10 of diamonds, changes the odds of lots of holdings.

steady advantage in the size and number of pots that they win. Moreover, it is very difficult either to detect with certainty or to prevent. Suppose Al and Ben are really playing in partnership in a limit poker game. Suppose Al has a lock and wants to make the most of his hand. He can only raise the amount of the limit unless someone reraises. If he can signal Ben to raise him, the contributions by an unlucky player—call him Colin—caught in the middle will surely rise. Or, if Colin can be expected to drop out if two others are raising each other, the partnership can get him to fold hands with which he might otherwise win. The possible methods of signaling are limitless, so this sort of collusion is virtually impossible to detect if done skillfully. The possibilities for undetected collusion are especially great in Hi-Lo games, where there are two legitimate raising hands; partners can let each other know whether their hands are competing or complementary, and then mercilessly squeeze someone in the middle.

My first experience with collusion (the first one I am aware of, that is) came in a rather clumsy scheme used by two Air Force officers who were passengers on a Navy ship. The game being played was 7-card Hi-Lo, and the colluders made bets that ended in odd numbers when they were going low, and even numbers when they were going high. If they had done no more, I doubt that I would have caught on. But they also "graded" their holdings: a bet ending in 1 or 3 was a very good low hand, one ending in 7 or 9 a weak one, and so on. I became intrigued by their bizarre bets and raises, figures like $23 or $38. By the third day of an eight-day voyage I had deciphered the code and was able to profit from it.[8]

Collusion is usually spotted indirectly rather than directly. Here are two suspicious situations: first, if the same two players seem too frequently to be part of the group of three or four in which there is a lot of final-round raising but only

8. It ended up paying for my first automobile.

one of their two hands is left at the showdown; second, if you find that the contested hands you win are typically characterized by fewer raises and reraises than the ones in which you turn out to be second-best. (This can, of course, result from the way you manage your play, but if the pattern persists you may wish to leave the table.)

There are also less blatant forms of partnership cooperation. Al, who has folded, or is planning to fold, may let Ben know what his hole cards were. Or if he is sitting next to Colin, who is careless about concealing his cards from a folded player, he may signal his partner about Colin's holding.

Collusion in any of these forms seems more likely the greater the number of players who move in and out of the game, and thus is more likely in casino and club games than in home games, but in my experience it is not unknown even there. In casino games, another possibility is a dealer colluding with a player (perhaps an off-duty dealer) sitting next to him. He may deal in such a way as to flash the cards as he deals them. The casino tries to make dealer-player collusion relatively unpromising by rotating dealers on a regular basis, often every half-hour, but this does not prevent it, especially in the late night hours when there are few tables in action and the same dealer returns frequently.

4. Running in Chips

Most poker games use chips instead of cash, a good practice for many reasons. Typically, players buy chips from the bank, and redeem them at the end of the session. Casinos take great pains to be sure their chips are not counterfeited, but casual games do not. Another of my Navy experiences alerted me to the possibilities. A more or less continuous poker game had gone on for months while we were at sea, and people often kept chips rather than turning them in to the banker (me, in this case). We played with a set of brightly colored plastic chips that someone had brought on board many months before. After a port call and then a return to sea, I began to suspect that there were more blue chips ($5 face value) in circulation than I remembered. Eventually I expressed my doubts and asked everyone to cash in. Sure enough, we discovered that there had been an inflation of the currency by an extra thirty blue chips. Someone—we never discovered who—had found identical chips ashore and was gradually introducing them into the game ("running them in").[9]

The potential problem this represents (I have not encountered it since) can readily be solved by buying individualized chips from a reputable gambling-supply store, which will keep your design on file and not sell chips so designed to anyone but you.[10] This is probably worth doing, either as an individual or by having the members of the poker group chip in to buy a set. A fine set can be acquired for less than $100 and will add a touch of elegance to the game in any case. This will not prevent someone picking up a chip at the end of one session, after it has been redeemed, and reintroducing it at the next one, but if the chips are kept in a case that just holds them, any shortage will become visible to other players.

DEALING WITH CHEATERS

All of the above is systematic cheating and requires both intent and preparation. It is, as such, rare in the Thursday-

---

9. Inflation of the currency is in the grand tradition of kings and princes (and, more recently, of irresponsible governments) who have long met their financial needs by simply creating new money and introducing it into circulation. Thereafter our shipboard game shifted from the use of chips to cash—an *ad hoc* version of a balanced-budget amendment.

10. One such is the Gamblers General Store, in Las Vegas (1-800-322-CHIP).

night poker games with which I am familiar, though it is not unknown. If it occurs, what does one do? Since intentional cheating is typically easier to suspect than to prove, it is probably unwise to make a direct and public accusation of the player. In any case, what you want is to have it cease, and also to have the perpetrator leave the game.

Either or both of these results can usually be achieved by plainly if subtly letting the person suspected know that he is being closely watched. Here is another example from my own experience. A fellow player named Earl confided to me that he suspected that a player whom I'll call Eddie, who regularly dealt 5-card stud, was dropping out of the hand before his deal, gathering the discards and arranging them on the top of the deck. With a sloppy shuffle and a crimp cut, he then dealt and had a remarkable propensity to have an Ace in the hole. He was a business colleague of Earl's, and it did not seem either wise or pleasant to confront him. After I watched and confirmed his suspicions, Earl made a point of standing up when it was Eddie's deal and saying something like, "Well, it's john time, I never can beat Eddie's Aces." By the third time this occurred, Eddie gave him a long look, and Earl looked straight back. Eddie dropped out of the game shortly thereafter. Eddie and Earl have served together in the same firm ever since without another word being said, but without confrontation.

PETTY DISHONESTY

Why do people fail to tell the waiter who has undercharged them for a meal? Why do lost wallets get returned, if at all, with the cash gone? "Human nature" is the answer usually given. Well, the same human nature is present in the people who play in poker games, and each of the following kinds of small-bore dishonesty occur often enough to be worth mentioning.

Shortchanging the Pot

Do players typically bet, call, or raise by throwing chips into the pot? If the bet is $12 and there is already $52 in the pot, can you tell if the player actually put in $12 or instead put in one $5 chip and six $1 chips? No, you usually can't, and human nature being what it is, a player (particularly one who is losing for the session) may be tempted to undercontribute. Similarly, if everyone must ante at the start of each hand, is the sum of the antes ever less than the required total, with everyone claiming to have anted? Usually someone, perhaps unsure or simply impatient to get play going, makes up the shortfall. These problems can easily be avoided if the table adopts the practice of having players place their bets or antes in front of them, to be gathered into the pot only at the end of each betting round. An alternative is to watch closely, and if in doubt to count the pot, but this is often unpleasant for the person who believes he has spotted someone shortchanging the pot.

At a table where players are allowed to play light by drawing chips from the pot to be made up at the end of the hand, it is easy, intentionally or not, to get confused and draw chips out on one round and put them back on the next. This happens so often that I would suggest never allowing light playing. It is better to let the player out of chips borrow from someone else at the table and repay at the end of the hand.

Routine means of preventing this sort of shortchanging the pot are desirable because people do make honest mistakes, and when they do so they should not be faced with the implication that they had acted dishonestly. But such means also have the effect of eliminating a source of temptation to petty dishonesty.

Using Privileged Information

Take this quiz:

1. If the dealer flashes the down cards that he deals to other players, do you both warn him that he is flashing cards and insist that any flashed cards you have seen be turned face up for all to see?
2. If your neighbor is careless in the way he holds his cards and you see cards in his hand that would lead you to fold when you had planned to call, do you still call?
3. If, while still in a hand, a neighbor shows you the cards that he is about to fold, thinking that you too have dropped, do you insist they be turned up for everyone to see?
4. If the person sitting to your left is known to be impatient and often bets out of turn, do you sometimes deliberately delay your own action, waiting for the extra edge you can gain by knowing what he is going to do?

Plainly there are morally right answers to each of these questions, but I am not certain that they are the answers I would give if I answered honestly. Perhaps failing to act in the morally correct way should not be construed as cheating, since the situation was not of your making, but in fact each represents an opportunity for you to gain an edge over the other players that is not due to your skill or to the effects of chance.

If you see other players taking advantage of such fortuitous opportunities, what should you do? The best answer seems to be to attempt to eliminate the opportunities by saying to the careless player something like, "Please, Tom, hold your cards up—you may not care if Ted sees them, but I do." This may even affect the way Ted behaves.

A FINAL WORD

I believe that the vast majority of people who play poker are honest and play in honest games. Obviously there are occasional exceptions, but they should not be allowed to spoil the game for you. Occasionally you may be unable to avoid an unpleasant situation, and then the best advice is simply to find another poker game. (You probably do not realize how many different games there are in your neighborhood, since you are happily ensconced in one. But the fact is that generally it is not hard to find a group of congenial poker players of about your own level of ability and with objectives that match your own. Ask at work, at your barbershop, or at the golf club where you play.)

APPENDIX TO CHAPTER 17:
IRREGULARITIES AND DISPUTES

While cheating is an infrequent source of tension in Thursday-night poker games, misunderstandings about the rules governing play and occasional disputes about individual behavior do occur. While there are a number of published sets of suggested rules for poker, the fact is that the typical Thursday-night poker game does not need a detailed set of rules of behavior complete with penalties and other sanctions. There is no *official* set of rules of poker because there is no official body that regulates the game. Moreover, the rules that are appropriate for one group of players are not usually appropriate for another in a different game at a different place.

What is needed first is everyone's clear understanding of the local rules and expectations on basic issues. Beyond that, what is required is an accepted method of dispute resolution for those almost inevitable times when two players disagree. These matters are commonly established either by the traditions (or "common law") of the particular game, or by consensus of the players present. There is no higher outside tribunal, nor should there be. If your group cannot manage to agree quickly on basic matters and procedures, it is inherently unstable and probably ought to be broken up and reconstituted.

Among the basic matters on which a consensus is required are what games may be played if it is dealer's choice and the stakes and betting rules. Here are some specific points that need to be understood by all the players. It is worth taking half an hour at the beginning of some session to put them on the table for the group to discuss.

1. Is the dealer constrained to choose only among a particular set of games, or is he free to choose any that are not specifically prohibited? Are there rules governing the introduction of new games? Can the dealer modify the games regularly played, or do so only with the consent of a majority of the other players?
2. Are wild cards ever permitted? If so, what are the restrictions on them?

3. Are Hi-Lo games permitted, either generally or specifically? If so, are the way in which hands are to be declared and the definition of what constitutes the best low hand matters of the dealer's choice, or are they governed by specific understandings?

4. What are the antes required of each player? What are the betting limits, minimum and/or maximum? Are there blind or forced bets? How many raises are permitted on any given round? Are limits on the number of raises waived when there are only two players remaining in contention? If so, does this happen as soon at the third player folds or only on the subsequent betting round?

5. Is the game table stakes or may players introduce new funds during a hand? If table stakes, may chips be taken off the table (rat-holed) by a player who is staying in the game? Is there a minimum buy-in or a minimum re-buy if a player loses all his chips?

Beyond these basics are literally dozens of other situations that may need to be resolved from time to time, such as what to do if a card is inadvertently exposed, or if there is a misdeal, or if a player misstates the quality of his hand or the amount of the bet or raise he is making. Rather than trying to anticipate all such questions and codify a set of answers to hypothetical problems, it is better to have a well-defined procedure for the resolution of a dispute. Once it is resolved, it should provide a precedent for future like situations.

Any dispute-resolution procedure that the group agrees upon will do. Here is one possible mechanism (it is two-tiered): first, if there a consensus among all, or all but one, of the players not involved in the dispute, that consensus governs; second, if there is not a consensus, a designated player (for example, the senior in age, or in years in the game) not directly or indirectly involved in the dispute is given the (unappealable) authority to decide according to what he believes to be appropriate, giving due regard to the past practice in the game.

In all of this, it is well to remember that you are playing for recreation, in a game among friends, and that it is important to give others the benefit of the doubt. Thus, motives and experience matter. It may help to offer a specific example. Suppose a player opens at Jackpots, draws one card, and at the time of the showdown has a flush. Obviously no four of his present cards contain a pair of Jacks or better. The player claims to have split his openers in order to draw for the Ace-high flush he ended up with. The usual practice in splitting openers is for the player to retain the discarded card in front of him, in order to be able to produce it on demand. For an experienced player, this practice is so well-known that his failure to do so should probably cause him to forfeit any chance of winning the pot. But for a newcomer to the game who simply did not understand the way in which to proceed, or who simply forgot to retain his discard, I would rule that he should be allowed to take the pot this one time. (Of course if the flush did not contain even one card as high as a Jack, the hand should be disqualified.) But if any player regularly opens without having the requisite openers, planning simply to throw his hand away unless he ends up with a hand that meets the opening requirement, a more severe penalty might well be appropriate, such as a warning that if it ever happens again he will be asked to leave the game.

The point is not that my resolution of this matter is correct, but that it—or some other that seems both humane and fair—is necessary. It is impossible to codify how to handle all the variety of problems that may arise, and it is not desirable to have a set of rules so rigid that while they unambiguously resolve all disputes they do not take account of individual circumstances. **A rigid procedure is preferable to rigid rules.**

18

♠ ♣ ♥ ♦

CASINO POKER

When Hugh gets invited to a conference in Las Vegas he decides to go a day early and try his hand at poker. He's considered one of the best players in his regular game at home, and his buddies have spoken enthusiastically about their trips to gambling casinos.

He finds the casino astonishing, with its endless rows of slot machines, the absence of windows, the shouts from the craps and roulette tables, and the glare of television from the sports bar. But the poker room is something else: perhaps thirty oval tables, with seven to ten players at each, the professional dealers, and a staccato voice calling Jimmy R. to an opening at table 21, or a dealer asking for a ruling at table 5.

When an opening occurs at a low-limit ($5/$10) Holdem game, Hugh sits down, buys $100 worth of chips, and, playing carefully, finds it lasts for about two hours. The second $100 lasts longer, but the third goes in twenty minutes. Shaken, he quits, wondering whether it was just bad luck or whether this is a different ball game from the Thursday-night game at home, where they often play Holdem, and for higher stakes than the ones here.

Once back home Hugh reflects on his trip, decides he enjoyed the game, but should have played more patiently and folded those borderline hands. But he knows he'll try again. On his second trip he again loses $300 (the amount he set himself as a limit), but this time it takes two and a half days. On his third trip he comes out $140 ahead; his patience, and that book he bought, seem to have paid off.

Hugh becomes a semiannual visitor, each time staying three or four days. Playing his cards carefully, it is challenging and not expensive as vacations go, but he doesn't understand why he's not even breaking even on average. He learns to spot, and feels superior to, the tourists who drop in, play poorly, and lose their stakes in a couple of hours. He recognizes some players who always seem to have a big stack of chips in front of them and who abruptly, and without comment, pick them up and disappear.

Why, he wonders, is he a regular winner at home, yet struggling just to break even here? After all, he's been playing poker for more than thirty years, is way above average in intelligence, and has learned a lot each trip . . .

Playing poker in a casino *is* different from playing at home, even if the games played are familiar and the stakes more or less the same.

CASINO VERSUS THURSDAY-NIGHT POKER

Here are five of the ways these differences work against the Thursday-night poker player.

1. The House "Take"

Casinos charge in one form or another for the privilege of playing at their tables and using their cards and dealers. In the typical low-stakes casino poker game this house *take* (also called *rake, cut, vigorish,* or *vig*) is usually a few dollars out of each pot. In a $5/$10 limit game, it amounts to about 3 percent of the average pot; in smaller-stakes games it can amount to as much as 8 percent. If you add to this the *toke,* the tip that it is customary for the winner of a pot to give to the dealer, a reasonable estimate is that, on average, only about 96 percent of the amounts bet are returned to the players.[1]

This doesn't sound like very much to pay for all the services the casino provides, but it is worth a second look. For this is a percentage taken by the casino on *every dollar bet*, not merely on a player's original stake. As the game progresses, a player wins some pots and this has the effect of recirculating the money, so he ends up, after a few hours, having bet a multiple of the amount of his original stake. To see quickly how this affects the aggregate house take, consider a slot machine that, over time, pays out $96 for each $100 put into it. On average, the player who starts with $100 gets back $96 after his original coins are all entered. If he then keeps playing—and he does!—this $96 becomes (again, on average) $92 after it is reinserted. And that $92 becomes $88 on the next cycle. If the player plays long enough, subject to a modest take of 4 percent, his original $100 will shrink toward zero. See Table 18.1.

After twenty repetitions, an original stake of $100 is down to $44, and if the take were 10 percent, it would be down to $12. It is not surprising that slot machines are big moneymakers for gambling casinos.

Poker isn't like the slot machine in many ways, but it is in this one: the longer you play, and the more hands you play, the greater the casino's take. This makes casino poker a negative-sum game. If in an average poker session at a reputable casino you recirculate your money five times, and the aver-

1. The practice of tipping is well established and allows the casinos to pay their dealers, who are highly skilled, wages near the minimum allowed by law. But when you think about it, it is odd: the dealers, if they are honest, are providing services to all players, not to the winners of a particular hand. Interestingly, dealers prefer to work in low-stakes rather than in high-stakes games, because the tips are greater in dollars per hour. I do not know whether this is because there are no small-value chips (such as $1 ones) in play in high-stakes games or because higher-stakes players take a more realistic view of the services that dealers provide.

Table 18.1 Effect of the House Take on Funds Returned to Players

Number of Cycles	Percentage of Stake Remaining (for Takes of 4% and 10%)	
	4%	10%
1	96	90
2	92	81
3	88	73
4	85	66
5	82	59
6	78	53
7	75	48
8	72	43
9	69	39
10	66	35
. . .	. . .	. . .
20	44	12

age take is 4 percent, the sum of your winnings will be 18 percent less than the sum of your losings. This is what keeps casinos in business, and what permits them to provide services and free drinks to anyone who plays. Anything that keeps the money turning over generates revenues for the casino. The take is a much smaller percentage of the totals bet as the stakes go up.[2] For the occasional player this advantage is, however, almost surely offset by the greater skill of the players encountered in higher-stakes games.

2. From the casino's point of view, this is sensible enough: the costs of devoting a table to $5 limit poker are as great as for $100 limit poker. Each requires the same space and a full-time dealer. Indeed, because the pace is usually faster in higher-stakes games, more hands are played per hour. In very-high-stakes games the take usually is a fee for using the table rather than a subtraction from the pot, because the smallest-denomination chip in play is larger than the planned take on any hand. Typically this fee is collected every twenty or thirty minutes.

Table 18.1 suggests one reason why even a better-than-average poker player has to work hard to break even if he plays for long stretches of time, as most amateurs do when they go to a casino on a poker holiday. Notice that, per hour, the looser you play—that is, the more hands you play and the longer you stay in a given hand—the greater the amount of turnover of your money, and thus the greater the effective house take. **It is more expensive to play loosely when there is a house take than when there is none.** This is one reason why small-time pros, who must overcome the house take to make money, are so conservative about how long they stay in hands.

2. Increased Number of Players

A typical casino will put seven to ten, or even more, people at a table.[3] If you play in a seven-person game you'll be dealt the best hand 14.3 percent of the time. If you are in a ten-person game, it will happen only 10 percent of the time. This difference is compounded by the fact that the more players there are, the better the winning hand will tend to be. Each of these facts decreases the value of a given holding—say, a 10-high straight, or Aces-up—since there are more hands that can beat it. Adjustment to these decreases in value is required, but is often neglected.

To suggest the magnitude of the required adjustment, consider Holdem. As was shown in Table 15.2 on page 309, the best holdings (Premium and Good) in which both cards are ten or higher occur about 14 percent of the time. They prove to be the best of seven hands about 25 percent of the time, but such hands are the best of ten hands 30 percent of the time. More importantly, when what were de-

3. One of the reasons a casino runs a specific single game at a given table is that it can adjust the number of players to the rules of that game. Holdem permits ten- and twelve-person tables, while 7-card stud is usually limited to eight.

fined in Chapter 15 as Poor holdings are folded, the percentage of time the hands classified as Good or better win rises from 40 percent to 55 percent. **The greater the number of players, the more conservatively you have to play to achieve the same level of success.**

3. The Nature of Your Opponents

There is a poker maxim that says if you can't identify the pigeon at the poker table, it's you. Actually the mix of players at a casino table is more complex than this, and consists (in addition to a possible pigeon or two) of: pros who specialize in the particular game and stake level being played; what I call "slumming pros," who are just passing through the game you are in; dealers who have just come off duty; regulars who seem to live in the place and play poker to pass the time of day or night; and occasional players such as Hugh.[4]

It is not possible to generalize about the proportions of each, for it varies from casino to casino, from stake level to stake level, from chosen game to game, and indeed by the hour of day or night. Here is my sense of the clientele at a game with a limit of $12 or less at a Las Vegas casino. These are the games that attract tourists most often. You can be reasonably sure that some of those playing are pros who are at their workplace; indeed, probably about a third to a half of the players fit this description. They tend to play silently, conservatively, and quickly, and for long periods of time. If

---

4. In some casinos there are *shills,* house players who are playing to provide whatever is considered the minimum number of players. Shills are required to identify themselves as such, if asked. If in doubt, ask the floor man. As to style of play, shills are not very different from the small-time pros, although they are playing with the house's money. There may also be what are called *proposition players,* who play with their own money but are paid a small salary by the casino to play for a specified shift in whatever game needs them to fill out the table but must give up their seat anytime a player is waiting to enter the game.

they are losing, they are surly and complain about their incredible bad luck. Moreover, they don't like one another—they are, after all, competing for shares of the same pie—and they let it show. They tend to win regularly enough to more than cover the house take, and if they get into a losing streak, they depart.

"Slumming pros" tend to talk a lot to each other, but not to you, and not about poker. They discuss their sports betting, both past and prospective, their golf games, and sometimes even their business and love lives. (You can get distracted listening to them!) This group is particularly tough to play against, since it consists of men—always men—who are sitting in a game that is really too small for them. They fall into two distinct types: first, those who are waiting for a game they prefer but which is either full or has not yet been organized; second, those who have lost heavily in their preferred games and are trying to rebuild their bankrolls so they can get back into the bigger game. The former are particularly likely to be found in the morning or early afternoon (when there are not yet enough players for the higher-stakes game) and will leave suddenly when the opportunity arises. The latter show up in the early evening, and will leave when and if they achieve some predetermined level of winnings. Slumming pros can be spotted by the apparent lack of attention they give to the cards and to the others at the table: they are regularly scanning the room, checking with the card-room manager, and often popping up from the table to make a phone call, place a bet in the sports bar, or investigate a shout or a dispute at another table. But their lack of attention doesn't mean they play badly. They know the game thoroughly, and without investing much energy they play few hands, raising rather than merely calling when they do, and win with regularity. With three or more of them in the game, the effective stakes rise substantially because of raises in the early rounds, and it is a good time for the

tourist to take a walk, go for a meal, or else to play extremely carefully, paying close attention to who it is that is
betting, calling, or raising.

Off-duty dealers are easy to spot by their casino-
provided shirts and by their small talk with the on-duty
dealer. They do not seem to me to play very well, although
they plainly know the game and each other. Why this is so
I do not know, but I expect that fatigue and boredom are
factors, and since they are usually playing with the money
they have collected as tokes, they do not seem to treat it
very carefully. Moreover, they engage in a kind of genteel
reciprocity with one another, not raising even when they
have an unbeatable hand. They tend to be killing time, not
playing serious poker. There are exceptions to this, particularly dealers not in uniform, mostly female, who sometimes play on their days off. They're in it for the money,
and they tend to play seriously, silently, conservatively,
and well.

The large group of resident regulars is more heteroge-
neous. It includes a sprinkling of apparently quite well-off
women (to judge from their expensive and flashy jewelry) of
middle age or older, who play competently but not aggressively. This group also includes a lot of male retirees who
come in the late morning and play to pass the time till late
afternoon; they know one another, talk a good deal, and are
reasonably friendly except when they are losing. (Some will
even get curious about you once they have seen you for the
third or fourth time and have decided that you are neither a
dolt nor a hustler.) It takes some practice to distinguish
them from the small-time pros.

And then there are the tourists, of both sexes but mostly
male, often here at a convention or accompanied by their
spouses on a business or vacation trip. You can identify
them pretty quickly because one of their companions will
come around and ask how they are doing, or when they

want to go to dinner, within an hour of their sitting down. Many of them are clear losers, playing too loosely in unfamiliar games. When one of them sits down, looks of anticipation are exchanged among the pros. Some are atrociously bad, some have been drinking, and they are likely to lose a couple of hundred dollars quickly. Others are better, lose a hundred quickly, but learn enough to make the second hundred last longer.

One group of tourists tends to do better, particularly if there are no slumming pros in the game. These are young, college-age men who have come to gamble on the weekend or at the time of a school vacation. They are likely to have studied the game and are looking to build a stake, which they will subsequently lose in the bigger games that are their real goal. They often come in pairs and play in partnership. They are nothing if not attentive, have great stamina, and will quickly learn who are the pros and who the tourists. They play long hours, often through the night.

All of this is important to you when playing casino poker, because whether to call, raise, or fold in a given situation depends critically upon who your opponents are. You must adjust your play to the particular set of other players in the game. For example, with even one typical tourist in the hand, it is impossible to bluff, though you need not assume that he has the quality of hand that will beat you. The pros, by contrast, always seem to have what you fear they have, except perhaps when you first sit down and they are testing you. Pros tend to characterize a tourist as either a *rabbit,* who folds at the slightest provocation, or a *calling station,* who grimly stays as long as there is any chance of winning.

At higher-stakes tables the proportions change sharply. If tourists are present, they tend to be big spenders or inveterate gamblers, and they become the sought-after targets of the pros.[5] The higher the stakes, the greater the proportion of pros, who are doing a lot of playing against each other. The occasional player who wanders in is likely to be caught in a crossfire of players who know each other's habits. Such games are challenging, but the higher the stakes, the tougher the going.[6] In them, indeed, *you* are likely to be the pigeon.

4. Conditions of Play

The physical aspects of playing at a casino poker table are significantly different from playing at home. The games are played at large oval tables at which you sometimes can't even see the faces of all of the other players. The poker room is windowless and the time of day, season, and

5. One experience of mine is revealing. An extremely wealthy businessman from Texas, whom I think of as "The King," periodically comes to Las Vegas to gamble, but from time to time chooses to play poker in relatively modest-stakes games. He plays poker very aggressively, and badly, raising at every opportunity no matter what he is holding until he loses a few thousand dollars, and then leaves cheerfully, with big handshakes all around the table. The pros and regulars love him and flatter him outrageously. The first time he sat down at a table where I was playing, a spectator leaned over and asked me quietly if I didn't want to take a dinner break. When I said no, he offered me a $100 bill to do so in order to play in my seat for the next hour. Curiosity kept me from accepting.

6. In preparing to write this chapter I played in a series of successively higher-stakes versions of 7-card stud, expecting to find the players increasingly more conservative as the stakes rose. This was not the case: loose play was, if anything, more common, but it was for the most part informed and skillful, with a good deal of deliberate deception. I was quickly in over my head, in large part because, unlike my opponents, I could not distance myself from the size of the bets, even when I figured that the pot odds were in my favor. At my final table, with antes of $25, and limits of $150 and $300, players often had $300 to $500 each in the pot before they seriously considered whether to fold. Proportionally, this is only a little looser than the way I play in a game with limits and antes one-tenth as large, and I was aware that it was only the color of the chips that had changed. But the fact remained that I was uncomfortable with these stakes, and I realized that I was not playing my usual game. I left in a cold sweat after sitting in for only one round of seven hands. Luckily I was the winner in one of them, and thus emerged only slightly dented.

weather are always the same. There is a high level of background noise, and a steady flow of people in and around the room. These are all strange and distracting, and anything that breaks your concentration on the poker game itself is not helpful.

Perhaps the biggest hazard for the newcomer is the rapid pace of the casino game. Since the take and the tokes are functions of the number of hands played, both the house and the dealers want to keep the pace as brisk as possible. There are no long pauses for shuffling, dealing, and pushing the pot to the winner, nor the friendly between-hands small talk of the kind found in your Thursday-night game. Neither are there frequent pauses during play for thinking, nor for postmortems on how a hand was played. All this means less time for evaluating your options and for figuring out what to do—precisely when your unfamiliarity makes such evaluations more necessary. Regulars and pros consider these factors automatically and quickly; occasional players do not. The result is the sort of unthinking play that leads to mistakes that cost money. While it is permitted to call time and slow the pace of the game, the player who does so more than very occasionally will feel the social pressure of dealers and of other players.

Different betting rules concerning the nature and size of blind bets, and different betting patterns, require adaptation, and yet there is often little time to make the adjustments needed. To take one important example, most casino games are what in earlier chapters I characterized as aggressive games, whereas most Thursday-night games are restrained. Professionals playing with tourists in low-limit games do not count on a few big kills to make their winnings, but instead on regularly winning on the hands where their opening cards are well above average. They are conservative in the number of hands they play, but very aggressive in how they play the ones they do play. They bet them heavily from the start, and are content to take a small pot quickly. They will benefit even more if the tourist, instead of folding mediocre cards in the face of aggressive betting, hangs in there and contributes. **The player who follows stay/fold rules that are correct at home will stay too often, and too long, in the casino game.**

Another important difference in the conditions of play is that the game itself is already in progress when the player joins it. At home all players start, warm up, get tired, and stop together. In a continuous game, players will be in all states of play, and this will affect how they play. The newcomer is usually so busy managing his own cards that it will take some time before he adjusts to the nature of his opponents. (Good advice, which is difficult to follow, is to sit and watch, playing an absolute minimum of hands for at least half an hour.) Moreover, the cast of characters is steadily changing, as some players leave and their places are filled by others. You need to relearn and reevaluate continuously, and you cannot simply store up information to use an hour or two later.[7]

All of this confirms that the demands on the attention and skills of the occasional player are large and, combined with the pace of the game, are likely to lead to more than an occasional foolish play. (I have even found myself making mistakes reading my hand, a type of mistake I virtually never make at home.) In this respect, the regulars and pros have a huge advantage: they know this game and they know one another's habits and foibles. They size up the table at a glance. As specialists in this game, at this casino, with this level of stakes, their experiential advantage is enormous.

---

7. I have a vivid, painful memory of being bluffed out of a good-size pot because I failed to notice that the player sitting in the number-six seat, whom I'd pegged as a very conservative player who didn't bet unless he had the nuts, had left and that his place had been taken by another, whose first hand it was, and who was plainly testing me.

5. Worries About Honesty

While it is clear that today major casinos want to prevent cheating, or anything else that discourages people from playing, it is virtually impossible for them to prevent it altogether. Casinos cannot, to take one example, prevent buddies, or even husbands and wives, from playing at the same table; this makes collusion an ever-present danger. Dishonesty, particularly collusion, does occur and is difficult to discover and police. When it happens it adds to the reasons why the occasional player has a hard time breaking even.[8]

I do not believe dishonesty is so disabling as to make casino poker an unwise activity, but caution is advised. I regard it as an occasional nuisance, an additional tax on my money, rather than a reason not to play.

ENJOYING CASINO POKER

Until you understand and adjust to the fact that playing poker in a casino is not the same thing as playing it at home, it can prove stressful. But once you do, it can be both challenging and fun.

The most important aspect of this adjustment is developing a realistic set of aspirations for your poker holiday. If you expect to enhance the family fortune, or even to win enough to make it a costless vacation, you are almost surely doomed to failure. If you are content to break even at the table, or to lose no more than you would if you spent the time at another leisure activity, you will be on the way to enjoyment. You will probably do better than this some of the time, and this will provide a sure sense of accomplishment. But you need also to expect to do somewhat worse without

---

8. My experience suggests that collusion rises in frequency as the stakes rise, but only if there are occasional players in the game. Regulars and professionals know each other too well to be victimized very often by collusion.

feeling inadequate. Unless you are willing to adopt both the commitment and tactics of the professional and to make poker-playing a major activity of your life, you are not likely to do much better than break even in the long run. This will mean winning some of the time, but losing about as often. If you become better than most of the tourists, though not as good as the pros, you ought to be satisfied. At this level you can enjoy yourself, and lose neither your self-respect nor more money than you can afford to spend.

But even to achieve this rather modest plateau requires some extra discipline for the player who finds himself a regular winner at home. Here are eight operating rules based on those that I have developed for myself when going to Las Vegas for a four- or five-day poker holiday.[9] I developed these rules the hard way, by violating them and suffering the consequences.

Rule 1: Choose a game you can afford.   It is essential to have a notion of the maximum amount you are willing to spend on a given holiday, as well as at an individual poker session. Watch the play at a given table long enough to be sure that even if you don't win a pot in the first hour of play, you will still have chips in front of you, and that if you have a run of bad luck you won't spend your whole bundle in the first session. It is best to err on the side of a too-small game. When you find yourself winning, you may feel comfortable moving up to a higher-stakes game, and if you find yourself bored, you will also need to move to a different game. But you must find a game where you do not gulp at the thought of losing a hand, or where you are constantly wondering if you can really afford the money you are spending. Abstracting from the inherent value of the chips—from what

9. It is possible to stay too long. For me, after the fourth day, the adverse effects of fatigue outweigh the benefits of having adapted to the conditions and gotten into the rhythm of the game.

economists call the utility of money—is always necessary to enjoying poker and to playing it well.

Some good poker players set themselves session limits and will stop playing when they either win or lose a pre-specified amount. I do not do this, preferring to think of separate sessions as all parts of the same long poker game. (But see Rule 8, below.)

Rule 2: Understand the game you choose. This rule refers not only to the game itself (say, Holdem) but to the rules under which it is played—including such factors as the number of players, the required blind bets, and the rules about which player must bet first. Even when you thoroughly understand the rules, you will not be wholly comfortable with the fast pace of the casino game, and thus you are liable to make costly mistakes. But if you are struggling merely to understand the rules, or are unsure of them, you will have no chance, and not much fun. The dealer is not permitted to help you correct your obvious mistakes due to misunderstandings of the rules as he is when you play blackjack, because in poker you are playing against other players, not against the house.

You may wish to learn to play a new game, or one that is rarely played at home. The best way to do this is first to read a book that is designed to teach you that game.[10] A second way is to watch long enough at least to appreciate the game's obvious features. A third and more expensive way is to sit down at the table and play. This is a perfectly possible way to learn, but unless you are prepared to pay the tuition involved, you would do well to begin with the other approaches. Even if you do so, you will surely pay tuition when first you try to put what you have learned into practice.

10. Not surprisingly, such books have been written for every game that is played at the casinos. The Gambler's Book Store, in Las Vegas, is a good source for such books and will provide a catalogue upon request (1-800-522-1777).

Rule 3: Budget your playing time.   If you are on a limited holiday, the temptation is to play poker virtually every available waking minute; after all, that may seem the best way to get your money's worth from your investment in travel and hotel room. One of the things that is wondrous about gambling casinos is that they operate around the clock, making it possible to play at all hours. But the temptation to do so should be resisted, for without lots of practice you cannot maintain your concentration for twelve or more hours a day over three or four days. Concentration is the key to playing poker competently. Your own lack of self-control can be as much of an opponent as the other players are.

My rule is to budget myself to two five-hour sessions in any twenty-four-hour period and then to stick to that even if I don't feel tired at the end. Professionals can play for longer than this, and often do, but they have trained for endurance and are actually investing less energy in the process than most amateurs are. This rule, or some variant on it, is usually violated by most amateurs on holiday. Look around the table when you are playing poker, especially late at night: the grim-faced losers will frequently have been at the table for hours and are playing listlessly, waiting for their luck to change. It is easy to slip into this mode when fatigue sets in. A good working rule is not to allow yourself to play any longer at one session in the strange environment of the casino than you do in a poker session at home. You can always come back a few hours later and start again.

A corollary is not to play poker the first minute you arrive. Get acclimated, unpack your bag, explore the casino, and then watch the action and remind yourself of the rules you are going to impose upon yourself. Particularly if you have traveled east to west and changed time zones, you may find that adrenaline is masking the fatigue of a day that began a long time ago.

Once you decide that ten hours per day is enough time to play poker, there is lots of time for doing other things. You can spend some of it sunbathing or going to a show, sight-seeing or playing a round of golf. If you do, you are likely to find that your return to the game is more fun—and more profitable—than if you do nothing but sit at the poker table.

Rule 4: Take frequent breaks during a poker session. During a five-hour poker session, you should plan to take at least three breaks from the table. You can usually arrange to do so for periods up to an hour without losing your place at the table. Ask the dealer how to do it.[11] Breaks are important, both physically and psychologically.

It is usually a good idea to take a break if you have made a serious mistake, or when you find yourself losing concentration and thinking about something wholly unrelated to the poker game. Also—perhaps especially—when you have experienced a shocking, and what you believe to be an undeserved, loss, a break is in order. Such situations occur (some idiot stayed in when he had no business doing so and got the only card that could beat you), and they tend to evoke unhealthy reactions and cause you to go *on tilt*, to play badly because you are angry or are seeking revenge.

In any of these situations, get up, go to the john, take a walk outside and do something else for a while. One friend of mine buys a roll of quarters and plays video poker; another goes for a half-mile walk; a third goes into the sports bar and forces himself to concentrate on whatever event is drawing the most attention, even though he really doesn't care about the outcome.

When is it time to return? I set a minimum of fifteen minutes, but that is because I am impatient. A half an hour is better. You'll know; it's when, after thinking about some-

11. If you want to take a break for a meal, most casinos will provide you with a card that will enable you to bypass lines and be able to eat in leisure within the permitted time away from the table. Again, ask the dealer how to arrange this.

thing else, you return to thinking about poker and are full of good intentions about how you're going to play better now.

Breaks of this sort are dictated by your state of mind rather than by the clock. They become essential whenever you are on a losing streak and are tempted to stay and even raise on marginal hands just to change your luck. They are not recommended at those rare and wonderful moments when everything is going your way and you feel you are the master of the universe. If you're on a rush, enjoy it to the full, but recognize it as a sometime thing that will end soon enough. And when it does, take your break.

Rule 5: Remind yourself regularly to play more conservatively than you do at home.   In preparation for a casino poker session, you are likely to have developed intended rules of when to stay and when to fold. But they are easy to forget. During the play, ask yourself occasionally if you are adhering to them. Typically, you get careless and play looser than you intend as the session progresses, and as the time since the last break increases. Because the pace of a casino game is so fast, it is in fact easier to fold a hand and wait for the next deal than it is at home, where the hand that you have dropped out of seems to go on forever. Patience is thus easier in a casino game, and it is more essential.

Rule 6: Use your non-playing time to study your opponents.   Use the time during the hands you don't play to watch and classify your opponents. Who are the pros? Who is playing ultraconservatively? Who is the pigeon? Who is flashing his cards? Who is winning even though playing too loosely? Poker is played against people, and you need to know who's who in the hands you do play.

Rule 7: Control what you eat and drink while playing poker.   Not drinking alcohol is the first rule, and it seems so obvious as to hardly warrant comment, but it is violated surprisingly often by amateurs, perhaps beguiled by the frequent opportunity to order free cocktails from the attractive waitresses who prowl the casino. Drinking lots of fluids is desirable and will increase your stamina, so bottled water, fruit juices, and soft drinks are a good idea. When you feel you need a drink to mask your fatigue, or to compensate for your bad luck, you are ready to take a break instead. Try fresh air. While coffee may seem innocuous, too much need for it suggests that you have played too long. After all, fatigue is a symptom, and your body is telling you something. As to food, try to avoid both an empty stomach and an over-full one. A full breakfast is usually sensible. Save your big meal of the day until after you have finished playing.[12]

All of this is an aspect of the fact that you will not play well if you are physically or emotionally distressed in any way. You can't control all aspects of life, but you can avoid dietary sources of discomfort.

Rule 8: Walk away from a game as soon as you feel something is wrong.   You can't play well if you suspect cheating or collusion, or where you feel you are the only outsider in a group in which each knows the others' every move. Nor can you do so if a new player has entered the game and altered its rhythm, say by betting and raising at every opportunity. Even if you had to wait to get into the game, do not stay if you feel uncomfortable for any reason. There are other games and, if necessary, other casinos. Anyway, things may look very different in an hour or two. This is a hard rule to follow, but it is important. If you are psychologically stressed—and any of these ingredients can cause stress—you will neither play well nor enjoy the process.

Following these rules, or something like them, is no guarantee that you will win at casino poker, but they will surely help you to have a better time and to come closer to winning than if you neglect them.

---

12. Casino restaurants tend to be open at all hours.

APPENDIX TO CHAPTER 18:
A NOTE ABOUT TOURNAMENT POKER

Most poker, casino and Thursday-night, is what I shall call *rubber poker,* in which every hand is an entity unto itself. But increasingly popular in major casinos are poker tournaments in which players all start with the same fixed stake, and play until it is gone. One by one, players are eliminated until only one is left. This is *knock-out poker.* As players are eliminated, the sizes of the antes and required bets rise, as do the betting limits. Either one grand prize goes entirely to the winner, or, more commonly, prizes are scaled to the order of finish. The World Series of Poker is the most famous of these tournaments, but others occur now at all levels of stakes, and for many varieties of games. Indeed, some casinos provide free tournaments to players who play there with some regularity.

Tournament poker is exhilarating and can be fun for the occasional player. The big advantage is that the rules covering the entry fee and amount of required buy-in make the maximum possible loss definite, and thus presumably controllable by the player according to his purse. The big disadvantage is that he has almost no chance of winning, or, usually, even of finishing in the group that shares in the prize money. This is because the strategy and tactics required are wholly different from those that apply to the same game played in a rubber poker game, even at the same casino.[13]

It is beyond the scope of this book to discuss how to win at tournament poker, but it is worth suggesting why it is a different game. The basic operating principle for coming out a winner in an ordinary poker game is to pay attention to the pot odds and bet when they are more favorable than the probability of winning. As mentioned, this means concentrating on the expected value of a decision, and choosing decisions for which the expected values are positive. In the long run you will be a winner if you bet whenever the expected value is positive, and fold whenever it is negative.

---

13. The art of tournament poker is the subject of Tom McEvoy's *Tournament Poker* (Las Vegas: Poker & Plus Publications, 1995).

If you treat every hand as simply one in a long string of hands, this is reasonable behavior for a risk-neutral player. If you are using expected value as the operating rule, you should play a given hand the same way whether you are winning or losing at the time, whether it's the first hand or the last of the evening. Each hand is a separate event, and its winnings or losings are part of the aggregate that determine your winnings or losings.

By contrast, in knockout poker survival is the key objective in the early stages. If you can survive while other players knock each other out you will be on the road to victory. Proper play of a given holding will be different at the beginning of a tournament than in the middle or near the end, and it is surely affected by the size of your remaining stake relative to that of the other remaining players. Of course a player is not allowed simply to sit by and watch the others compete. Antes and blind bets are required, and they will eat up the stake of anyone who plays too conservatively. As the number of players left decreases, the size of these required bets rises steadily and eventually dramatically, thus making a waiting strategy increasingly prohibitive.

To see the difference between rubber and knockout poker, suppose all the cards have been dealt and you hold a hand that has a 50-percent probability of winning; and suppose that there is $100 in the pot and that you have $100 in front of you. Your only opponent, who has $1,000 in his pile, bets $100. Using expected value, you would call at once—the pot odds of 2 to 1 in your favor are better than the probability odds against you. Your expected value is +$50. In rubber poker, if you call that kind of a bet four times, you can expect to win $200. In a knockout tournament, if you call and beat your opponent, you'll end up with $300, and he'll be down to $900. But if you lose, which is an even-money bet, you'll be wiped out.

In knockout poker, if you accept an even-money chance of being eliminated four times, your chance of surviving all four is only 1 in 16; that is, you will find yourself wiped out 15 out of 16 times. You must weigh your chances of being knocked out by calling each bet against your chances of being wiped out by the antes and required bets. The larger the compelled contributions are, the more attractive it is to call bets where you have some chance of winning. Indeed, as your pile dwindles, you will tend to call even a long-shot possibility, since it may be your best chance of survival, small though it is.[14] The tactics required for winning at tournament poker are centered on avoiding positions where another player can put you in an all-in situation. Mathematically this implies that your objective is not to maximize your winnings, but to minimize your chance of being behind by the amount of the original stake. How to do this depends crucially on the rules and structure of the tournament game, such as the antes and blind bets.

One of the things that makes knockout tournament poker difficult and outside of the experience of most poker players is that as the number of competitors decreases, the required antes, bets, and stakes increase. **This leads to ever-heavier betting on ever-poorer hands.** Most importantly, it leaves the inexperienced tournament player at a decisive disadvantage in comparison to the professional in evaluating the changing worth of a given hand.

14. The critical timing of stay/fold decisions occurs in many other situations. For one example, George Washington reported that during the Revolution he was frequently forced to make his military decisions on a similar basis. His famous attack across the Delaware River on Trenton, on Christmas Night of 1776, was made only after he concluded that the desertions from his army were occurring at such a rate that it would surely be defeated if he did nothing, and even the slim chances of victory in his daring attack were better than none. The rest, of course, is history.

Glossary
♠ ♣ ♥ ♦

ACES-FULL	Full house with three Aces.
ACES-UP	Two pair, headed by Aces.
ADVERTISING	Getting caught in a bluff early in a session for the purpose of getting called on good hands later.
ALL BLUE	Flush in spades or clubs.
ALL-IN	In table-stakes poker, a player who has no chips remaining to put into the pot.
ALL PINK	Flush in hearts or diamonds.
ANTE	Required payment to the pot before the deal. May be required of each player or only of the dealer.
BABIES	In lowball poker, cards below a 6.
BACKDOOR HAND	In Holdem or Omaha, a winning hand that requires using both of the last two common cards.
BACK-TO-BACK	In 5-card stud, having the first two cards be of the same rank.
BAD BEAT	Losing with a hand that by all odds should have been a winner.
BET	1. To put chips into the pot. 2. The first bet in a betting round.
BICYCLE	See *wheel*.
BLIND BET	A required bet before the cards are dealt.

BLUFF	To bet or raise on a hand that the player does not believe to be the best hand, in the hope of inducing all opponents to fold.
BOARD	The showing cards.
BOAT	Full house.
BRING IN THE HAND	Open the first round of betting.
BUG	The Joker that may be construed either as an Ace or as a wild card to complete a straight or a flush.
BULLET	An Ace. Also called *bull*.
BUMP	To raise. Also a raise.
BURN	To remove the top card from the deck facedown before a card is dealt.
BURY	See *burn*.
BUST	1. Worthless hand. 2. To receive a card that ruins a hand.
BUTTON	Token that indicates the position of either the dealer or the player who is required to act first in a betting round.
BUY	1. To use the option to receive a card. 2. To receive a needed card.
BUY-IN	The minimum amount required to enter play at a table.
CALL	1. To meet a bet by a previous player. 2. To be in at the showdown of a hand.
CALLING ERROR	Calling the final-round bets with a second-best hand.
CALLING STATION	Derogatory term for a player who calls too many bets.
CAPPING THE RAISES	Taking the final permitted raise in a betting round.

CARDS SPEAK	In Hi-Lo poker, the rule that players need not declare which way their hands are to be considered.
CASE CARD	Last available card of the required type.
CHASING HAND	Hand that has slim prospects of becoming a winner.
CHECK	Declining to bet when one has the option to open.
CHECK AND RAISE	To raise after checking earlier on the same round of betting. Called *sandbagging;* also *check-raise.*
CLOSED CARDS	Down cards, seen only by the player to whom they are dealt.
COLD DECK	Stacked deck used by cheaters.
COMMON CARDS	Cards that are dealt up and are part of every player's hand. Often called the *widow.*
CONSECUTIVE DECLARATION	See *sequential declaration.*
COUNTERFEIT	To turn a leading hand into a loser.
COUPLE	Two-card combination.
COWBOY	1. A King. Also called *K-boy.* 2. Reckless and aggressive player.
CRIMP CUT	A cheating *cut* that occurs at the specific place where the person shuffling the cards intends.
CUT	1. To divide the deck before the deal and after the shuffle so as to determine randomly the first card to be dealt. 2. The house *take.*
DAMES	Queens. Also called *girls, hookers, ladies,* or *whores.*
DEAD HAND	Hand that must be abandoned because of some irregularity.

DEALER'S CHOICE	Game in which the dealer is permitted to choose the variety of poker he is going to deal.
DEALING SECONDS	Cheating by dealing the second card rather than the top card from the deck.
DECLARATION	In high-low poker, indication of the direction in which the player chooses to have his hand considered.
DEUCE	A two.
DOG	See *underdog*.
DOOR CARD	The first up card for each player in any stud game.
DOUBLE-SUITED	In Omaha, a holding that has two cards in each of two suits.
DOWN CARD	Closed card.
DRAW DEAD	To pay to get a card when in fact there is no card that can make the hand a winner.
DRAW OUT	To get a card that turns a losing hand into a winning one. Also to *hit*.
DRAWING	1. Seeking to improve one's hand on the next round. 2. In draw poker, replacing some of the cards originally dealt.
DRAWING HAND	Hand that must improve to have a chance of winning and has a credible chance of doing so.
DRIVER	Player who is aggressively pushing the betting.
DROP	Fold.
FACE CARD	Any King, Queen, or Jack.
FAIR GAME	Game of chance in which the expected value is zero.
FALSE CUT	A cheating cut that leaves the cards in their original position.

FAMILY POT

Hand in which all players have stayed through the first betting round.

FAST PLAY

To be aggressive in the betting of a good hand.

FEATHER MERCHANT

Derogatory for a timid player.

FIFTH STREET

1. The round of betting after the fifth card has been dealt to each player in stud poker. 2. The final betting round (the *river*) in Holdem or Omaha.

FILL

Receive a card that completes a hand of straight or better.

FISH

See *geese*.

FLOP

1. The first three common cards exposed in Holdem or Omaha.
2. The round of betting that ensues.

FLUSH

Five cards of the same suit.

FOLD

To give up on a hand.

FOLDING ERROR

To fold what would have been the winning hand.

FORCED BET

Required bet of prescribed minimum size, the alternative to which is to fold but not to check.

FOUR FLUSH

Four cards of the same suit, without a fifth one.

FOURTH STREET

1. The round after the fourth card has been dealt to each player in stud poker. 2. The next-to-final betting round (the *turn*) in Holdem or Omaha.

FREE CARD

Card received at no cost (without betting) because all players checked on the previous round.

FREE RIDE

Receiving a free card.

FREEZE-OUT

Form of poker in which a player who loses his whole stake must drop out of the game.

FULL BOAT	Full house.
GARBAGE	Worthless cards. Also called *trash* or *rags*.
GEESE	Derogatory term for poor players whom pros treat as targets. Also called *fish, pigeons, sheep,* or *suckers*.
GIRLS	Queens.
GUTS	Draw poker with no opening requirements.
HAND	1. A player's best five cards at the time of the showdown. 2. The whole set of cards a player may choose among. 3. The whole sequence from the deal to the showdown.
HI-LO	Poker game in which the pot is split between a winning high hand and a winning low hand. Also called high-low.
HIT	To draw out, or to *fill*.
HOGGING	See *scooping*.
HOLDING	The closed cards a player is dealt.
HOLE CARD	Down card.
HOOK	A Jack.
HOOKER	A Queen.
HOUSE TAKE	See *take*.
IMMEDIATE POT ODDS	The ratio of the size of the existing pot to the amount the player must pay to stay in the hand.
IMMORTAL	An unbeatable hand. Also called the *nuts,* or a *lock*.
IMPLIED POT ODDS	The ratio of a player's possible winnings on a hand to the anticipated subsequent cost of determining whether he has a winning hand.
IN THE HOLE	Closed cards.

INSIDE STRAIGHT	Four-card straight that only four cards can fill.
JACKPOTS	Draw poker with a pair of Jacks or better required to open.
JACKS	1. Two or more cards of the rank of Jack. 2. Jackpots.
JACKS-OR-BACK	Variation on Jackpots in which if no hand is opened for high, it is played as lowball draw.
JACKS-OR-BETTER	Jackpots.
JACKS PROGRESSIVE	Variation on Jackpots in which if a hand is not opened, the opening requirements increase on successive deals to Queens, to Kings, and to Aces.
JAMMED POT	Pot with multiple raises.
JOKER	Distinctive fifty-third card sometimes used in play.
K-BOY	King.
KICKER	An unmatched card held with one or more pairs.
KNOCKOUT POKER	1. Poker in which *freeze-out* rules apply. 2. Tournament poker in which play continues until there is only one player left.
LADIES	Queens.
LEADING HAND	Hand that is believed to be the best at the moment.
LIGHTS	The chips owed by a player who has *played light*.
LIMIT POKER	Fixed-limit poker games in which there is a specified maximum bet on each round.
LIVE CARD	Card that is available to be paired or received because few like it have shown.

LOCALS	Casino players who are regulars in a given game.
LOCK	Hand that is unbeatable. Also called the *nuts*.
LOOSE	Style of play that is not as conservative as experts advise.
LOWBALL	Poker games in which the lowest hand in rank is the best hand.
MADE HAND	Hand that is already as good as it can be expected to get.
MECHANIC	Crooked dealer who skillfully manipulates cards.
MEET	*Call.*
MISDEAL	Irregularity that requires a redeal.
MONSTER HAND	Extraordinarily powerful hand.
MULTI-WAY HOLDING	Holding that has alternative ways to become a winning hand.
NEGATIVE-SUM GAME	Game in which the sum of the winnings will be less than the sum of the losings.
NO-LIMIT POKER	1. Poker played subject only to *table-stakes* rules. 2. (archaic) Poker played where any size of bet is permitted and a player unable to meet the outstanding bet within a reasonable time limit is forced to fold.
NUT FLUSH (STRAIGHT, ETC.)	Best possible flush (straight, etc.)
NUT HAND	The best possible hand.
NUT-NUT	Hand in Hi-Lo that is the *nut hand* in each direction.
NUTS	Unbeatable hand. A *lock*.
OFF-SUIT	Two cards of different suits.
ON THE BUTTON	In the last betting position.

ON THE COME	Needing to improve the hand to have a chance of winning. A *drawing hand*.
ON TILT	Playing badly because of anger, usually caused by a recent bad beat.
OPEN	1. In draw poker, to make the initial bet subject to minimum requirements. 2. To initiate the betting.
OPEN CARDS	Showing cards; up cards.
OPEN PAIR	Showing pair.
OPEN-ENDED STRAIGHT	Four-card straight where any of eight cards can complete it.
OPENER	Player who opens a hand of draw poker.
OPENERS	Cards that meet the minimum requirements for opening a draw-poker hand.
OUTS	Combinations of cards that can lead to an alternative winning hand if the primary winning combination does not work out.
OVERCARD	Higher card.
OVERPAIR	Higher pair than a showing pair.
PAINT	Face cards.
PASS	*Check.*
PAT HAND	In draw poker, a made hand on the deal.
PIGEON	See *geese.*
PLAY LIGHT	Situation in which a player is permitted to call a bet without sufficient chips to do so on the understanding that he will make up any shortfall at the end of the hand.
POCKET CARDS	Hole cards.
POCKET PAIR	Pair in the hole.
POSITION	Seating in relation to the dealer, which affects the order of betting.

POSITIVE-SUM GAME	Game in which the sum of the winnings is greater than the sum of the losings.
POT	1. The sum of all prior bets and antes. 2. The amount available to be paid to the winner after all bets have been completed.
POT ODDS	See *immediate pot odds* and *implied pot odds*.
POT-LIMIT	Form of poker where the maximum size of any bet is the amount currently in the pot.
PROBE BET	Bet that is designed to elicit information.
PROGRESSIVE JACKS	See *Jacks progressive*.
PROPOSITION PLAYER	Player using his own money but employed by the house to play at tables where he is needed to fill out a game.
PROS	Professionals.
PUT ON A HAND	To correctly determine an opponent's hand. (*To put him on his hand*.)
QUADS	Four of a kind.
QUASI-BLUFF	Blufflike bet made with a mediocre hand that might still be good enough to win in a showdown. Also called *semi-bluff*.
RABBIT	Timid player who is likely to fold regularly in the face of aggressive betting.
RAGS	Worthless cards.
RAISE	1. Make a bet that is larger than the previous bet in the same round. 2. The amount of the increase over the previous bet.
RAKE	The amount of the house's deduction from the pot, charged for the privilege of playing. Also called *take*, *cut*, *vigorish*, or *vig*.

RAT-HOLING	Taking chips off the table in a table-stakes game.
READING CARDS	Correctly inferring closed cards in others' hands.
RELEASE	Fold.
RERAISE	To make a second or subsequent raise in a given round of betting.
RISK-AVERSE	Willing to pay a premium to avoid variance in the outcome of uncertain events.
RISK-NEUTRAL	Neither risk-averse nor risk-seeking. Concerned only with expected value.
RISK-SEEKING	Willing to pay a premium over expected value to have variance in the outcome of chance events.
RIVER	1. Last round of betting in Holdem and Omaha. 2. The (fifth) common card received just before this betting round. Also called *Fifth Street*.
ROCK	1. Player who bets or raises only when holding the nuts. 2. A very conservative player.
ROLLED-UP	Holding three of a kind in the first three cards in stud poker.
RUBBER POKER	Game in which every hand is a separate event. Contrast with *knockout poker*.
RUNNING PAIR	Two cards of the same rank received in succession.
RUSH	Period in which the player wins a series of pots.
SANDBAG	See *check and raise*.
SCARE CARDS	Showing cards that suggest a strong hand.
SCOOPING	Winning both halves of a Hi-Lo pot. Also called *hogging, sweeping,* or *swinging*.

SECOND-BEST	A good hand that fails to win the pot.
SECOND-DEALING	See *dealing seconds*.
SEE	*Call.*
SEMI-BLUFF	See *quasi-bluff*.
SEQUENTIAL DECLARATION	In Hi-Lo, declaring for high, low, or both in sequential order.
SET	Three of a kind.
SHEEP	See *geese*.
SHILL	Casino employee playing with house money.
SHOWDOWN	1. The end of a hand, when all remaining hands are exposed and the winner is determined. 2. Game of poker with only an ante but no subsequent bets required, so all hands are in at the end.
SHOWING CARDS	Cards that are dealt face up.
SIDE POT	Secondary pot made necessary when one or more players is all-in and cannot meet the full amount of a bet. All additional bets are contested for only by the remaining players.
SHINER	Reflecting device used by cheats.
SIMULTANEOUS DECLARATION	Contrast with *sequential declaration*. All players indicate simultaneously whether they are going high, low, or both by an appropriate signal.
SLOW-PLAY	1. To *check* with a leading hand. 2. To refrain from aggressive play with very good cards.
SMOOTH	Low hand in which the four lowest cards are as small as possible. E.g., 8, 4, 3, 2, A, is called an 8-smooth.

SPLIT OPENERS	In draw poker, to open with a pair but then discard one of them in order to draw for a straight or flush.
SPLIT PAIR	In stud, a pair with one of the cards in the hole, the other showing.
STAKE	The amount of a player's money or chips when he enters the game.
STAKES	The betting rules governing the game.
STAND PAT	In draw poker, to draw no cards.
STAY	*Call.*
STEAL THE ANTE	Make a first-round bet that causes all opponents to fold.
STRAIGHT	Five cards in sequence.
STREETS	Betting rounds. See, e.g., *Fifth Street.*
STRING BET	Bet or raise made in two installments, and generally disallowed.
STUD POKER	Poker in which some of the cards are dealt up.
SUCKED IN	Induced to call a later bet because of a foolish earlier call.
SUCKER	See *geese.*
SUITED CARDS	Cards of the same suit.
SWEEPING	See *scooping.*
SWINGING	See *scooping.*
TABLE STAKES	1. The betting rule that a player need never meet a bet for an amount larger than all the chips or money he has on the table. 2. (rare) The only limit on size of bet is the amount of a player's chips or money on the table. This is now usually called no-limit.

TAKE	The amount of the house deduction from the pot.
TAP	1. To bet all one's chips. 2. To bet an amount equal to all of an opponent's chips.
TELL	Any involuntary giveaway of the quality of one's hand.
TIGHT PLAYER	Conservative player. A *rock*.
TOKE	Tip to a casino dealer by the winner of a hand.
TOUCHING CARDS	Cards adjacent in rank.
TRASH	See *garbage*.
TREY	A three.
TRIPLETS	See *trips*.
TRIPS	Three of a kind. Also called *triplets*, or a *set*.
TURN	1. The next-to-last round of betting in Holdem and Omaha. 2. The fourth common card received just before this betting round. Also called *Fourth Street*.
TWO PAIR	1. Hand that contains two pairs and a kicker. 2. Holding that includes two pairs.
UNDER THE GUN	In first position after the dealer, and re-quired to act first.
UNDERDOG	Not the favored hand.
UNDERPAIR	Pair lower than a showing pair.
UP CARD	Showing card.
VIGORISH	See *rake*.
WHEEL	The low hand 5, 4, 3, 2, A; also called *bicycle*.
WHORES	Queens.

WIDOW	The common cards produced on the *flop*, *turn*, and *river* in Holdem and Omaha.
WILD CARD	Card that may be given any desired rank or suit by the player holding it.
WIRED	See *back-to-back*.
ZERO-SUM GAME	Game in which the sum of the winnings and the sum of the losings are equal.

Some Additional Reading
♠ ♣ ♥ ♦

There is an enormous number of books about poker. The Gambler's Book Store catalogue lists nearly a hundred, and many others are advertised in every issue of *Card Player* magazine. They are of three main types: books about poker and poker players; general guides to "How to Win at Poker"; and game-specific treatments of how to play given hands. They vary in level from primers to manuals for the tournament professional. Here are fourteen (listed alphabetically by author) that I have either enjoyed or learned a good deal from, or both. The brief comments are intended to give you an indication of their scope and level.

A. Alvarez, *The Biggest Game in Town* (Boston: Houghton Mifflin, 1983; 185 pages).

> Alvarez is a poet, freelance writer, and avid amateur poker player. The book is about big-time poker pros gathered in Las Vegas for the 1981 World Series of Poker. The contents appeared originally in *The New Yorker* in somewhat different form.

Nesmith C. Ankeny, *Poker Strategy: Winning with Game Theory* (New York: Basic Books, 1981; 189 pages).

> Ankeny is a professor of mathematics at MIT. This is an intriguing account of how to use game theory to play draw poker against one, or at most two, opponents. Its limitation to draw poker is one drawback; another is his "basic truth" that "The object of poker is to win the antes."

Doyle Brunson, *According To Doyle* (Secaucus, N.J.: Gambling Times Books, 1984; 165 pages).

> "Texas Dolly" Brunson is one of the great gambler–poker players and a two-time winner of the World Series. This shot-

gun collection of forty-eight short anecdotes full of wisdom
and sensible advice is fun and easy reading.

Doyle Brunson *et al.*, as told to Allan Goldberg, *How I Made over
$1,000,000 Playing Poker* (Las Vegas: B&G Publishing, 1978; 605
pages); retitled: *Super/System: A Course in Power Poker.*

Interspersed with the author's autobiographical accounts and
the game-specific advice provided by his collaborators are
Brunson's comments and advice on how to win at no-limit
poker, at which he was an undoubted master. Enough of the
advice is applicable even to Thursday-night games to make
the book worth skimming, but whether it is worth the $50
price is moot. It is surely necessary for the amateur who as-
pires to play high-stakes poker with the pros.

   Game-specific chapters, mostly by others, account for
about 90 percent of the book. They are by Mike Caro on
draw poker; David Reese on 7-card stud; Joey Hawthorne on
lowball; David Sklansky on 7-card Hi-Lo; Bobby Baldwin on
limit Holdem; and Brunson himself on no-limit Holdem. All
are by well-known expert players and are directed to the kind
of aggressive high-stakes games played in Las Vegas casinos.
The book has been called the bible of the professional poker
player.

Michael Cappalletti, *Cappalletti on Omaha* (Las Vegas: Gamblers
Book Club, 1992; 69 pages).

Cappalletti writes a biweekly column on Omaha in *Card
Player.* This is a collection of forty-eight of those columns,
which are somewhat uneven in quality. Given the slim writ-
ings about Omaha, it may be worth reading as a complement
to Bob Ciaffone's much better book on the subject.

Bob Ciaffone, *Omaha Holdem Poker* (Las Vegas: Harris Printers,
1992 [fifth edition]; 69 pages).

A brief but excellent book on the high-only version of
Omaha, a game that I believe is ideally suited to Thursday-
night poker.

David M. Hayano, *Poker Faces: The Life and Work of Professional
Card Players* (Berkeley: University of California Press, 1982; 205
pages).

Professor Hayano is an anthropologist who spent years doing field work in the card parlors of Gardena, California. The result is an insightful study of the life and mores of small-time poker pros that won't help you play poker better but will help you understand some of your opponents if you choose to play in low-stakes casino games.

Anthony Holden, *Big Deal: A Year As a Professional Poker Player* (New York: Viking, 1990; 306 pages).

Tony Holden is a British journalist and writer and by reputation a first-rate amateur poker player. This is an account of his year-long quest to play in and try to win the no-limit Holdem game at the World Series of Poker. It provides substantial insights into how tough life is in both high-stakes and tournament poker.

A. D. Livingston, *Advanced Poker: Strategy and Smart Winning Play* (N. Hollywood: Wilshire Book Co., 1971; 227 pages).

An introduction to playing poker that, despite its title, is really for advanced beginners or intermediate players. Part I contains solid but well-known general advice; Part II contains 33 pages of tables about probabilities, some of which are very useful; and Part III gives rules and brief accounts of dozens of varieties of poker games, from Anaconda and Baseball to Woolworth and Zig-Zag. It can serve as an encyclopedia for dollar-limit and smaller poker games.

Albert H. Morehead, *The Complete Guide to Winning Poker* (New York: Simon & Schuster, 1967; 284 pages).

Perhaps the best book for beginners ever written, it suffers only from having been written in 1967, before the now-common widow games were being played.

Edwin Silberstang, *Winning Poker for the Serious Player: The Ultimate Money-Making Guide!* (New York: Cardoza Publishing, 1992; 221 pages).

A good recent, intermediate, general introduction to poker, with lots of specific advice about how to play given hands. What detracts from it, in my view, is the author's premise that "The only purpose in playing poker is to make money."

David Sklansky, *Hold'em Poker* (Las Vegas: Gamblers Book Club, 1976; 65 pages).

A brilliant, insightful analysis of how to win in high-stakes Holdem. While it is at a more advanced level than is appropriate for most Thursday-night players, it gives a scary glimpse into the subtleties of the game and the psychology of high-stakes play.

David Spanier, *Total Poker* (New York: Simon & Schuster, 1977; 255 pages).

An English journalist's collection of anecdotes about poker and poker players that is fun to read. Chapters on Presidential poker and on poker in the movies add spice to generally sensible advice.

Herbert O. Yardley, *The Education of a Poker Player* (New York: Simon & Schuster, 1957; 129 pages).

The justly famous, and now classic, autobiographical account of poker playing by one of the world's most famous cryptographers. His anecdotes and characters are unforgettable, even if the advice he gives about how to play the game is much too conservative for Thursday-night games.

About the Author

PETER O. STEINER served for twenty-three years at the University of Michigan as professor of economics and professor of law; for eight years he was also the dean of the College of Literature, Science and the Arts. After receiving a Ph.D. from Harvard in 1950, he taught economics and statistics at the University of California at Berkeley and at the University of Wisconsin at Madison, before moving to Ann Arbor in 1968. He is the co-author of a textbook, *Economics,* which is currently in its tenth edition.

Mr. Steiner retired from teaching in 1991, but his serious poker playing began during World War II aboard the aircraft carrier U.S.S. *Independence* and has been a profitable hobby ever since. He and his wife have five children and four grandchildren.

About the Type

This book was set in Galliard, a typeface designed by Matthew Carter for the Merganthaler Linotype Company in 1978. Galliard is based on the sixteenth-century typefaces of Robert Granjon.